Exploring Inner Experience

Advances in Consciousness Research

Advances in Consciousness Research provides a forum for scholars from different scientific disciplines and fields of knowledge who study consciousness in its multifaceted aspects. Thus the Series will include (but not be limited to) the various areas of cognitive science, including cognitive psychology, linguistics, brain science and philosophy. The orientation of the Series is toward developing new interdisciplinary and integrative approaches for the investigation, description and theory of consciousness, as well as the practical consequences of this research for the individual and society.

Volume 64

Exploring Inner Experience: The descriptive experience sampling method
by Russell T. Hurlburt and Christopher L. Heavey

Exploring Inner Experience

The descriptive experience sampling method

Russell T. Hurlburt
Christopher L. Heavey
University of Nevada, Las Vegas

John Benjamins Publishing Company
Amsterdam / Philadelphia

∞™ The paper used in this publication meets the minimum requirements of American National Standard for Information Sciences – Permanence of Paper for Printed Library Materials, ANSI Z39.48-1984.

Library of Congress Cataloging-in-Publication Data

Russell T. Hurlburt
Exploring Inner Experience : The descriptive experience sampling method / Russell T. Hurlburt and Christopher L. Heavey.
p. cm. (Advances in Consciousness Research, ISSN 1381–589X ; v. 64)
Includes bibliographical references and indexes.
1. Introspection. I. Heavy, Christopher L. II. Title. III. Series.

BF316.H87 2006
153--dc22 2006040657
ISBN 90 272 5200 9 (Hb; alk. paper)

John Benjamins Publishing Co. · P.O. Box 36224 · 1020 ME Amsterdam · The Netherlands
John Benjamins North America · P.O. Box 27519 · Philadelphia PA 19118-0519 · USA

Table of contents

Preface

There is a strong, widespread resurgence of interest in inner experience (thoughts, feelings, sensations, etc.). In applied psychology, the cognitive approach, now the dominant force, rests largely on questions such as "What were you thinking when you...?" In psychological science, researchers are now asking participants in brain-imaging studies to report whether they were forming mental images when they were in the fMRI scanner. In everyday life, the first question a TV reporter typically asks the victim/witness/participant/athlete is "How were you feeling when..."? This resurgence of interest in inner experience is legitimate; it is becoming increasingly apparent that any attempt at understanding a person without considering thoughts and feelings is likely to be sterile.

However, this resurgence of introspective reporting is *not* accompanied by an increase in the sophistication of methods that guide that reporting. That is a grave mistake, because historically introspection has been a spectacular failure. A century ago, introspection, which had been a mainstay in early psychology's exploration of consciousness, was so thoroughly discredited that introspection was banned from psychology. This ban was so complete that from then up to the present day, the term "introspection" does not even appear in most textbooks of psychological method except as a historical footnote describing introspection's inadequacy.

Thus the history of introspection demonstrates without ambiguity that introspection is not trivially easy. There is simply no reason to believe that questions such as "What were you thinking/feeling when...?" can be answered any better in 2006 then they were in 1906 unless psychological science figures out how to do a better job of asking such questions. Unfortunately, the resurgence in introspective questioning has largely disregarded the history of such questions, and there has been little effort to fashion better introspective methods.

This book argues that it is indeed possible to make accurate introspective observations if, but only if, an adequate method is used, and it lays out the parameters of such a method. It shows that accurate reports about inner experience can be obtained by focusing on one single moment at a time, and by asking the one legitimate question about inner experience: "What are the details of your inner experience *at this very moment*?" It argues that faithful descriptions of individuals can be built up bit by bit from a mosaic of such truly described moments. A method designed to incorporate those principles was developed by the senior author in the 1970s. Called Descriptive Experience Sampling (DES), this method uses a random beeper to cue people to observe moments of their inner experience as they move through their natural environments.

An example

We will discuss the DES method in detail during the course of this book, but here is a preview. On October 16, when the beeper sounded at 18 seconds after 2:47 in the afternoon, 9-year-old Jimmy was in his bedroom playing with his cars. The DES interview revealed that instead of paying attention to the cars that were arrayed on the floor in front of him, he was at that moment seeing in his imagination an image of a big hole he had been digging for the last several days in his backyard. The hole in his image was about a foot deep, and his red tricycle was seen to the left of the hole, with its front wheel partly down into the excavation. The imaged scene was viewed as if from a perspective standing on his back porch.

"Was this hole in your imaginary picture just like the real hole in your backyard?"

"Yes," he said, "except that the real hole has more toys in it. If you had beeped me in a couple minutes, I would have had time to finish the picture."

Jimmy's story illustrates why accurately observing inner experience is necessary to an effective science of psychology. If Jimmy was right (and we think he was) when he said that he had put only his tricycle in the imaged hole because he hadn't yet had time to elaborate the entire image, and that if we had beeped him a bit later, there would have been more toys in the imaged hole, it suggests that seeing an image may be a skill that is acquired gradually. As children just begin to acquire this skill, it may take many minutes to construct an image, to "draw in the details," so to speak. The image-making skill may be like the skill of riding a bicycle – it is acquired only with painstaking difficulty, but once acquired, it is impossible to remember what it was like not to have the skill. An adult can pretend not to have the bike-riding skill, based on observations of children attempting to acquire it, but there is absolutely no reason to believe that the *experience* an adult has while feigning skill acquisition (pretense, controlled wobbling) is anything at all like the actual experience a child goes through in real skill acquisition (terror, pain, out-of-controllness?). Furthermore, because images are covert, we don't get a chance to see children going through the skill-acquisition efforts.

As a result, most adults, including most psychologists, presume that children's images are like their own – they seem to happen in an instant, and appear fully formed. Jimmy's image suggests that is not true for at least some, perhaps all, children. Psychology doesn't have a basic science of the image, answering questions such as, "Is image-making a skill that has to be acquired gradually?" "Does everyone have images?" "At what age do images begin?" "Are the first images in color or black-and-white?" "Are the characteristics of early images schematic or simplified in other ways?" Science has rarely, if ever (at least not in the last half century or so), tried to answer those questions. There is little or no mention in the psychological literature that the image-making skills may need to be acquired.

How could psychology have overlooked such an obvious question about children's images? Because, as this book will show, psychologists rarely ask about inner experience with adequate care.

A crisis for psychological science

Psychological science has never fully explored inner experience. As we shall see, in the first part of its history, one of psychology's main aims was the exploration of consciousness; however, its introspective methods were not adequate. In the second part of its history, largely as a result of the failures of introspection, psychological science has sharply avoided the study of consciousness, with the result that fundamental questions cannot be answered. For one obvious example, the diagnosis of Obsessive-Compulsive Disorder requires determining whether a person has recurrent unwanted thoughts, impulses, or images. But when a patient says, "I have recurrent unwanted thoughts," there are at least two possibilities: she does in fact have such thoughts, or she thinks she has such thoughts but is mistaken. Modern psychology has great difficulty distinguishing between these very different alternatives because modern psychological scientists do not ask about experience with adequate care. As we shall show, the technology exists to make those observations, but very few people are using it.

Psychology's interest in consciousness is dramatically increasing, largely due to the recognition that science cannot understand what is going on with a person, or what he or she is doing, without access to inner experience. However, even now, when psychology studies consciousness it usually declines to investigate how consciousness is really experienced. Instead, it measures blood flow in the brain or reaction times and tries to infer the characteristics of consciousness. Brain scan and reaction time techniques are important, but sterile unless a tight connection to inner experience is explored.

Thus we believe that psychology is in the midst of a crisis that involves a fundamental mismatch between a topic of central interest to psychology and society – inner experience – and the inadequacy of our knowledge about it and our methods of exploring it. In the pages that follow we will explore this crisis and its history and present the DES method, which we believe can lead psychology out of this crisis by avoiding the shortcomings of previous introspective methods and providing accurate descriptions of inner experience.

A note to non-professionals

This book is written primarily for professionals, but we think the layperson will find it interesting and entirely accessible. Ours is a psychological age. We accept psychological explanations for personal successes and failures, family relationships, the success or lack thereof of sports teams, and the rise and fall of the stock market so readily that it is hard to imagine a world where explanations for such events might be non-psychological. And yet, psychological explanations were unheard of before about a century ago. Throughout human history, except for the last 100 or so years, people explained such events by saying, "It was the will of the gods," or "He had too much black bile." However, the psychological explanations we give are only as solid as the science upon which they are built. Thus if psychology is indeed experiencing a crisis of knowledge and method related to inner experience, then some of what we take for granted about ourselves and the world may be partially or even entirely incorrect.

In particular, if psychology hasn't adequately understood inner experience, it is likely that you as an individual reader also haven't really understood inner experience. That's important, because inner experience is a fundamental topic, underlying all culture, religion, philosophy, and so on. It is important to recognize that the crisis found at the heart of psychology is also a crisis for modern Western culture and its individuals. If you are a part of modern Western culture, you are likely to be estranged from important aspects of your own personal life and situation. Clinical psychology, as we shall see, thinks it can ignore asking carefully about the inner experience of its clients, and therefore often constructs partially correct or largely incorrect understandings of the client. In the same way, and for the same reasons, lay people construct partially correct or largely incorrect understandings of themselves and the people around them. Our society, like our psychology, is quite cavalier about the narratives we advance and believe about others and ourselves.

About this book

This is a very optimistic book. We believe that it is possible to get a pretty accurate look at inner experience. Not a perfectly accurate look, but a pretty darn accurate look. We show one way (DES) that it can be done, and confidently expect other ways to appear. We show that an accurate view of inner experience is a necessary part of a science that intends to deal with the truth about individuals.

The book is also necessarily confrontational. If psychology remains blind to inner experience, it will remain estranged from personal truths and will be limited in the extent to which it can advance.

Exploring Inner Experience is a compromise between two overlapping but different intentions, which we might call the "analytical" and the "skill" intentions. An analytical approach to DES involves setting DES in the historical context and examining how DES is similar and different to related approaches such as introspection, phenomenology, and qualitative investigations. By contrast, a skill approach involves discussing how to do DES and giving some practice in understanding the important features of the DES techniques.

At this stage of development of the science of inner experience, these two conceptions have considerable overlap: an analytical approach must include enough of the skill details to make the method intelligible, while a skill approach must include enough analysis to help users understand the methodological rationale. This book is somewhere in the middle of the compromise between the two approaches but closer to the skills end. There are, we think, a growing number of investigators poised to begin attempting inner-experience investigations, and we think a discussion weighted in the skills direction has more value than one weighted in the analytic direction. Thus this book includes case studies, exposition, comparison, examples, repetition, practice, more exposition, more repetition, and so on, in a style designed to develop the skill of observing inner experience. At the analytic end, we do discuss reliability and validity, and we do compare DES to other systems.

It is in the nature of compromise that no one is entirely happy; those who would prefer a more analytical approach may be put off by the repetition, while those who would prefer a skills approach may find too much theory. That unavoidably reflects, we think, the way the field is at this time.

One more appeal

Consider these quotations:

> When we utter a word, we cannot help but mentally see an image of its written version. In our heads, what we have said ... is that sequence of written symbols. When we say "dog," a little picture of that word flashes through our minds, *Sesame Street*-style... Imagine saying "dog" and only thinking of a canine, but not thinking of the written word. If you're reading this book, it follows that you couldn't pull this off even at gunpoint.
> (John McWhorter, respected specialist in language development, 2003: 3)

> Human beings talk to themselves every moment of the waking day.
> (Bernard Baars, noted expert on consciousness, 2003: 106)

These claims are made by current leaders in their fields, but they are not true. The fact is, as DES shows, that seeing a mental image of the written version of a spoken word is very rare; and that while some people talk to themselves frequently, many people talk to themselves rarely if at all.

Why do these scholars allow themselves to write such untruths? Why do their editors not remove it? Why do their publishers elect to print it? Why haven't reviewers taken them to task for their misstatements? Why haven't psychologists stood up and said, "This is not true!"? Primarily because all those people haven't taken inner experience seriously enough to recognize untruth when they see it. This is not a particular criticism of McWhorter or Baars – their view of inner experience is by no means less well informed than that of most of their colleagues. We are clearly *not* singling out these authors in this regard – there are heaps of books that make similar mistakes.

It is surprising that, of all people, linguists and psychologists don't make it their business to know whether language exists inside the head, and if so, how. Our intention is to point out that the disregard of inner experience is a pervasive and unfortunate characteristic of our science and our culture. We believe it is remediable, and this book is aimed in that direction.

Russ Hurlburt and Chris Heavey
October, 2005

CHAPTER 1

Inner experience

Inner space is the real frontier.
Gloria Steinem

The exploration of inner experience has fallen into disrepute, and this book is intended to contribute to its restoration. By "inner experience" we mean anything that is going on in your awareness at any particular moment. A thought, feeling, tickle, sensation, kinesthetic awareness, image, perceptual awareness, whatever is "before the footlights of consciousness," as William James said. We'd like to throw the net as widely as possible at the concept of inner experience. Your inner experience is whatever is in your awareness at any particular moment.

Some observers have preferred the terms "consciousness," "conscious experience," "experience," or "in awareness" to the term "inner experience," because "inner experience" seems to favor "inner" experiences such as thoughts and feelings over "outer" experiences such as visual perception and sensation. We believe that there is no best term; all have their advantages and drawbacks. Suffice it to say that by "inner experience" we mean *anything* that emerges, or coalesces, or becomes a phenomenon, or is experienced, out of the welter of inner and outer stimuli that simultaneously impinge on a person.

That definition may seem loose or vague, but it turns out, as we shall see in the next section, that the definition can be quite unambiguous in practice.

Descriptive experience sampling

We have been exploring inner experience since the early 1970s using a method we call Descriptive Experience Sampling (DES). DES gives people a beeper that emits a beep through an earphone at random times. If you're a DES subject, you wear this beeper in your own natural environments, as you engage in your everyday activities – at work, at home, driving between the two, playing tennis, writing a paper, cooking dinner, reading, and so on. Your task is simply to pay attention to whatever you were experiencing at the moment you hear the beep, and to jot down in a notebook the characteristics of that experience. If you were thinking, we want to know the details of the thought. If you were feeling some emotion, we want to know how that felt; if you were visually focused on the external environment, we want to know what you were seeing; if you were seeing an inner image, we want to know about that experience; if you were hearing some external event, we want to know what it sounded like; and so on.

As you may have noticed, the DES method follows directly from the definition of inner experience: DES tries to describe whatever is in your awareness at any particular moment. We use the beeper to define the particular moment, and simply ask you to report what's in your awareness at that moment.

The overwhelming majority of people who have engaged in this kind of study do find it easy to pay attention to what's going on at the beep, despite the fact that prior to sampling, *they don't think they can do it*. Prospective DES subjects often try, as informal preparation for their sampling participation, to pay attention to their inner experience and find that paying attention to be very difficult. But during sampling, most find that paying attention to their awareness at the moment of the beep turns out to be an easy thing to do. The turnaround is striking: most subjects go from believing they can't do it at all to finding that it's easy.

The beeping process itself is easy. It's the *simulation* of the beeping process that is difficult. In the simulation, prospective subjects must pretend they are being beeped, which is something like asking, "What's going on in my inner experience right now?" What's actually going on in experience right then is the question itself, "What's going on?" However, that question is ruled out, and it therefore seems that there *isn't anything* apprehendable in awareness at that particular moment, and therefore that the attempt to apprehend inner experience is difficult or impossible. That's a mistake – a mistake shared by many influential philosophers, but a mistake nonetheless.

It turns out that, for most people, actually wearing the beeper makes it easy to "catch awareness in flight." Once subjects get the hang of it, the beep frees them from having to *ask* what's going on; with a little practice, they easily develop the skill of letting the beep cause them simply to *pay attention* to whatever happens to be ongoing in awareness.

This book shows that DES is an effective way of exploring inner experience, and that the descriptions it provides are largely accurate characterizations of ongoing inner experience.

The ancient history of inner experience

Inner experience is one of humankind's oldest and most important topics.

- *Gilgamesh* is thought to be the oldest existing narrative, transmitted orally for thousands of years beginning in roughly 2700 BC. Much of that narrative consists of considerations of inner experience, such as Gilgamesh saying, "How can I rest, how can I be at peace? Despair is in my heart" (Mack 1997:32).
- Buddha said: "The mind is fickle and flighty, it flies after fancies wherever it likes: it is difficult indeed to restrain. But it is a great good to control the mind; a mind self-controlled is a source of great joy." (*Dhammapada*, Verse 35, about 500 B.C.; Mascaro 1973)
- Confucius said, "In the Book of Poetry are three hundred pieces, but the design of them all may be embraced in one sentence 'Having no depraved thoughts.'" (*Analects*, Book 2, about 500 BC; Leys, 1997)
- Then Jesus called to the crowd to come and hear. "All of you listen," he said, "and try to understand. Your souls aren't harmed by what you eat, but by what you think and say".... And then he added, "It is the thoughtlife that pollutes. For from within, out of men's hearts, come evil thoughts of lust, theft, murder, adultery, wanting what belongs to others, wickedness, deceit, lewdness, envy, slander, pride, and all other folly. All these vile things come from within; they are what pollute you and make you unfit for God." (*Mark* 7:14–23, about 29 AD, *The Living Bible* translation)
- Aristotle wrote: "It is not possible to think without an image. For the same effect occurs in thinking as in drawing a diagram. For in the latter case, though we do not make any use of the fact that the size of the triangle is determinate, we none the less draw it with a determinate size. And similarly someone who is thinking, even if he is not thinking of something with a size, places something with a size before his eyes, but thinks of it not as having a size." (*On Memory,* 449^b30, about 330 BC; Sorabji 1972)

Thus throughout history, the world's deepest thinkers have recognized the central importance of inner experience.

The recent history of inner experience

Over the past century or so, however, inner experience has lost its central importance in Western science. In broad strokes, the history of psychology began with an unquestioned acceptance of the importance of consciousness. Much of early psychology (from the establishment by Wundt of the first psychological laboratory in 1879 to the early 1900s) involved the development of introspection, a set of techniques for the careful, systematic observation of consciousness.

However, introspective psychology was soon embroiled in a bitter controversy, primarily between E. B. Titchener at Cornell and a group of German psychologists loosely called the Würzburg School. Titchener held the sensationalist position that all thoughts had at the core some sort of image. Sometimes this image was clearly available to consciousness, but at other times it was only dimly perceived. By contrast, the Würzburgers held that their introspections revealed a form of thought that had no imaginal core whatsoever; they named this newly discovered form "imageless thought." Titchener disagreed, and the two laboratories conducted 20 years of introspective research aimed at settling the issue. In the end they were unsuccessful; both sides continued to maintain that their positions were correct. This apparently unresolvable conflict at the heart of introspection served to discredit introspection as a psychological method, and it was banished from the psychological arsenal.

There were other contributors to the demise of introspection (Danziger 1980), most important for our purposes being Freud and the behaviorists. Freud believed that the unconscious held the most important features of a person; therefore introspection, which could examine only conscious contents, was a feeble tool (although the case of Donald that we will discuss below shows that Freud was somewhat mistaken in this view). The behaviorists, seeing the difficulty that introspection had in deciding between two views of inner events, advanced a psychology that focused only on externally observable behavior and ignored inner experience altogether.

For a variety of reasons, first the Freudian and then the behavioristic approaches came to dominate the psychology of the second half of the 20th century. Both those positions powerfully criticized the study of consciousness. Introspection was completely discredited; the word "introspection" and any technique to which it referred were banned from scientific psychological discourse.

At the same time, much of clinical psychology, under pressure to understand what their clients were telling them about important aspects of their lives, could not surrender to the anti-introspection onslaught of psychological science. Clinical psychologists recognized that they had to inquire about thoughts and feelings if they were to understand their clients, and this (among other things) brought them into substantial conflict with their research-psychologist colleagues. Tavris characterized this conflict as a war:

> Indeed, the split between the research and practice [clinical] wings of psychology has grown so wide that many psychologists now speak glumly of the "scientist-practitioner gap," although that is like saying there is an "Arab-Israeli gap" in the Middle East. It is a war, involving deeply held beliefs, political passions, views of human nature and the nature of knowledge, and – as all wars ultimately do – money and livelihoods. (Tavris 2003: B7)

Throughout the first three-quarters of the 20th century, this war was hard fought, full of vitriolic argumentation on both sides. But in the last quarter of the 20th century, the amount of vitriol has substantially lessened and there is surprisingly little modern debate about this conflict. Our interpretation is that neither side can claim victory because *both sides are correct about the shortcomings of the other*: the researchers are correct to point out the unreliability of the clinicians' introspective methods, and the clinicians are correct to point out the sterility of a science that overlooks inner experience. Because neither side can admit the correctness of the other's critique without weakening their own position, the argumentation has been stalemated. Modern clinicians act as if there were no methodological flaws to their introspective questions, and modern researchers act as if avoiding inner experience is good science.

A principle casualty of this stalemate has been the careful examination of inner experience. The clinicians can't examine the adequacy of their introspective questions, lest they fuel once again the researchers' attacks. The researchers can't examine whether inner experience is important lest they give clinicians the upper hand. There is therefore very little, if any, scientific discourse over the adequacy of introspective methods, with the result that there are, currently, two widely disparate views on the exploration of inner experience, the clinician's view that it is easy (just ask about it) and the scientist's view that it is impossible.

We believe that this account of the history of psychology explains the remarkable advance of cognitive psychology over the last few decades. Searching the psycINFO database of all psychological articles reveals that the terms "cognition" and "cognitive" appeared as keywords in only about one half of one percent of all articles in the middle third of the 20th century (1920–1960), but now those terms appear in about 15 percent of all articles (a 30-fold increase). The study of cognition has clearly become a dominant force both in clinical and in scientific psychology. Our interpretation is that the current investigation of cognition is psychology's attempt to fill the vacuum left by the war: it seems to explore inner experience scientifically, and thus seems to satisfy both the clinicians and the scientists. However, an examination of the articles shows that this new science of cognition is proceeding without any actual examination whatsoever of the experience of thinking. Cognitive science infers the existence of cognitive structures but for the most part does not seek to explore them using introspection or any other direct observation technique. Thus the satisfaction that cognitive science provides is an illusion: it *seems* to explore inner experience without *really* exploring inner experience, an attempt that we think can provide only a limited understanding of human experience.

The only way, as it seems to us, to end the war between the clinicians and the researchers is to solve the problems that drove them to war, that is, to improve the methods of exploring inner experience. We think that is doable, and we show how in this book.

An example

We have seen that inner experience has been important since before the dawn of recorded history, but that this importance has been undermined over the last century. Here's an example from our own sampling research to illustrate why we should continue to view inner experience as being fundamentally important. Hurlburt and Sipprelle (1978; see also Hurlburt 1997) described a university professor we will call "Donald." He was tenured, he was successful, had a loving wife and family, a perfect life, so it seemed, except he suffered from extreme anxiety, so much anxiety that he wouldn't drive his car anymore because he was afraid he would black out and kill somebody or himself.

In an attempt to understand the mystery behind Donald's anxiety, Hurlburt and Sipprelle asked Donald to wear a beeper for a few days and to write down his thoughts each time the beeper beeped. Donald did so and brought a typed transcription of beeped experiences to his next meeting with Hurlburt and Sipprelle. Upon inspection of the transcription, the investigators noticed an obvious theme emerge from the data: Donald was angry with his children in many of his reports. More surprising, however, was that when Hurlburt and Sipprelle pointed out this theme to Donald, he denied the existence of such a theme *despite the fact that he had faithfully collected and transcribed his own experience at the time of each beep.*

Hurlburt and Sipprelle went through Donald's transcribed thoughts with him one by one. One beep involved thinking that son Johnny has the radio turned up too loud, and Donald acknowledged that he was angry at that moment. Another beep involved thinking that son Billy had gotten ice cream on his shirt again, and Donald acknowledged that he was angry at that moment, also. It developed that at approximately a third of his thoughts (which is a very large percentage for any content theme), Donald was angry with his kids. As Hurlburt and Sipprelle pointed out particular events moment by moment, it became easier for Donald to acknowledge that he had in fact been angry *at that moment*, and by the time he had finished reviewing the series of such moments, he had come to realize, to his great surprise, that he was in fact frequently angry. Hurlburt and Sipprelle reassured Donald that anger with kids is perfectly natural, and apparently as a result of the new awareness of his experience, his anxiety disappeared.

This example illustrates four of the recurring themes of this book. First, retrospective self-accounts are often substantially incorrect. When Donald retrospectively generalized about himself, he systematically neglected his anger, seeing himself as having a perfect, loving family with no anger involved. Second, a method that examines a series of randomly chosen moments may discover important characteristics of a person. Donald's anger was easy to spot against the random background of the other beeped experiences. Third, the DES method does *not* explore the unconscious, even though it reveals important aspects that were heretofore hidden. Donald's retrospective hiddenness was by no means unconscious: Donald *knew* he was angry at his kids *at every moment in which that anger occurred.* His anger was missing from his retrospective general account of himself, even though he was well aware of it each time it occurred. And fourth, it demonstrates how important it is to have an accurate view of your own personal inner experience. Donald's debilitating anxiety was apparently the result of his substantial attempt to overlook systematically the fact of his anger. (As with all case studies, there are, of course, alternative explanations.)

Another example

Recall that in the Preface we discussed Jimmy's image of a hole he had been digging in his backyard, and concluded that image-making may well be a skill that requires practice and time to develop. Here's another image from a young teenager that again illustrates that image-making practice.

Wendy had an image of her junior high orchestra. She played viola, and the image was viewed from her usual place – the violins and conductor/teacher were ahead of her, the flutes off to the left, and so on. It was as if she were sitting in the orchestra – she saw and heard the orchestra playing a piece they had performed in a recent concert. Asked whether there were any differences between the imaged scene and the real orchestra, she replied that everything was the same except that the orchestra in her image sounded better than her real orchestra. She had been "playing with this image," she said, for a few months. Each time she had replayed it, she had improved the sound: one time she corrected a squeak in the clarinets; another time she put a violin passage into better tune; and so on. Now, as the result of these repairs, she was hearing her orchestra but without nearly as many mistakes. It was definitely *her* orchestra, but better than she had ever heard it.

We take this as an example of Wendy playing with images in order to become more skilled in their properties, to learn what she can and cannot do with them. This is serious kids' work in the sense that Wendy is developing an important skill, but she perceives it as "playing" in much the same way as kids play with blocks to learn the serious skills of coordination, balance, sequencing, and so on. She meant to be taken literally when she said she had been working on this image for "months."

Adults take for granted that their image-making abilities were always the way they are now – that images come apparently immediately, fully formed. We will see that because psychology has not developed techniques for the accurate exploration of inner experience, psychology also accepts this common-sense view without much discussion. However, Wendy and Jimmy's images suggest that image-making is a complex skill that has to be learned with practice, and a science of psychology that fails to explore such basic principles is bound to be limited.

Characterizing inner experience

Here's a typical example of a DES summary report, to give a hint about the individualistic nature of this method.

Violet has visual images in 75% of her samples – a high frequency by comparison to most subjects. But it is the idiographic characteristics of those images that are striking. First, the images come at her, one after the other, and by "come at her" she means to be taken literally – her images seem to travel toward her from the front-right portion of her visual field. Sometimes an image is replaced by the next image that comes a second or so later; sometimes an image moves off to the left before it is replaced by the next image coming from the front/right.

Often her images are of verbal content. For example, when she thinks about errands she has to do, or about bills she has to pay, she sees a series of images of buildings with the company signs and/or logos: "WAL*MART" in the proper red color with the Walmart star seen between the syllables, "UMC" and the top of the University Medical Center with the sign letters in light blue (just as they are on the real building), and so on.

Often her images are exceedingly complex, visual collages. For example, she was putting on makeup and had just read a reference to Bobby Brown's song "My Tenderoni." That produced a visual collage of scenes related to Zack, a character in the TV show *Saved by the Bell.* When Violet was younger, she had had a crush on Zack; during that time, whenever she had heard "My Tenderoni" on the radio, she had told whoever was listening that the song was to Zack dedicated from Violet. Now, at the moment of the beep, she was seeing a complex collage of Zack-related scenes: a video replay of a *Saved by the Bell* episode where Zack and Slater are coming down the stairs; a still picture of a poster of the *Saved by the Bell* cast; a moving image of Violet telling her sister that "My Tenderoni" was from her dedicated to Zack; a moving image of Violet's sister making fun of her for the Zack crush; a non-moving image of her sister looking at a magazine. This complex visual display was a single multifaceted collage of images, not a series of images. The various scenes, still and moving, had fixed positions in the collage – the poster to the right, Zack and Slater to the upper left, and so on.

Violet's images seem related to her level of stress. When she is "stressed out," the images come faster and more insistently. And the images seem out of her control – they come at her unbidden. For example, at one beep Violet is thinking about disciplining her niece and is seeing an image of a sequence of scenes in an Albertsons grocery store; her niece flopped on the floor in a tantrum over not getting a ball; then Violet flopping down beside her; then the niece kicking Violet in the leg; and so on. She'd like to stop this image sequence, but she can't.

Violet believed that similar situations always evoke a nearly identical sequence of images. For example, if a new disciplinary occasion were to occur, the same Albertsons sequence would be replayed, but the new situation might get added to the end of the Albertson's sequence to become a new sequence of images to be played the next time niece-discipline becomes an issue. Thus Violet believed she has "a record" for all of her acquaintances – a series of visual scenes that gets replayed. Casual acquaintances have short records; long-term relationships like parents and sisters have long records. Whenever, for example, Violet gets mad at her father, the same long sequence of mad-at-father images comes flying at her. This can last for a day or longer, and Violet seems powerless to stop it.

The aim of this book

This book will show that it is possible to examine inner experience and report it with substantial accuracy. We will describe in detail one method for such examination, the Descriptive Experience Sampling (DES) method. Furthermore we contend that it is important to draw a bright-line distinction between descriptions of inner experience that were collected under carefully crafted situations such as the DES beep on the one hand and descriptions of inner experience that are retrospective or general on the other. We shall see that clearly maintaining that distinction is a key to obtaining accurate views of inner experience because individual moments can be described with accuracy whereas retrospective or general accounts are often inaccurate, sometimes strikingly so (as in the case of Donald described above). The discussion of Violet's experience illustrates this issue. Until the last paragraph of our discussion of Violet, everything that we said about her experience was based on beeped samples; we will show that such reports should be believed at a high level of confidence. However, Violet's report in the last paragraph that "similar situations always evoke" identical images is a general, retrospective self-characterization that extends well beyond the sampling data. We will show that such a retrospective characterization should be viewed with substantially more skepticism than are the carefully elicited descriptions of particular samples.

Unfortunately, much of current psychological science rests on precisely the kind of retrospective characterization about which we are skeptical. For example, the diagnosis of obsessive-compulsive disorder requires determining whether the person has obsessions, "recurrent and persistent thoughts, impulses, or images that are experienced, at some time during the disturbance, as intrusive and inappropriate and that cause marked anxiety or distress" (American Psychiatric Association 2000: 462). Thus diagnosis requires determining the characteristics of the person's inner experience. Such determination is often done using clinical interviews, but there is substantial analysis showing the limitations of clinical interviews. The gold standard of psychological assessment of Obsessive-Compulsive Disorder, the Y-BOCS (the Yale-Brown Obsessive-Compulsive Scale, Goodman et al. 1989) uses questions such as:

"How much of your time is occupied by obsessive thoughts?" The interviewer must then score the answer based on the following scale:

0 = *None*
1 = *Less than 1hr/day or occasional occurrence*
2 = *1 to 3 hrs/day or frequent*
3 = *Greater than 3 and up to 8 hrs/day or very frequent occurrence*
4 = *Greater than 8 hrs/day or nearly constant occurrence.*

To give a truly veridical answer to this question, the patient would have had to have kept track of all his minutes during the day, logged those that were occupied by obsessive thoughts, and counted up those minutes. Clearly that is not what people do. Instead, they try to figure out the answer using some unspecifiable process. Such a process is doubtless substantially influenced by a variety of cognitive distortions and heuristics, so the answer to the question may have very little to do with the actual number of hours involved.

It is possible to retort that the Y-BOCS shouldn't be interpreted as really asking about inner experience: it is not the individual items on the Y-BOCS that are important but the sum of all the items on the test. That is, the value of the Y-BOCS lies in its validity, not in its accurate reporting about inner experience. That is entirely true, but it makes our point. As far as validity is concerned, it doesn't matter whether people answer such questions accurately; it matters only whether they answer such question in the same way as do other people who are thought to suffer from obsessions or compulsions. It follows that the proper interest of the Y-BOCS user is not in the inner experience of the respondent but only in his or her classification or diagnosis.

The distinction between *actual* inner experience and what one *thinks* inner experience is, in a nutshell, the theme of this book. It is possible to obtain accurate descriptions of inner experience if you use an adequate method and you avoid being seduced by similar-sounding but fundamentally different reports of inner experience. Furthermore, we propose that obtaining accurate descriptions of actual inner experience is of crucial importance to psychological science.

CHAPTER 2

Amy's inner experience

This book is about why inner experience is important and how to go about accessing it. Our concern in this chapter is not so much with the specifics of the DES method; they will be discussed in detail in later chapters. Instead, we wish to illustrate the "big picture" questions: whether inner experience can in fact be observed accurately and whether its observation is important. As a way of illustrating this, we tell the story of Amy (not her real name), a 22-year-old college student who had sought therapy from her university's psychological services center to help her deal with what she saw as a compulsion to lie – she couldn't stop herself from saying things that weren't true. She lied even about inconsequential things like what she had for lunch or whom she had seen at the library. She saw no motivation for the telling of these untruths and often didn't realize that they were falsehoods until corrected by someone who knew the facts under consideration. She worked hard at not lying, but lied "all the time" anyway. It's not that she tried to lie, or that she seemed to have a motivation to hide something; she "just lies." Even when she was in the act of trying to talk herself out of lying, arguing with herself about it, untrue words come out of her mouth.

Amy was also struggling with the question, "who am I?" Some friends had wondered whether Amy was bisexual, and Amy worried that they could be right. This worry was not self-generated – she didn't seem to have bisexual feelings or actions. But because her friends asked about her sexuality, she called her sexuality into question, as if she didn't have any independent way of confirming or disconfirming their claims. Amy was also worried about her identity in general. She said her mother did not know who her father (Amy's grandfather) was, so Amy didn't know what her own ethnicity was. Her own father was from Puerto Rico, so she was sure of being part Puerto Rican, but because she didn't know her mother's lineage, she didn't "know what to make of myself." Her behavior, as we observed it, confirmed this "who am I" bewilderment: she was tentative, nervous, almost mousy; she spoke softly and was often on the verge of tears.

Amy believed she lies "all the time" and worries about it obsessively, and her obsessive worry was documented by the Yale-Brown Obsessive Compulsive Scale (Y-BOCS), a scientifically validated and widely used test for Obsessive-Compulsive Disorder. These are statements about Amy's inner experience, and the question that this book is asking is, Are Amy's claims true? And what difference does it make?

One possibility is that Amy's claims are correct: she *actually does have* repetitive thoughts about lying. But another possibility is that she does *not* have such repetitive thoughts, but instead is more accurately characterized as being *afraid she is having* repetitive thoughts. We asked her about this distinction, and she just was not sure of what to make of it. She believed that she is a repetitive, compulsive liar, and she believed she worries about it all the time, but she diidn't trust her own self-characterizations. In general she was simply unsure about what is true and what is not true, even, or perhaps especially, about her own experience.

Amy's therapist referred Amy to our inner experience research project because he knew of our interest in Obsessive-Compulsive Disorder. We explained the DES procedure to Amy – that she would wear a beeper and when it beeped, she should pay attention to her experience that was ongoing at the moment of the beep, and take notes about it in the notebook we provided. That same day or the next day we would discuss the details of those experiences. Amy agreed to participate.

Sampling day 1

On the first sampling day, we discussed two samples. It was evident that the sampling procedure caused Amy some anxiety, that she had difficulty zeroing in on what was to be done, that she could not easily let the DES process "just happen." We discussed the first beep for nearly 30 minutes and were never clear about what had actually been ongoing in her experience. As best we could determine (but with little confidence), here is her experience that was ongoing at her first beep:

> Amy was sitting in her political science class, and she said that at the moment of the beep a stream of thoughts were ongoing: "What am I doing here [in the DES study]? What will it show for me? Will it shed good light or bad light?"

When a DES subject, as Amy did here, reports thoughts that are related to the sampling procedure, part of the DES procedure is to determine, if possible, whether these are ongoing thoughts "caught in flight" by the beeper, or whether the thought actually took place after the beep as a reflection on the process triggered by the beep. That is, DES tries to make a bright-line distinction between ongoing thoughts (that were ongoing in the last undisturbed moment before the beep; that would have been happening anyway even if the beeper had not beeped) and triggered-by-the-beep thoughts. We tried to make this distinction with Amy, but to little avail. She, and we, could not ascertain whether the "What am I doing here?" line of thinking was ongoing in the last undisturbed moment before the beep or was triggered by the beep.

This was the first sample on the first sampling day, and it is not uncommon for us to have to give some careful instruction to DES subjects about the distinction between ongoing thoughts and triggered thoughts. Most of those subjects, once we explain the distinction, say something like, "Oh, I understand now. I can't recall whether this particular thought was ongoing before the beep or was triggered by the beep, but I'll pay better attention next time."

But the situation seemed different for Amy. It was as if the distinction between ongoing-at-the-beep and triggered-by-the-beep was hard or impossible for her to grasp, despite our repeated attempts to clarify the distinction in various ways.

It is also standard DES practice to inquire about the characteristics of a thinking process. Amy reported that the "What am I doing here?" thoughts were represented in her own voice just as if she said them out loud, a phenomenon we call inner speech, but she was not convincing in that regard. It was difficult for us to be confident that she actually understood what "the characteristics of a thought" might mean.

It is unwise to make too much of the first sample or the entire first sampling day. We typically consider first sampling days as part of the DES training, and we discard any data that might appear on the first day. But it is noteworthy how difficult it was for Amy to be clear about her experience at this beep, or to express understanding of how she might improve for the next sampling attempt, despite our skillful efforts at helping her.

She was equally unclear in her description of the second beep, again despite our concerted efforts. We recapitulated the sampling instructions and the distinction between ongoing-in-the-last-undisturbed-moment-before-the-beep and triggered-by-the-beep, and encouraged her to "hang in there" on the possibility that the sampling process would become easier.

Sampling day 2

Here's the first sample from the second day:

> Amy reported that at the moment of the beep she is saying to herself, "Oh God, Amy, you have to get a job," and that the beep came while she was saying the word "God." She said that she was saying this to herself in an inner voice that was just like her own external voice, and described that voice's inflection. But as the exposition interview progressed, she also said that other words, like "C'mon, Amy," were expressed at the moment of the beep, and she also described this get-a-job thought as a more general thought process that did *not* involve words at all. And then she also said she was *seeing* some of the words that indicated that she needed to find a job. As a result of these inconsistencies, we never were confident about her ongoing experience at the beep.

Thus the discussion of this sample started out like a clear example of inner speech clearly apprehended and clearly described, and it seemed that our previous day's discussion of paying attention to experience had borne fruit. But as her description became more and more inconsistent, it became impossible to be confident that this description actually captured anything of her experience at the moment of the beep. She could not be pinned down, and we were left not knowing whether her ongoing experience was of spoken words (and if so, what those words were), seen words, or of no words at all.

In all of the beeps from this sampling day, there was never what we judged to be a sufficient comprehension of what we meant by the moment of the beep, as if Amy was unable to aim her reporting at some specific instant. Perhaps she still didn't understand the instructions; perhaps she didn't have an adequate focus. Throughout the 45 minute interview, we stressed, repeated, reiterated, gave examples of, answered questions about, and otherwise explained the important distinction between catching ongoing thoughts in flight and having the beep trigger thoughts, but we could not be confident of the effect of this instruction.

Sampling day 3

> Amy and her friends had just arrived at a park where they will have a potluck dinner. Amy is looking around the crowded park for a place to set up her stuff. She sees some picnic tables and swings – looks like a good

> place. Also she has heard the rest of her group opening the car trunk and getting out their stuff, and she knows that they are getting stuff ready.

This is a complicated scenario, and it's hard to be confident about exactly what was happening here at the moment of the beep. Certainly it is possible that all these things (the seeing of the tables/swings, the recognition of a good place, the hearing of the trunk opening, the knowing that they are getting ready) were being experienced simultaneously, but Amy could not convincingly say that she was aware of all of that or just one or two aspects at the moment of the beep. It was impossible to get her to focus on exactly what was happening at the moment of the beep.

We continued our effort to help Amy understand what we meant by the moment of the beep. For example, we snapped our fingers and momentarily later said "Beep!" and explained that the snap is what we mean by "the moment of the beep" – the last undisturbed moment before the beep arrives. Such an explanation typically is easily understood by others, and it seemed to make sense to her, but it did not make the sampling task much easier.

It is quite unusual for a DES subject to get to day 3 with as little clarity about the sampling task as Amy was showing. Could it be that Amy had relatively normal inner experience but that she simply didn't understand the sampling instructions? That might have seemed likely on the first sampling day, but it was now growing more and more implausible: we had explained the task in too many different ways, and Amy herself was too intelligent. Could it be that Amy would never be able to sample adequately? That seemed possible, even likely, given that we had made so little progress.

Sampling day 4

Here's the fourth sample from the fourth day:

> Amy is reading. She's in the middle of paragraph: "In [beep] adopting the constitution...." She said she was speaking the words to herself in her own voice while reading the words. She said she was also concerned with the time, wondering how late it is, whether she has time to get to class, and thinking that she should look at her watch when she has finished reading this paragraph. This was described as being a "jumble" of simultaneous thoughts, but Amy wasn't confident about this – it might be just one thought with several aspects.

Amy understood that we wished her to be careful to identify the exact moment of the beep, and she did so by saying that the beep came just before the word "adopting." However, this report of the beep was given with little apparent confidence, and she was equally unconfident about the rest of her "jumble" of thoughts, so there was still little reason for us to be confident that the description adequately characterized Amy's experience. Despite four days of concerted efforts, describing a moment continued to be difficult for Amy. At the conclusion of the day's sampling she did say that the sampling task was getting easier for her, but we were still not convinced that she had actually grasped the time-triggered nature of sampling.

Sampling day 5

The fifth sampling day was apparently a breakthrough for Amy. For the first time, she seemed to be confidently discerning at what moment the beep actually took place. Her reports were much more definite and non-contradictory.

Furthermore, her reports were now mostly about feelings. Until this time, reports had been mostly about thoughts. Feelings, if they occurred at all, were only hinted at or reported tentatively. However, on sampling day 5 feelings were prominent and clear.

Here are a few samples from day 5. Notice their relative clarity and emotion-focus:

1. Amy and her roommate are watching TV. Their dog walks by and gives Amy a "weird" look. Amy wonders what the dog is thinking – whether he blames her, whether he likes her roommate better than Amy (Amy does the punishment), whether he feels upset towards her. She's looking at the dog, noticing his look. [Amy seems relatively confident about this.]
2. Amy is studying in the living room with her roommate, who is helping her. Amy has read a sample problem and its multiple-choice answers, and is now confused, frustrated because the answers seem all the same. This frustration is felt as pressure in her fingers. She is taking a deep, labored breath. She is also noting that her roommate is getting frustrated with her – her voice is becoming higher pitched and stronger, as if she's nagging, "Aw c'mon, Amy!" but there are no words. [Notice the clear apprehension of bodily sensations (fingers, breathing), a first for Amy.]

3. Amy is watching *Matlock* on TV – a murder scene. Her roommate had commented about what is likely to happen next. Amy had nodded in agreement, but she's thinking that it could be different from the roommate's prediction. That thinking was, however, before the beep. At the moment of the beep, she is just watching the show. [Note the clear distinction between what was before the beep and what was at the moment of the beep, a first for Amy.]
4. Amy's roommate had asked her about the beeper procedure. At the moment of the beep Amy is feeling an overwhelmingly happy, joyous feeling because the roommate is interested in Amy. At the moment of the beep Amy is talking, telling her about sampling interviews, and those words are clear and under her control. Amy doesn't know precisely what those words are because she's "riding the strong feelings" and didn't stop immediately to write down the words. It is hard for Amy to describe the bodily involvement, if any, of the feelings, even though the feelings themselves are strongly felt. [Note the clear feelings; as we shall see, it is not particularly unusual for DES subjects to have difficulty describing the bodily characteristics of feelings.]

On her fifth sampling day, Amy was beginning to sound like most subjects do on their second day. For the first time she was able to recognize when the beep occurred, and was able to describe the ongoing phenomena. That change might have been because she had simply finally understood our questions, but we think that is unlikely for the reasons we stated at day 3. Therefore we believe either that she had finally begun to have experience (that is, that experience had been initially nonexistent); or that she had finally begun to acquire the skill of observing her experience (and that that skill acquisition took longer for Amy than for other subjects); or that her inner experience itself had undergone some transformation so that it was now easier to report; or that she had finally learned how to report experience that had always itself been clear. Any of those alternatives (except the last one for reasons that we have discussed) seemed plausible.

A skeptic might advance a fifth alternative: that Amy had merely given in to our pressure to sound clear. That is of course possible, but we think unlikely. First, there's no reason to believe that Amy would know how to sound clear. Our questions are quite detailed, and it would take substantial skill to be able to guess what the right answers would be if she didn't herself have access to clear experience. Second, the abrupt shift to the report of feelings would be surprising if someone were simply now attempting to sound clear but all else had stayed the same.

Sampling day 6

Coincident with Amy's increased sampling clarity as we saw in day 5, Amy's life outside of sampling was now changing quite dramatically. At the beginning of our interview about the samples from day 6 she reported that her relationship with her roommate has become far better than it ever had been, but that her relationship with her mother seemed to have worsened dramatically: Amy had always been quite compliant, but now found herself confronting her mother about problematic issues. Perhaps coincidentally, one of the major confrontations with her mother took place while Amy had been wearing the beeper. Here are some samples:

1. Amy is in the midst of the confrontation with her mom, who had left the room to get a drink of water. During the confrontation, Amy's mother had told Amy about two things that are still "sticking in Amy's mind": that Amy's dad had cried when Amy left for school; and that Amy's dad had seen his brother Marc (Amy's uncle) and Marc's daughter Frances showing some affection to each other, and Amy's dad realized that he had not done that with Amy. At the moment of the beep Amy is seeing an image of her dad looking at Marc with Frances sitting on his lap. This image is seen clearly and was described clearly: Marc is facing to the right, Frances is also facing right but not as much, and is wearing a blue shirt, and so on. Amy is also feeling a very strong sadness, experienced as a heaviness in her heart pushing down and inward (perpendicular to her body). She's also aware of tears coming. [She's trying to resist the tears, but that is not in her awareness at the moment of the beep.] The image is just about ending and the feelings are coming on strong. [Note that this is Amy's first sample that includes an image, and note also the clarity and power of the image. Also, Amy describes her feelings in much clearer physical detail than they were in day 5. Note also the confidence that Amy has in discriminating between events in her awareness (tears coming, for example) and events in her body but not in her awareness (resisting the tears). This is a substantial increase in clarity of report for Amy, even over day 5 but dramatically so over the earlier samplings.]
2. Amy is still talking with her mom, who is now more calm. Amy is watching her mom's expression as it is changing from calm to sad (tears etc.). That's all that's happening at the moment of the beep: Amy is watching her mom's expression. Amy herself will also become sad as a result, and her mom will become angry at Amy and herself,

but those events are after the beep. [Note the confident clarity with which Amy reports the temporal sequence.]

3. The beep comes 20–25 minutes after the end of Amy's talk with her mother. Amy is in her room by herself, and she feels good – at ease with herself – like a weight has been lifted off her shoulders. The center of awareness is in her shoulders but extends throughout her body where the weight had been (but is no longer) crushing down from her shoulders throughout her body. She feels like she can do anything.
4. Amy's mom stayed in Amy's apartment overnight. Amy is now in bed, lights off, and at the moment of the beep she's reflecting/rejoicing in the comfortableness. She feels comfortable in her body, and simultaneously she is liking that feeling. The feeling of comfort is the same as in the previous beep except a little bit stronger, and now includes the feeling of rejoicing in it.

At the end of this session, we commented to Amy that she seemed much clearer than we had ever seen her. She said she herself feels clearer, both in the sampling task and in general. Furthermore, she feels better about herself and her life situation.

We noted her gutsy decision to wear the beeper during the confrontation with mother, and expressed our appreciation for sharing those moments with us. We also recalled that she had told us at the beginning of the session that her relationship with her mother had *worsened*, and yet the samples evidenced a decided *improvement* in her relationship. Yes, they had been angry and sad, but also they had been comfortable. Faced with the evidence of her own beeps, Amy easily agreed; her relationship with her mother *was* much improved.

A discrepancy between a general report (e.g. my relationship with my mother has worsened) and the actual sampled experiences (improved experience of relationship) is not at all uncommon in DES, and we do not attribute that to Amy's characteristic lying. Instead, as we shall see repeatedly in this book, people's general beliefs about themselves and their situations are *often* untrue.

This example gives some insight into why general beliefs can be false. Certainly Amy's recent relationship with her mother had been confrontational, and Amy certainly had the general belief that confrontations were bad. On that logic, her general belief that the relationship with her mother was worse makes sense. But that logic singles out only one characteristic of the relationship (the confrontation) and ignores the other contrary and compelling evidence (the comfortableness). In Amy's own judgment, the actual comfortableness with her mother far outweighed the confrontation, and yet her general belief had apparently followed primarily from the confrontation.

Sampling day 7

Amy's experience during her samples continues to be clear.

1. Amy is watching the TV movie *Sixth Sense*. Her roommate always wants to know when a scary part is coming, and Amy had just warned her about an upcoming scene. At the moment of the beep Amy is just watching the movie, seeing her roommate out of the corner of her eye with blanket pulled up to her eyes. Amy is not sure whether she is seeing her roommate at the exact moment of the beep, or maybe her focus has just left her roommate. She has some kind of knowing that the roommate will pull the blanket up further if it gets scarier. [The inability to be sure about where the focus was at the exact moment of the beep is quite different from Amy's earlier unclarity. Now, the beep occurs during a rapidly changing situation, and Amy could not be sure precisely where the beep occurred. This is more the sign of an accurate observer being careful not to over-specify than of a person who cannot fathom the task.]
2. Amy's Mom had telephoned. The call was over, and Amy now feels bad that she didn't go to see her Mom on her last day before she returned home to Puerto Rico. This feeling is experienced as a heaviness in her chest. Amy is in the midst of replaying in images a series of conversations they had had, one after the other, and at the moment of the beep she's seeing the image of their first conversation, viewed from across the room. The image was an accurate portrayal of the scene as it had happened, viewed from a perspective external to Amy: Amy herself is to the right, Mom to the left, and her roommate in the center.
3. Amy is still watching the movie. She's wondering whether there are really people who are similar to the one being portrayed in the movie, and she says out loud, "Do you think there could be anyone who is similar to this boy?" The thinking and the saying seem to be separate processes.
4. Amy is now in the library computer lab working on her homework. Prior to the beep, people's cell phones had been ringing frequently, and that had disturbed her, but then subsided. Now, again! the cell

phone from the guy behind her rings and he doesn't answer it. At the moment of the beep irritation is flaring up in her – hotness in her body, fingertips tingling, sweaty palms. She feels like her body turns and picks up the phone and throws it away – like she's separated from her body. It doesn't really do that, of course, and she knows it, but she is imagining her body going through that motion.

5. She is still at the computer lab. She has typed some words, but at the moment of the beep the words on the screen have lost their meaning – "they might as well be Greek." She is seeing the words but she doesn't know what they mean. She's in suspended animation – as if she's waiting for the meaning to appear. A small part of her knows that she is confused.

Amy's samples continued to be quite clear, and they continued to be populated by bodily sensations and feelings. Amy reported that it seemed to be the experiences themselves that had become clear. That is, Amy herself recognized the improvement in clarity, and observed that the change seemed to be in her experience itself rather than in her way of apprehending it.

Amy reported that outside of sampling she was much improved. She still lied sometimes, but the difference was that now she knew when she was lying. She would discover halfway into her speaking that what she was saying was not true. Sometimes it was too late to correct it, but now at least she knew that it was a lie. In previous times, she would often not have known that she had lied until her roommate or someone in a position to know reported to her later that there had been a discrepancy.

Overall, she reported that her life was much better, specifically that her relationships with her roommate and her mother were much improved. She attributed these improvements to her therapy and her conversations with her roommate and mother.

Our original research contract had been to sample for as many sessions as were needed to get a sense of what Amy's experience was like, and it seemed that we had reached that goal. We therefore began the necessary termination arrangements. However, Amy did not want to stop sampling. She recognized it as having been good for her to examine carefully what was really happening with her, and was reluctant to discontinue what had become important to her. We agreed to sample with her at least one more time the following week.

Sampling day 8

Amy reported that her life situations have continued to get better. Her communication with her friends and mother were much easier. She was more open, and she found it easier to talk about little things that happened.

1. Amy is at the computer lab doing homework. The lab assistant is nagging her, doing silly things. Amy has just pushed her keyboard away and has put her head in her hands, and is now saying innerly to herself, "He's irritating me! He's irritating me!" over and over. This inner speech is in her own voice, and the "He's" is accented. She's also feeling irritated, a tingling burning in her fingers, as if they wanted to flex but couldn't.
2. Amy is talking about buttons with a friend and the lab assistant. The lab assistant is saying to her friend that both she and Amy have an accent (both are Puerto Rican) when they say the word "button." At the moment of the beep Amy is innerly saying to herself, "Button, button, button" over and over, and wondering what portion of her speaking, which seems entirely natural to her, has an accent. She's also feeling a bit quizzical.
3. Amy has gotten hungry and gone to a vending machine. She had taken a dollar bill out of her pocket and ripped the bill. At the moment of the beep she's thinking that this is too much, that she's having a bad day, but at the same time that it's not that bad. This thinking is not in words, but is clearly thought. She's also feeling a little overwhelmed.
4. Amy is working in computer lab, and her friend had just let out big sigh and cursed. Amy had asked what's wrong, and she had said it's about her paper. Amy is now feeling happy that it's not about her.

This last beep gave us some insight into Amy's honesty issues. When Amy first described this beep, she said that at the moment of the beep her attention had been split between (a) her own happiness at not being the target of her friend's curse; and (b) sadness for her friend's difficulty with the paper. But the sampling interview revealed that in actuality she was *not* sad for her friend at that moment, she was just happy/relieved for herself. The sadness was an abstraction – the way she *should* feel – whereas the happiness was a concrete, real experience. Prior to sampling, it seemed that Amy didn't have access to her own experience (or didn't have experience at all), and therefore didn't have the ability to distinguish between an abstract possibility and a concrete reality. Now she was acquiring that skill.

Amy seemed to be confident in her newly won skill, and now did not feel the need to continue sampling and so we said goodbye.

Questions and answers

Q: What do you think changed for Amy?

A: It seems there are four possibilities. (1) Nothing changed except her reports; (2) her skill at engaging in the sampling task improved, whereas everything else stayed the same; (3) her access to her inner experience improved; and (4) her inner experience itself changed. We'll discuss each.

It seems that if either (1) or (2) is correct, then we are hard pressed to explain (except as coincidence) the bona fide improvement in her life situation. It seemed that something had fundamentally changed with Amy herself, not merely with her ability to perform the sampling task.

We will not be able to decide between options (3) and (4) at this point. Option (3) implies that Amy had clear inner experience both before and after sampling, as if the "inner movie is playing" but Amy couldn't see it clearly prior to sampling but that during the sampling period she somehow gained access to that already clear experience. Option (4) implies that Amy's experience itself went from unclear (or perhaps nonexistent) to clear during the sampling period. On the basis of our DES experience, we favor option (4), that Amy, prior to the sampling period, simply didn't create, much less observe, clear inner experiences. It is indeed possible to navigate through the world without entertaining specific thoughts, experiencing specific feelings, and so on.

We freely acknowledge that we cannot authoritatively say which of these options actually occurred for Amy. However, there can be little doubt that *some* fundamental change occurred in Amy's experience: she went from not having access to clear experience to having it.

Q: At the outset did Amy know she had unclear (or no) experience?

A: No. She had no way of knowing the difference between clarity and unclarity until she experienced clarity for herself. She used the same words as other people ("thinking," "feeling," etc.) and assumed that others meant the same thing that she did.

Q: What caused this change?

A: This is a case study, so we cannot answer this question with assurance. Amy's opinion was that the change was due to her confrontational/supportive/informational conversations with her roommate and mother, and due to her psychotherapy. Certainly those conversations could have led to Amy's gaining confidence in general, which could have led to her gaining confidence in her ability to apprehend her inner experience.

An alternative attribution (which we did not discuss with Amy) is that the DES procedure's probing for the details of her experience served as a "calisthenic" for clarity, and as a result Amy began to be able to apprehend her own experience, and as sampling continued she experienced an increase in clarity of experience that allowed Amy to become a much more accurate observer of herself and others, and that increase in accuracy of observation allowed her to engage in the confrontational/supportive/informational conversations effectively.

In any case study, chance or maturation might have been the important factor: Amy's experience may have been destined to clarify itself at that point in time regardless of the sampling procedure or the conversations.

There is no way of determining which explanation is correct – perhaps both played a part. But whether by cause, effect, or by chance, the sampling process did allow us to see in some detail the relationship between clarity and mental health, at least in this single case.

Q: Please clarify why you think clarity of inner experience is related to Amy's truthfulness.

A: We think (and this is the point of this book) that truth fundamentally inheres only in particular moments. It is possible to have general understandings, but for those general understandings to be true and understandable, they should be real generalizations from a series of particular moments. At the outset, Amy apparently was not clear about what was going on with her at any particular moments; this made it impossible for her to be confident about her general characteristics.

Recall that Amy's friends asked if she was bisexual, and that worried Amy – were they right? The way a healthy person answers such questions is to observe a long series of actually occurring, concrete moments, noticing the feelings/sensations that occur. After a sufficiently long sequence of accurate observations, it is possible to advance a real generalization: I either do or do not have frequent bisexual thoughts or fantasies. Amy couldn't perform such a real generalization because she apparently didn't have access to the basic data on which to build the generalization.

Amy's lies were not just about general characteristics – they were about specific events such as what she had for lunch. It may be that healthy people recall what they had for lunch by trying in some way to reconstruct lunch – perhaps a visual image, perhaps a recreated taste sensation, perhaps a recreated kinesthetic sense of preparation, and so on. It is our impression that Amy had no such direct experiences (no images, no direct, much less recreated, taste experiences, and so on), or if she had such experiences, she didn't have clear access to them. Therefore she was always at risk for saying things that weren't true.

Furthermore, healthy people can check the truth of what they are saying against the experiences they are having while saying it: when something is exaggerated, minimized, or otherwise misrepresented (purposefully or not), it "doesn't feel right," giving people who are motivated to convey themselves accurately real-time information that can then be used to refine or correct the ongoing utterance. Amy apparently didn't have access to experience, much less real-time "doesn't feel right" experience at the beginning of sampling, and acquired that skill (somewhat slowly) as sampling progressed.

It's only in the moment that you can know what's actually happening with you. And if you don't know what's happening with you, you simply are unable to be honest or dishonest about it. For whatever reason, Amy had lost (or never acquired) that ability to be honest with herself – lost what was happening at the moment – even lost what a moment itself really was. And as a result, she became estranged from the only place where she could find the real truth about herself.

Q: Do you think unclarity of inner experience is a characteristic of all Obsessive-Compulsive people?

A: Not all. We have sampled with *some* other Obsessive-Compulsive individuals who show this characteristic inability to apprehend inner experience. But we have also sampled with Obsessive-Compulsive individuals who don't. Apparently there are at least two different kinds of obsessive-compulsive individuals.

A look ahead

Certainly it is unwise to expect too much from a single case study, so we're not expecting the reader to be convinced of anything at this point. We have the remainder of the book to be persuasive. We, however, have been making such observations for 30 years, and we feel entitled to our opinion that Amy's experience did change dramatically over the course of her sampling. Let's for the moment assume that that opinion is true (readers can judge for themselves in 200 pages). So what?

First, Amy's example shows that inner experience is fundamentally important to individuals. Without clear inner experience, Amy was adrift, tentative, and withdrawn, literally unable to tell the difference between true and false statements about herself, and nebulously sad. When her experiences clarified, she became stronger, more direct and even constructively confrontational, much more animated, and happier. We do not underestimate the importance of her psychotherapy and her conversations with her friends and mother, which Amy herself found important. But how did those therapeutic and personal interactions have their effect on Amy? We think they contributed to the clarification of Amy's inner experience, which then contributed to her improvement. Second, Amy's case shows that it is in fact possible to observe inner experience accurately, despite a century of opinion to the contrary. At the same time, Amy's case shows that inquiring about another person's inner experience is not trivially easy. For example, what would Amy have said if someone had asked her, prior to sampling, whether she had clear experience? She probably would have said, "Of course!" or "I think so," not because she meant to misrepresent, but because she didn't really know what the question referred to – she had nothing to compare. So whereas is it *possible* to observe inner experience accurately, it is *not* trivially easy. We will make that point in much more detail in the next chapter, but here we note that, as far as we know, Western psychological science has no other observational method that is sensitive enough to have discovered Amy's lack of clear inner experience.

Third, Amy's case shows that the accurate exploration of inner experience has substantial ramifications for psychological science. For example, as we discussed in the previous chapter, intrinsic to the definition/diagnosis of Obsessive-Compulsive Disorder is a characterization of inner experience as having repetitive, unwanted thoughts. Amy's case shows that there are probably at least two distinctly different kinds of people who get the Obsessive-Compulsive Disorder diagnosis: those who actually have repetitive, unwanted thoughts, and those who, like Amy, have no clear thoughts at all. And it shows that it is likely that methods do exist (such as DES) that can make valid discriminations between those two kinds of people. But for reasons that will become clear in this book, psychological science has eschewed the careful examination of inner experience and is therefore blind to such distinctions. This book will show that that blindness is unnecessary because it is possible to explore inner experience with accuracy.

Fourth, we wish to observe that the important feature of Amy's inner experience was *not its content* but its nature. It was *not* that Amy changed *what* she thought *about*; it was that Amy changed *how* she thought/felt/sensed. This is a radical point of view from the standpoint of modern psychology, which, to the extent that it focuses on thinking at all, is focused primarily on the content of thought. Even those features of cognitive therapy first advanced by Beck, such as overgeneralization and selective abstraction, refer to distortions of content. Based on our years of sampling, we have found that the *how* of experience is more important than the *about what*.

CHAPTER 3

Telling what we know

Describing inner experience

At the moment of the beep, Mort was working at his computer. The TV news was on in the background, and at the moment of the beep Mort was hearing Tom Brokaw say "…cancer." The word "cancer" seemed like it was at the end of a sentence, but Mort was not sure of the words leading up to it. That is, Mort heard Brokaw saying "da da da da da da da cancer," but Mort didn't know what the "da da da da" words were.

As he stopped to jot down what was happening at the beep, he realized that the word that was actually being said on the TV was not "cancer" but "canvas," and he realized that the speaker was not Tom Brokaw but Dan Rather. But those realizations came not at the actual moment of the experience, but only when brought up short by the beep's demand to respond. Also as part of the response to the beep, Mort saw his mistaking "canvas" for "cancer" and Dan for Tom as weird, bizarre.

At the moment of the beep, however, there was nothing weird or bizarre or incorrect. Mort was in fact simply hearing Tom Brokaw say "da da da da da da da cancer," nothing more, nothing less. The "canvasness" and the "Ratherness" of the experience simply didn't exist at the moment it was being experienced. It was *not* part of his awareness that he was mistaken. He was in fact mistaken, but had the beep not occurred, he probably would never have realized that.

This is a simple example, but it is instructive because this kind of mistake is not an uncommon occurrence. We think this kind of occurrence is vitally important in understanding human events. It is a commonplace to explain differences of opinion as being differences in interpretation of events, as if one person bends an interpretation one way and the other person bends it the other, and as a result they fail to communicate. This example shows that the problem can be much deeper, much more fundamental than mere difference in interpretation. Mort didn't misinterpret what he was hearing, *he got it wrong in the first place.*

People very frequently get it wrong, *and when they are in the process of getting it wrong, they have no awareness of the wrongness of their getting.*

Our society makes very little attempt to train its citizens in the skill of creating inner experiences that reflect actual occurrences. Other societies take great pains – Eastern meditational traditions, for example, whose core is the practicing of seeing the world without distortion. Our society does essentially nothing. For generations, it has nearly completely ignored the *existence* of inner experience, much less how one might go about training it to be congruent with reality.

We now turn our attention to beginning to answer the question, *Why doesn't psychology do a better job of exploring inner experience?*[1] At least part of that reason is that there is a chasm in psychological science, and people on both sides of this chasm lead you away from caring about inner experience. On one side are those who think that describing inner experience is essentially impossible and unnecessary – methodological behaviorism, for example. On the other side are those who think that describing inner experience is trivially easy and vitally important – cognitive psychotherapy, for example, which rests on the question "What were you thinking when . . .?" Although both positions contain an element of truth, neither leads directly to a thoughtful approach to understanding inner experience. In this chapter we reconsider these positions and show that for each it is possible to separate the kernel of truth from the chaff of overgeneralization and thereby to bridge the chasm. We argue that it is possible, but not trivially easy, to understand inner experience, and that doing so will advance cognitive science.

To examine this opinion more fully, we first consider three positions that hold that exploring inner experience is impossible. For each position, we show that although the essential criticism is fully justified, the criticism serves as a guide towards an adequate method of exploring inner experience rather than a categorical dismissal of such methods. We then cross to the other side of the chasm and consider positions, such as that of cognitive therapy, which holds that exploring inner experience is trivially easy – you just ask. Again we show that the core of that position is also fully justified even though the assumption of methodological ease is erroneous.

"Nisbett and Wilson said it couldn't be done"

The first position that holds that exploring inner experience is impossible is attributed to Nisbett and Wilson, whose 1977 review examined studies in which participants gave causal attributions for their behavior. Nisbett and Wilson observed that participants often said that their behavior was caused by mental events when in fact their behavior was the result of external manipulation. Nisbett and Wilson's conclusions were scathing and were very broadly written – overly so, in our opinion. For example, they wrote, "The accuracy of subjective reports is so poor as to suggest than any introspective access that may exist is not sufficient to produce generally correct or reliable reports" (Nisbett & Wilson 1977:233). Critics of introspective-like methods have rallied around the Nisbett and Wilson article, often taking it to be an unconditional refutation of introspection in general, not merely of the attribution of causation.

However, it does not seem to be widely known that even Nisbett and Wilson recognized the possibility of accurate reports about inner experience:

> We also wish to acknowledge that the studies do not suffice to show that people *could never* be accurate about the processes involved. To do so would require ecologically meaningless but theoretically interesting procedures such as interrupting a process at the very moment it was occurring, alerting subjects to pay careful attention to their cognitive processes, coaching them in introspective procedures, and so on. (Nisbett & Wilson 1977:246, italics in original)

Nisbett and Wilson's "theoretically interesting procedure" is essentially a description of DES. Our opinion is therefore that Nisbett and Wilson were basically correct when they observed that people are often (or usually) substantially mistaken about inner experience. However, that position is often overgeneralized to imply that *all* people are *always* substantially mistaken about inner experience when in fact Nisbett and Wilson themselves had explicitly acknowledged that DES-type investigations might produce accurate reports. Thus Nisbett and Wilson should be understood as contributing to knowledge about how to explore inner experience, namely that one adequate way might be to interrupt a process at the very moment it was occurring, to alert subjects to pay careful attention to their cognitive processes, and to coach them in introspective procedures.

"Introspectionists can't agree"

As we touched on in Chapter 1, others have held that introspection is futile based on the well-known dispute between German introspectionists (mostly in Würzburg) and American introspectionists (mainly E. B. Titchener at Cornell) about the existence of "imageless thought" a century ago. Titchener held the sensationalist view that thinking without images is impossible: every "experience has an elemental core and a meaning providing context. Perceptions have sensory cores and ideas have imaginal cores" (Wertheimer 1987: 111). However, the Würzburg introspectionists observed that some ideas had apparently no imaginal characteristics. They therefore concluded that they had discovered a new class of thinking, contrary to sensationalism, that they labeled imageless thought. Titchener disagreed, maintaining that imaginal cores always exist for all ideas even though these imaginal cores are sometimes dim and difficult to apprehend.

After 20 years of introspective research designed to settle the controversy over whether imageless thought exists, neither side could claim unequivocal victory. This failure to agree about so fundamental an issue discredited introspection and was one of the reasons for a demise so complete that the term "introspection" rarely occurs in modern textbooks of psychology or psychological method except as a historical reference to its use during the earliest days of psychology (Danziger 1980; Vermersch 1999).

However, Monson and Hurlburt (1993) reviewed the Würzburg and Cornell results and showed that the two factions "*did in fact agree with each other's reports of the phenomenon which was called imageless thought*" (p. 20, italics in original). Subjects in both the Würzburg and the Cornell laboratories reported identical observations, namely the existence of "vague and elusive processes, which carry as if in a nutshell the entire meaning of a situation..., such as 'a realization that the division can be carried out without a remainder'" (Titchener 1910/1980: 505–506). From the Würzburgers' theoretical perspective, these "vague and elusive processes" were imageless thoughts; from Titchener's theoretical perspective, they were not.

Thus Monson and Hurlburt showed that as long as the two sides remained at the level of description, they were in perfect agreement: "vague and elusive processes which carry ... meaning" exist. But when the two sides gave their theoretical interpretations of those observations, they differed dramatically. Therefore the imageless-thought debate should be understood as contributing to knowledge about how to explore inner experience: Psychological science should discriminate strictly between the description of inner phenomena and the use of those descriptions in psychological theorizing.

"Skinner said that inner experience is impossible to examine"

The final position we consider that holds that exploring inner experience is impossible follows from a pervasive but incorrect belief that Skinner held private events to be nonexistent or unimportant. Actually, Skinner quite explicitly denied that position:

> The statement that behaviorists deny the existence of feelings, sensations, ideas, and other features of mental life needs a good deal of clarification. Methodological [non-Skinnerian] behaviorism and some versions of logical positivism ruled private events out of bounds because there could be no public agreement about their validity. Introspection could not be accepted as a scientific practice, and the psychology of people like Wilhelm Wundt and Edward B. Titchener was attacked accordingly. Radical [Skinnerian] behaviorism, however, takes a different line. It does not deny the possibility of self-observation or self-knowledge or its possible usefulness. (Skinner 1974: 16)

In fact, Skinner believed that private events have the same essential nature as public events:

> We need not suppose that events which take place within an organism's skin have special properties.... A private event may be distinguished by its limited accessibility but not, so far as we know, by any special structure or nature. We have no reason to suppose that the stimulating effect of an inflamed tooth is essentially different from that of, say, a hot stove. (Skinner 1953: 257–258)

However, Skinner did identify three main limitations on the scientific use of private events: (1) that verbal behavior about private events may be impoverished because it is difficult for the verbal community to shape a person's speech about inner experience; (2) that it is impossible for a person to have access to his or her thinking in its entirety; and (3) that it is a mistake to give causal significance to mentalistic events. All three criticisms are entirely justified, but the first is most important for our purposes.

According to Skinner, a main difference between private events (like toothaches or thoughts) and public events (like hot stoves) is that the community of speakers has more control over the speech about public events:

> The verbal response "red" is established as a discriminative operant by a community which reinforces the response when it is made in the presence of red stimuli and not otherwise. This can easily be done if the community and the individual both have access to red stimuli. It cannot be done if either the individual *or the community* is color-blind. The latter case resembles that in which a verbal response is based upon a private event, where, by definition, common access by both parties is impossible. How does the community present

> or withhold reinforcement appropriately in order to bring such a response as "My tooth aches" under the control of appropriate stimulation?
> (Skinner 1953 258–259, italics in original)

If a community wishes to develop a differentiated usage of the talk "*I see red*," it can give a series of trials in which it presents external objects that are variously rose, auburn, russet, rusty, carnation, strawberry, cerise, and carmine, appropriately reinforcing or punishing talk about each specific variation of red. Thus the community can shape "*I see red*" with great precision and thus can reliably differentiate such statements as "*I see auburn*" from "*I see cerise.*" However, if the community wishes to develop a differentiated usage of the talk "*I am depressed*," it *cannot* present a series of internal states that are variously melancholic, downcast, downhearted, droopy, low, blue, bummed out, and down. It therefore cannot directly reinforce or punish talk about such states. It is forced to rely on public accompaniments of private events, such as withdrawal, failure to eat, or crying, to shape statements about the private events themselves. Even though such public accompaniments may in fact be correlated with depression, those correlations are far from perfect. Therefore talk about the experience of depression receives only impoverished differential reinforcement and is *not* likely to have the same precision as talk about external events.

Differential reinforcement

Skinner's claim that private events receive impoverished differential reinforcement is exemplified with particular clarity in our own DES research. With striking regularity, subjects early in their DES participation refer to their own inner experience as "thinking," saying things like, "*At the moment of the beep I was thinking that I don't want to take that exam.*" The DES procedure carefully examines the details of such experiences. In fact, there is substantial variability from person to person in what is intended by the phrase "*I was thinking. . . .*" For example, when Alice says "*I was thinking. . .*" she means that she was saying something to herself, in her own naturally inflected inner voice. When Betty says "*I was thinking. . .* " she means that she was seeing a visual image of something. When Carol says "*I was thinking. . .* " she means that she was feeling a sensation in her heart or stomach, and that she had no awareness of cognition whatsoever. Over the course of the DES training, subjects learn to differentiate the talk about such experiences, but until that time, the verbal community simply has not differentiated the term "thinking" much beyond the fact that it pertains to a private event.

> We speculate that there is a developmental reason for "thinking" to have such widely disparate meanings. We think it likely that as children acquire language, they hear their elders say, "I'm thinking..." referring to something inside the elder. Children, of course, have no way of knowing what that inner something might be. When they themselves begin to use the phrase "I'm thinking..." they refer to something inside themselves, and that something is likely to be whatever they frequently experience as ongoing. Thus children differentiate their use of "I'm thinking..." within their own experience, and that differentiation is never corrected because the elders don't know what the children are experiencing. That of course is precisely Skinner's point.

From this discussion, we suggest that Skinner should be understood as contributing to knowledge about how to explore inner experience: we should limit ourselves to talk that has been adequately differentiated. Thus a major aspect of DES training involves teaching subjects to differentiate their inner experiences adequately and to communicate accurately about those experiences. Once subjects are trained in DES, they can report, for example, whether or not at any particular moment they were engaging in inner speech, precisely what words were being spoken at that moment, and the perceptual characteristics of that speech. That communication about inner experience can then be shaped with the same level of precision as the communication about what you see at Buckingham Palace. However, it is far more difficult, if not impossible, to shape adequately such sentences as "*I am sad all the time*," an item from the most widely used depression inventory. Sampling frequently shows that individuals who endorse that item are sad at fewer than half their sampled moments. It is thus simply wrong to believe that endorsement of that item should be understood as a description of inner experience. If we want to know whether someone is sad all the time, there is no substitute for collecting a large number of random samples and inquiring whether sadness is present at each sample.

"Accessing inner experience is easy – just ask"

We now turn to the other side of the chasm, the position that holds that exploring inner experience is easy. Cognitive therapy is based on the premise that people can give adequate answers to questions such as, "*What were you thinking when you...?*" or "*How do you feel when you...?*"

DES demonstrates that the assumption that people know the characteristics of their inner experience is usually, to at least some degree, untrue and often dramatically untrue. Remember the example of Donald from the first chapter. Even though Donald was well aware of his angry thoughts toward his children when they were caught by the beep, he later was surprised by how frequently he was angry with his children even though he had written vivid descriptions of the angry moments! And Amy began sampling with the seeming inability to describe her inner experience at all and only after substantial practice was she able to capture moments of her inner experience. Hurlburt (1993, 1997; see Chapter 11) also used DES with Fran, a woman suffering from borderline personality disorder, and discovered that she nearly always experienced multiple visual images, usually with extremely negative content. Before sampling, Fran had no knowledge of the multiplicity of her visual awareness or its consistent negativity despite the ubiquity of both characteristics.

Most DES subjects, whether diagnosed with a disorder or not, are surprised by some aspect of their sampling results. Thus the cognitive therapy perspective exaggerates the ease of obtaining accurate inner reports. Nonetheless, it rests on the essentially true foundation that inner experience is important, and thus provides impetus for the study of inner experience.

Conclusion

We have considered three anti-introspection criticisms and shown that each involves an overgeneralization that has been overlooked in the history of psychological science. We have then refocused each position, showing that each provides valuable guidelines regarding how to gain access to inner experience. We concluded that the exploration of inner experience is neither impossible nor trivially easy, and that the three positions serve as valuable guides between those two extremes.

Explorations of inner experience have the potential to inform cognitive science broadly defined. For example, DES research has found that some individuals have predominately visual images with no verbal content; others have frequent inner speech with no visual imagery. Others usually experience cognition that contains neither images nor words, and still others have inner experience that almost never includes any form of conscious cognition at all. It is plausible that these kinds of individual differences will be related to many processes of interest to cognitive scientists – memory and reasoning, for example.

The DES method is clearly not the only avenue available for accurately exploring inner experience. For example, truly adept meditators in the Eastern tradition without doubt have a deeper and more accurate view of their experience than many nonmeditators. However, the DES examples do establish, in our opinion, that most ordinary people can, with some training, accurately observe and report the features of their experience. Furthermore, the results of such explorations can be dramatically productive for cognitive science. It is our opinion that science should do more of them.

Note

1. The remainder of this chapter is an edited version of Hurlburt, R. T., & Heavey, C. L. (2001). Telling what we know: Describing inner experience. *Trends in Cognitive Science 5*, 400–403. Revised with permission.

CHAPTER 4

Psychological science's prescription for accurate reports about inner experience

with Todd Seibert

Another vantage point from which to consider the issue of exploring inner experience is that of psychological science in general. In other words, what guidance can we draw from the accumulated body of psychological knowledge to help us gain accurate reports of inner experience? Of course, the interest in inner experience is not new; the founders of psychology used introspection to address the nature of consciousness and the components of mental life well over a century ago. Table 1 shows the frequencies with which terms occur as keywords in the journal articles cataloged by PsycINFO by decade as percentages of the total number of articles cataloged. It documents the early interest in inner experience: the column headed "Conscious*" reveals that a century ago (in the decade of 1900 to 1909), nearly a quarter (22.5%) of all articles used "conscious" as part of a keyword.

Table 1 also shows the precipitous decrease in the frequency of the use of "conscious*" and "introspect*" as keywords early in the twentieth century. The widely accepted explanation for this rapid change in the focus of psychological science was the failure of those using introspection to produce scientifically defensible results about consciousness (recall the disagreement about the existence of imageless thought that we discussed in Chapter 3). Here is a typical summary of the failures of that era:

> In spite of various improvements and safeguards, introspection had inherent defects and insurmountable limitations. It was often found unreliable. The results based on introspection in various laboratories were conflicting, and at times the findings of one laboratory were exactly the opposite to those of another, even when the conditions of experimentation were identical. Woodworth's subjects failed to confirm Titchener's subjects, and Titchener's own students reported results different from those of their master. The controversy

> about "imageless thought" provided another striking case of the unreliability of introspection.
>
> ...Because of the defects and limitations of introspection, psychologists restricted its use and put greater trust in more objective methods, particularly when they began to focus their attention more sharply on performance and overt behavior than on conscious states. (Misiak & Sexton 1966:47–48)

Danziger (1980) showed that there were factors other than its unreliability that led to the demise of introspection, but for whatever reason or set of reasons, introspection was thoroughly discredited. The fourth column of Table 1 shows that terms with the root "introspect" (such as introspection, introspected) now appear in less than one-tenth of one percent of psychology articles. When "introspect" does appear, it is often part of a historical critique.

Table 1. PsycINFO Keyword References as Percentages of Total PsycINFO References by Decade

Decade	Total	Conscious* %	Introspect* %	Cognit* %
–1899	384	14.06	.78	4.94
1900–1909	737	22.52	5.29	3.00
1910–1919	2434	9.61	4.77	2.42
1920–1929	19171	4.25	1.27	.55
1930–1939	58538	2.81	.57	.40
1940–1949	50886	1.92	.34	.37
1950–1959	82956	1.92	.14	.69
1960–1969	132116	1.36	.11	3.42
1970–1979	266341	.95	.08	7.88
1980–1989	438749	1.14	.10	9.95
1990–1999	590583	1.63	.08	13.12
2000–2004	271624	1.63	.08	14.32

The return to introspection

Despite the stunning demise of introspection and the systematic avoidance of studies of consciousness, the interest in inner experience has continued and is in fact growing. For example, as we discussed in Chapter 3, cognitive psychotherapy, now the most influential force in the practice of psychology (Simon 2002), is based squarely on introspection-like questions such as "What were you thinking/feeling when you...?" The Table 1 column headed, "cognit*" shows that interest in cognition and cognitive processes has grown steadily since the heyday of behaviorism in the 1940s and 1950s to the present. To be sure, much of the research exploring cognition eschews the use of self-reports of thinking or other aspects of subjective experience, but there are growing numbers of calls for self-reports to be gathered alongside objective data. For example, neuroscientists, historically among the most skeptical critics of self-report, are now asking their participants for introspective self-reports of inner experience while performing tasks in an fMRI scanner (Jack & Roepstorff 2003). Psychology is, in short, undergoing a resurgence of interest in inner experience and an increase in the use of introspective self-reports of it.

This renewed interest in self-reports of inner experience, however, has not been accompanied by sufficient discussion of the difficulties and risks of introspection-like reports. The failure of early 20th century introspection could not have been more spectacular, and criticisms of introspection throughout the middle of the 20th century could not have been more sweeping. Despite the unhappy history of introspection, psychology has not adequately discussed why questions about how sad you are, about the extent to which you are interested, distressed, or excited during the day, or about the characteristics of your thinking while you are engaged in tasks inside an fMRI scanner should be expected to be answered at the beginning of the 21st century with any more accuracy than they were at the beginning of the 20th century.

Early in psychology's history, the introspectionists recognized that introspection was problematic: "It was not uncommon for psychologists in this period [late nineteenth and early twentieth century] to begin their textbooks with cautions about the difficulty of accurate introspection (for example, Külpe 1893/1895; Titchener 1900, 1901), or even to challenge each other's work by suggesting that their opponents failed accurately to introspect (for example, James 1884; Angell 1897; Woodworth 1906; Titchener 1915)" (Schwitzgebel 2002:37).

The implication seems clear: For most of its history, psychology has concluded that introspective reports are substantially problematic, and yet psychologists are beginning to ask again for introspective reports. If psychology is to be more successful now than it was a century ago, it must ensure that its introspective methods are better now than they were a century ago. Simply asking people to report their inner experience wasn't good enough in 1900 as the introspectionists discovered, wasn't good enough in 1977 (at the time of Nisbett and Wilson's review), and there is no reason to believe that it is good enough today. Psychology has advanced since 1900 however, and this chapter shows how introspective methods can profit from that century of psychological science.

The lessons to be learned from the eyewitness identification dilemma

The history of eyewitness identification can serve to illuminate the dangers that psychology currently faces with regard to understanding inner experience. The eyewitness-identification history has six characteristics (Wells & Olson 2003): (1) The witness often has private access to an event; (2) there is often little independent corroborating evidence; (3) the stakes can be high (including the death penalty); (4) authorities and juries often use eyewitness identification; however, (5) developments in science (particularly DNA studies) exposed the substantial unreliability of eyewitness identification (Connors, Lundregan, Miller, & McEwen 1996); leading to (6) the subsequent scientific exploration of and improvement of eyewitness identification techniques (National Institute of Justice 1999).

Psychology is in an analogous situation with respect to inner experience. (1) The introspector has private access to an event; (2) there is often little independent corroborating evidence; (3) the stakes can be high (inner experience is considered to be substantially important in understanding issues such as depression and suicide); (4) scientists often use introspective techniques; however, (5) science (the introspection history; Nisbett & Wilson 1977) has exposed the substantial unreliability of introspection. Psychology should be, but largely is not, (6) undertaking the subsequent exploration and improvement of introspective techniques. This chapter contributes to that exploration by using psychological science to develop guidelines for methods of exploring inner experience that maximize the likelihood of gaining accurate reports.

Importance of the task and need for improvement

It is noteworthy that psychology as a field has more to say about altered states of consciousness than it does about unaltered everyday consciousness. For example, introductory psychology textbooks (e.g., Myers 2004; Weiten 2004) typically have chapters addressing consciousness in sleep, dreams, hypnosis, and drug-altered states, but no or almost no discussion of the contents and nature of ongoing unaltered consciousness. Similarly, much of what is written about consciousness derives from studies of individuals having suffered brain damage that alters normal consciousness (e.g., Sacks 1990; Damasio 1999). In general, psychology emphasizes internal states in psychopathology much more than in normalcy.

Undoubtedly a number of factors contribute to the lack of attention paid to typical consciousness. However, the lack of attention to normal consciousness is also likely to be at least partially due to the mistaken assumption that we are all familiar with our inner life and therefore there is no need to study something so familiar (Hurlburt 1993).

Beyond our lack of knowledge about unaltered consciousness, reports of inner experience are the basis for many important aspects of psychology. In Chapter 1 we discussed the Yale-Brown Obsessive Compulsive Scale (Y-BOCS) and its role in the diagnosis of Obsessive Compulsive Disorder. Here we address the issue in greater detail by considering the Structured Clinical Interview for DSM (SCID; Spitzer, Williams, Gibbon, & First 1990). The SCID is considered a state of the art method for determining if someone suffers from a mental disorder. A series of questions from the SCID used to evaluate for a diagnosis of Major Depression is, "In the last month has there been a period of time when you were feeling depressed or down most the day nearly every day? . . .Did it last. . .as long as two weeks?" Research on autobiographical memory gives substantial reason to question the accuracy of answers to such questions. For example, a person's current state has been shown to influence reports of past depression: people who are currently depressed appear to over-report past instances of depression, whereas those that are not depressed appear to under-report past instances of depression (Aneshensel, Estrada, Hansell, & Clark 1987).

It might be argued that the process of establishing the validity of the SCID and its component diagnostic modules support the accuracy of SCID reports. This is incorrect. Validity of a SCID diagnosis is established by examining those diagnoses within a web of theoretically interconnected concepts. For example, if those individuals who answer the SCID questions in a way that leads to a diagnosis of Major Depression also evidence behavioral indicators of depression (e.g., psychomotor retardation or agitation, disturbed sleep, etc.) or are rated by independent observers as being depressed, the validity of the SCID diagnosis of Major Depression is supported. SCID validity does not, however, directly address the veridicality of the answers to the SCID questions. In fact, the validity of the SCID indicates only that people who are judged to be depressed are likely to report that they have felt depressed or down most of the day nearly every day for a two week period. SCID validity does not indicate that such reports are true. It is quite possible that people who are depressed would mistakenly believe that they have felt depressed or down most of the day nearly every day for a two-week period. Thus, an item can substantially contribute to the validity of the SCID even though the answers typically given to the item are false.

Whether the items of a valid test such as the SCID are answered entirely veridically may not be critical to the diagnosis of depression. But to the scientific understanding of depression, and thence to exploring what is the best treatment for depression, the veridicality of the answers is critical. In other words, it may matter a great deal to the science of depression whether a depressed person actually does feel depressed most of the time or mistakenly thinks that he or she feels depressed most of the time. Ultimately veridicality should be considered a higher standard and the primary target of those wishing to understand inner experience.

Fifteen guidelines for the exploration of inner experience

We have seen (a) that the introspection of a century ago was fatally flawed; (b) that the modern interest in introspection-like techniques is high and growing; and yet (c) there is little modern reconciliation of (a) and (b). We are optimistic that such a reconciliation is possible, and this chapter is intended to contribute to it. What follows are 15 guidelines, distilled from 100 years of psychological science, intended to help introspection overcome its inherent challenges. It should come as no surprise that DES abides by these guidelines. In fact, it was developed with them in mind. Nonetheless, these guidelines are generic in nature and are useful for evaluating the likelihood of gaining accurate introspective reports when using a range of methods.

Guideline 1: The stakes are high

It is clearly not enough merely to want to know about inner experience. Nearly all psychologists want to know about inner experience, including most of those psychologists who suppressed the study of inner experience for methodological reasons. The issue is not desire for knowledge, but adequacy of method. The historical lesson is that, for legitimate reasons, psychology came to believe that it was better to do without desirable knowledge than to use inadequate methods to explore it, and psychology maintained that position for nearly a century.

The corollary to that is that if modern psychologists use questionable methods to explore inner experience, psychology may have an even more severe reaction to this second introspective era. Therefore, if psychology is to re-engage seriously in the study of inner experience, it has to develop adequate introspective methods.

Guideline 2: Skepticism is appropriate

Except for think-aloud procedures (e.g., Ericsson & Simon 1993; Davison, Vogel, & Coffman 1997), memory is central to all attempts to gain access to inner experience. However, psychological science robustly shows that human memory is prone to a variety of errors. For example, Schacter (1996) provided a summary, concluding that verbal reports can be inaccurate when imprecise words are used to describe non-verbal memories; reports can be distorted by pre-existing knowledge that distorts encoding; memory can be altered by the way it is cued; the retrieval environment can influence recall; memory can be influenced by a mediator (therapist or researcher); the more a false memory is discussed or analyzed (cued), the more confident the rememberer will be; confidence therefore does not necessarily imply accuracy; and the specifics of the context of the original memory is crucial to accurate retrieval.

There can be little doubt that researchers should always be skeptical regarding the accuracy of their subjects' self-reports: There is no reason to presume that the description of an inner experience created at some later time accurately mirrors the actual experience. That such recollection may be accurate is not denied, but whether or not a recollection is accurate is precisely the issue, and therefore cannot be presumed without evidence.

A corollary of this guideline is that introspective investigators should be careful not to overstate the accuracy of their conclusions. If the introspective enterprise is to surpass the "meager" results described by Titchener (1912), investigators must be bluntly honest about the possibility that introspective descriptions fail to mirror the targeted lived experience, and must scrupulously avoid locutions that imply, or seem to imply, more than a method deserves.

A second corollary is that skepticism cannot be resolved by appeals to felt certainty or confidence. Psychological science has established that confidence concerning recollections is devilishly disconnected from accuracy: "Study after study has observed low or even zero correlations between [actual] accuracy and confidence [about accuracy]; some studies have even documented negative correlations" (Reisberg 1997: 218).

The conclusion is clear: Psychological science convincingly demonstrates that science should be skeptical of subjects' ability to accurately recall, relive, or gain access to past experiences. This skepticism does not imply that science should simply discard all reports of past inner experience (a common overgeneralization). Instead, this skepticism demands that science explore the conditions under which introspective descriptions might be expected to be accurate, develop methods by which science can evaluate these observations, and fashion methods that live within the constraints of this skepticism.

Guideline 3: Introspect with little delay

From the earliest days of psychological research (Ebbinghaus 1885) to current studies of memory, evidence shows that forgetting occurs rapidly following an event (Rubin & Wetzel 1996; Wixted & Ebbesen 1991). Regardless of whether we attribute inaccurate recall to encoding difficulties, decay, interference, or retrieval failure, memory for an event that happened a moment ago is likely to be better than memory for an event that happened hours, days, weeks, or years ago. For example, Tourangeau (2000) summarized the attempts to provide mathematical functions to model the amount of information retained as a function of time. He concluded that "all four functional forms share several basic predictions – that forgetting increases monotonically over time, but that it occurs rapidly at first and then slows down" (p. 39).

Of particular importance to introspective reports is the encoding of inner experiences. It is well known that a if something is not encoded, it will likely not be recalled (Klatzky 1975); and that (b) meaningful chunks, not random details, are likely to be encoded (Bower 1970). Because the features of inner experience that might be requested by introspection (the colors in an image or precisely what was said in inner speaking, for example) are not usually the meaningful portions of an experience, those features are not likely to be encoded and therefore not likely to be reported accurately unless the introspection takes place very soon after the event. It is generally accepted that the encoding must take place within a few seconds of the event. There is typically a rapid decline in memory for something directly after its occurrence or presentation. This rapid initial decline holds across a variety of situations, procedures, and measurement variations and is even observed as occurring at a similar rate across species (Wixted & Ebbesen 1991).

Psychological research explores not only the temporal aspects of forgetting but the state-dependent aspects as well, with the same conclusion: A short interval between event and report is desirable. Recall is best when people's states at the time of recall are similar to their states at the time of encoding, and people's states are likely to be more similar the closer they are in time. Important aspects of state that can influence recall include the physical surroundings (Eich 1980), internal physiological state (Eich et al. 1975), and mood (Eich 1995). In fact, the impact of changes in mood on recall is greater when recalling internal mental events compared to external events: "Considered collectively, these results are compatible with the idea that internal events, by virtue of their close connection to current mood, are particularly apt to be forgotten following a shift in mood state" (Eich 1995:70). Salovey, Sieber, Jobe, and Willis (1994) reached similar conclusions in their review of the retrospective reports of pain. Thus the influence of state-dependent memory is particularly critical for the introspective enterprise. Although there is no definitive solution to this concern, relevant states such as context and mood may tend to vary less as the interval between event and report decreases.

We therefore conclude that psychological science suggests that introspective methods should keep the interval between an event and its report as short as possible. Because introspective methods often require inquiry about the features of an inner perception that are otherwise not likely to be encoded, the interval should be very short.

Guideline 4: Target specific, concrete episodes

Pearson, Ross, and Dawes (1992) reviewed studies that ask people retrospectively to characterize experiences over time and concluded that people may engage in theory-guided recall if they hold a theory that is salient and credible and if relevant memories are not easily accessed. However, the veridicality of these self-theories or beliefs about many aspects of one's own inner experience has been called into question by research (see Robinson & Clore 2002a for a review), so characterizations of experience over time are likely to be distorted by the person's self-theory.

Characterizations of experience over time are also likely to be distorted by features of the experiences themselves. For example, Kahneman and colleagues (e.g., Kahneman 1999; Redelmeier & Kahneman 1996) have found that people asked to characterize pain over time do not mentally calculate an average across actual events, but rather are unduly influenced by the peak level of pain and the current level of pain.

Characterizations of experience over time are more likely to rely on semantic memories (Tulving 1984, 1993), general knowledge about the self or world. Introspection should be careful to avoid the semantic memory of experience over time in favor of methods that target episodic memories tied to specific events. Introspection that targets specific, clearly identified moments will minimize the likelihood that participants engage in a process of aggregation or report based on semantic memories or self-theories. Similarly, targeting specific moments of experience will also minimize the operation of processes such as confirmation bias (Klayman & Ha 1987) and pre-existing schemata.

Guideline 5: Keep the target experience brief

From about the beginning of the rise of cognitive psychology in the 1950s, it has been known that there are "severe limitations on the amount of information that we are able to receive, process, and remember," as Miller summarized in his highly influential "Seven, Plus or Minus Two" paper (Miller 1956: 94). Although there are competing models about how information is stored in long-term memory, there is agreement that the ability to encode events such that they can be recalled later is limited by the time available for rehearsal (Atkinson & Shiffrin 1968) or processing (Craik & Lockhart 1972). Perhaps the clearest demonstration of this is the well-known primacy effect. When a person learns a series of new pieces of information, the information learned at the beginning of the series is more likely to be recalled than the material learned in the middle of the series, apparently because the time available for rehearsal or processing of new material decreases as the attempt to encode new information continues (Murdoch 1962). Thus there are substantial limitations on the amount of material that people can store in memory during a given period of time. Furthermore, when there is less information that must be rehearsed, the recall will generally be more accurate (Atkinson & Shiffrin 1968).

Extrapolating from this research suggests that there are likely to be severe limitations on the amount of introspective material that a person can be expected to remember. Therefore, if the object is to reveal the details of inner experience, it is desirable to keep the amount of material to be remembered as small as possible. This in turn generally entails keeping the target experience as brief as possible.

The introspectionists recognized such limitations a century ago. For example, Watt (1905), in his introspective analysis of problem solving, "fractionated" the problem-solving event into four parts, the preparation, the period prior to the presentation of the problem, the presentation of the problem, and the search for the solution, so that each part was no longer than a second or so.

The implication is that the shorter the experience to be introspected, the better. It is worth noting here that autobiographical memory researchers concur with this "the-shorter-the-better" principle, but often understand short as being in the range of two weeks or less: "In sum, these findings suggest that there is something like a 2-week time limit on the episodic self. For time frames longer than this as well as for generalized reports of emotion, we argue that the person must rely on more generalized beliefs about his or her emotions to make emotion judgments" (Robinson & Clore 2002b: 212). However, Hurlburt (1993 1997) showed that focusing on much briefer time frames (on the order of one second) allows people to report a substantial level of detail about the contents of their inner experience. Thus, to the extent that the object of the study is accuracy in reporting the details of experience, the duration of experience explored should be very short.

Guideline 6: Disturb the experience as little as possible

One potential concern with all forms of measurement is that the process of measurement alters that which is being measured. In fact, James (1890/1950) suggested that it would be impossible to capture ongoing inner experience because the attempt to capture it would destroy the experience:

> As a snow-flake crystal caught in the warm hand is no longer a crystal but a drop, so, instead of catching the feeling of relation moving to its term, we find we have caught some substantive thing, usually the last word we were producing, statically taken, and with its function, tendency, and particular meaning in the sentence quite evaporated. The attempt at introspective analysis in these cases is in fact like … trying to turn up the gas quickly enough to see how the darkness looks. (p. 244)

In contrast, John S. Mill suggested that it might be possible to capture ongoing experience by recalling that experience just after it has passed: "A fact may be studied through the medium of memory, not at the very moment of our perceiving it, but the moment after: and this is really the mode in which our best knowledge of our intellectual acts is generally acquired. We reflect on what we have been doing when the act is past, but when its impression in the memory is still fresh" (Mill 1882/1961: 64). We believe that Mill is correct in assuming that this method of measurement does as little to disturb the targeted experience as possible (see Hurlburt & Heavey 2004). Psychological science labels this concern "reactivity" and cautions that it can significantly distort results (Campbell & Stanley 1963). This concern is especially critical when examining something as evanescent as inner experience. To minimize disturbance to the ongoing awareness, investigators should use methods that are as open ended as possible and do not invoke processes beyond attempting to capture and report on the experience.

Guideline 7: Explore natural situations

When psychologists evaluate the extent to which research speaks to some truth of the world, they typically distinguish between internal and external validity. Internal validity addresses the extent to which the observed relationships are attributable to those causes identified by the researchers (Campbell & Stanley 1963). External validity "refers to the robustness of a phenomenon – the extent to which a causal relationship, once identified in a particular setting with particular research participants, can safely be generalized to other times, places, and people" (Aronson, Wilson, & Brewer 1998: 130). One central aspect of external validity is "the extent to which events occurring in the research setting are likely to occur in the normal course of the participants' lives, that is in the 'real world'" (Aronson et al. 1998: 131). This aspect of external validity is known as "mundane realism" (Aronson & Carlsmith 1968). Hormuth (1986) credits Brunswick (1949) with coining the term "ecological validity" to describe the notion that time samples should be taken in the environments that the subject naturally inhabits, rather than in experimental or otherwise artificial situations.

Although those exploring inner experience do not always seek to establish causal relationships, the analogy of internal and external validity is nonetheless clear and compelling. Guidelines 2–7 can be conceptualized as relating to the internal validity of introspective methods. That is, these guidelines seek to maximize the probability that the results of the introspective process mirror the truth of the lived experience. To maximize the generalizability of the results, the introspective process should be carried out in varied natural contexts, thus maximizing mundane realism and ecological validity. Given the important and varied findings from psychological research concerning the impact of context and situation on behavior, concerns about generalizability are critical.

Guideline 8: Minimize demands

Psychological science has long recognized that participants can be influenced by subtle characteristics of experiments. These observations date to at least 1911, when Pfungst suggested that Clever Hans, the horse that appeared to count, was actually being influenced by subtle cues from his owner. The expectations of a researcher that can influence the behavior of a participant, combined with the desire of participants to "please" researchers, have been called "demand characteristics" (Orne 1962) or the "Pygmalion Effect" (Rosenthal & Jacobson 1968).

An important part of these general demand characteristics is the robust finding that the form of a question can strongly affect the answer (e.g., Ceci & Bruck 1993; Schwarz 1999). For example, eyewitness memory research on the contaminating effects of information provided after an event has led to the general conclusion that it is desirable for witnesses to tell their stories in their own way, in their own words, before subjecting them to questioning. The accuracy of stories related in their own words is likely to be greater than the accuracy of stories told as a result of questioning (e.g., Hilgard & Loftus 1979;

Fisher & Geiselman 1992; Bruck & Ceci 1999). There are many other ways in which memory can be altered by outside influences including priming effects (Schacter 1996) and source misattribution effects (Zaragoza & Lane 1994).

Thus psychological science documents the many ways in which self-reports can be distorted by outside influences. These observations have led to such everyday methodological requirements as the need for double-blind testing when possible (Rosenthal 1976).

Explorations of inner experience are particularly susceptible to interviewer bias and other demand characteristics, and those demands often take place without the interviewer's knowledge. In some introspective situations it is possible to make double-blind observations, and that is clearly desirable. However, it is often the case that the personal nature of the interactions makes blindness impossible or artificial. In such situations, researchers can attempt to "suspend" or "bracket" preconceptions that might otherwise distort the process.

A presupposition is a preconception, something that is taken for granted, a notion about the world that is so fundamental that it exists prior to critical examination. Presuppositions interfere with the ability to see or otherwise experience the world accurately. Phenomenologists, following Merleau-Ponte, recognize presuppositions as a feature of the human condition but try to limit their distorting influences. They refer to this limiting as the bracketing of presuppositions, the attempt to take the presupposition out of play, to act even-handedly as if it may or may not be true. The bracketing of presuppositions is difficult; double blind experimentation is one attempt to avoid this difficulty. But in those cases where double blind experimentation is impossible, bracketing of presuppositions may be the best alternative. There is, unfortunately, no generally accepted method; we return to this discussion in Chapter 10.

Guideline 9: Terminology is problematic

As we discussed at length in Chapter 3, verbal behavior about private events may be impoverished because it is difficult for the verbal community to shape a person's speech about inner experience – recall Skinner's critique, which we support, that it is easier to establish careful speech about the external characteristic "red" than about inner characteristics such as "depressed". Thus it is crucial that substantial care is taken to illuminate to the fullest extent possible the meanings of words used to represent inner experience.

Guideline 10: Don't ask participants to infer causation

Also as discussed at length in Chapter 3, Nisbett and Wilson (1977) convincingly established that people cannot reliably infer causation. The studies Nisbett and Wilson reviewed showed that people are often incorrect when identifying the causes of their own behavior and are unaware of these errors. Thus, because participants cannot be expected to attribute causation with accuracy, modern introspective techniques should avoid asking "why" questions.

Guideline 11: Abandon armchair observation

It follows from the previous guidelines that casual observation about inner experience is not likely to yield scientifically valid results. Merely asking someone about their inner experience is simply not good enough. Furthermore, asking someone to perform armchair observations about their own experiences is problematic, even if that observation is done with careful instruction or by sophisticated observers:

> I have conducted this brief examination of our introspective knowledge of visual imagery to promote the more general thesis that we can be, and often are, grossly mistaken about our own current conscious experiences even in favourable circumstances of quiet attention.... We must abandon not only research paradigms in psychology and consciousness studies that depend too trustingly on introspection ... but also some of our ordinary assumptions about our knowledge of our own mental lives and what it's like to be ourselves. Human judgment about anything as fluid, changeable, skittish and chaotic as conscious experience is bound to error and confusion. (Schwitzgebel 2002: 50)

We wholeheartedly support Schwitzgebel's conclusion, but we note that it, like many others, is itself at least partially based on armchair observation:

> Finally, in introspecting my own imagery, I do not find myself in the position of feeling that I know exactly what the experience is like, fumbling only because I am unable to put my knowledge clearly into words or because I am unsure of the standards of reporting. Rather, I am unsure about the *experience itself*, about how much detail is filled in at any particular time, about how narrowly the imagery experience confines itself to what is in the scope of my immediate attention, about how much visual imagery is like visual perception.... The introspection of visual imagery feels difficult if one sets to it conscientiously. We should not be surprised if people go easily awry.
> (Schwitzgebel 2002: 49–50, italics in original)

We believe that armchair observation is just as risky when used to discredit introspection as it is when used to provide the "true facts" of inner life. It is in fact difficult, if not impossible, to ask yourself to observe yourself and then act as if the asking and the observing do not affect that which is observed. We believe that armchair observation should be either abandoned altogether or treated with the highest skepticism.

Guideline 12: Separate report from interpretation

There is one part of the psychology literature where introspective reports have been accepted as informative (although certainly not conclusive) throughout the past century. Reports of experience by those suffering from brain damage and disease have consistently contributed to neuroscience's understanding of brain processing.

Neuroscience has made effective use of introspective reports because they have appropriately separated the introspective report from the interpretation of that report. It is the patient's job to provide the introspective reports, and the neurologist's job to provide the interpretation. Just as a neurologist would not ask her patient to speculate on which lobe of the brain is involved, psychologists should not ask introspectors to provide anything more than descriptions of phenomena.

It is reasonable to marvel at how the science of psychology has arrived at a place where introspective reports from seriously disturbed or damaged individuals are credited, whereas introspective reports from "normal" individuals are dismissed. It is certainly difficult to conclude that these individuals provide reports that are more accurate than their non-brain damaged/non-disturbed counterparts.

Guideline 13: Introspection has limitations

Science should recognize that introspective techniques are not useful in all situations, and that it may not be obvious where introspection is or is not useful. We give two examples: imageless thought and processing outside of awareness.

The alert reader may be noticing that classical introspection observed many or most of these guidelines and still disagreed vehemently about the existence of imageless thought. However, as we discussed in Chapter 3, the introspectionists could agree about the phenomena associated with imageless thought but could not agree about the interpretation of those phenomena.

The mistake, as we see it with a century of hindsight, is that the introspectionists required too much of their observations – they wanted to resolve an issue in their theory of mind, and introspection was simply not equipped to meet that challenge. Introspective techniques that are useful for observation may not be useful for deciding some theoretical issues (Shanon 1984).

Second, there is no reason to believe that introspection can explore all aspects of human behavior, which is so complex that at least part of it must occur outside of awareness (Skinner 1953). In skilled performance, for example, the brake and the accelerator may often be in the center of awareness early in driving skill acquisition, but rarely or never once driving has become automated.

Furthermore, there may well be high level processes that are unconscious and therefore beyond the reach of direct observation. Freud, as is well known, understood the unconscious to include thoughts that were kept out of consciousness by dynamic forces such as repression. Views of the unconscious have matured over the past century; Wilson (2002), for example, held that the unconscious comprises many adaptive processes rather than repressive ones, and that people are unaware of these processes because that is the more efficient way of processing information. For example, Gilbert, Pinel, Wilson, Blumberg, and Wheatley (1998) gathered evidence that "people are generally unaware of the operation of the system of cognitive mechanisms that ameliorate their experience of negative affect…, and thus…tend to overestimate the duration of their affective reactions to negative events" (p. 617). Thus most observers agree that "there is a great deal about ourselves that we cannot know directly, even with the most painstaking introspection" (Wilson 2002: vii). Such aspects may have to be explored indirectly, as Freud understood when he used free association and more sophisticated researchers understand when they use modern techniques such as the Implicit Association Test (IAT, Greenwald, McGhee, & Schwartz 1998), which employs reaction times to explore characteristics that the self may be unwilling or unable to report directly.

Considerable research, not *a priori* analyses, will be required to determine which processes are amenable to introspection and which are not. Hurlburt (1993, 1997), for example, showed that some processes that seemed to be unconscious were simply characteristically neglected and were easily discoverable by an introspective method that followed the guidelines presented here.

Guideline 14: Value prospective research

A prospective study collects data from a group of participants and examines their progress or status over time. Later, meaningful changes (e.g., the development of some disorder) may occur for some but not all of the participants. By contrast, a retrospective study asks participants to recall events that occurred prior to the actual occurrence of the condition.

Thus prospective studies gather presently-occurring data that might be relevant to some future condition; retrospective studies start with presently-occurring conditions and ask for recollections of past events. Giele and Elder (1998) caution researchers

> not to make too rigid a division between retrospective and prospective designs because, in practice, nearly all social surveys elicit some information about the distant past, for example, questions about the respondent's place of birth or the socioeconomic status of his or her family of origin. Moreover, prospective studies are almost invariably in the business of collecting retrospective data, albeit over a shorter recall period. Even measures about current occupation usually refer to the week preceding the survey, measures of current educational attainment often refer to qualifications that were obtained many years earlier...
>
> So what does differentiate prospective designs from retrospective ones? Retrospective designs can, on the surface, cover a longer time span than usually is practical with prospective designs. However, prospectively collected data are generally considered to be more reliable than recall data because of the limitations and biases of the human memory. In addition, prospective designs can increase the validity of the data because they can tap a far wider range of information on other life events or changes that might relate to the topic at issue but are not memorable at a later point in time. (pp. 106–107)

Thus, as Giele and Elder (1998) and many others have observed, prospective studies have two advantages: greater accuracy and wider range of information. The impact of greater accuracy can be substantial. For example, Wilson (2003) summarized the situation in criminal justice by saying "prospective studies have largely revolutionized our understanding of what is happening." We have already seen that retrospections of inner events may be particularly problematic; it follows that the advantage in accuracy that prospective studies enjoy may be even greater in introspective studies.

It is the other characteristic of prospective designs – the possibility of tapping a wider range of information – that we wish to highlight here. A prospective study can gather observations relatively irrespective of theoretical perspective, collecting evidence that may or may not be related to some later question. Those observations can later be "mined" (or "prospected") for informative relationships, as was done in the well known "Nun Study" that used prospective data to search for precursors of Alzheimer's disease (Snowdon et al. 1996).

We believe that, particularly at this early stage of the science of inner experience, this ability to allow the emergence of perhaps unexpected relationships or characteristics is especially important. We therefore think that it is a mistake to presume that a person's inner experience has some particular characteristics until after that person's experience has been carefully examined. It has been common, for example, to examine images by asking people to form images. We believe that there is a substantial risk in that procedure if the aim is to introspect accurately. There may be substantial individual differences in the ability to form images (Hurlburt & Heavey 2002). Asking a person to form an image is perhaps more likely to elicit a report of an image than it is to elicit the actual formation of an image.

A better procedure, by analogy to a prospective experiment, is to put participants into situations that the investigator may have reason to believe is likely to elicit images (say, a mental rotation task; Cooper & Shepard 1973) and then even-handedly to inquire about *whatever* characteristics of inner experience might appear. Then if images appear, fine; but if the participant reports some other form or experience, fine as well.

As the history of flashbulb memory shows, the prospective/retrospective distinction is likely to be especially important when studying personal experience. Brown and Kulik (1977) coined the term "flashbulb memory" to denote their observation that people had clear memories of the assassination of John F. Kennedy: 13 years after he had been shot, 99% of people could recall where they were and what they were doing when they had heard of the event. But that was a retrospective study. Several teams of psychologists used the event of the Challenger Space Shuttle disaster to perform a similar study prospectively. For example, Neisser and Harsch (1992) asked students the day after the disaster when and how they had heard of it. Then they contacted those same students 2.5 years later and asked the same questions, finding that over 40% were clearly inconsistent on the two occasions. The more fleeting the phenomenon, the more desirable is a prospective study.

Despite their well-known advantages, prospective studies are rare in psychology; a PsycINFO search similar to those described above reveals that since 1993, the keyword "prospective stud*" appears in only 2482 out of a total of 702,393 articles listed, or about 3.5 times per thousand articles. However, because experiences are evanescent, and because private theories/explanations of experience (either the researcher's or the participant's) may influence the recollections of prior activities in substantial ways, introspective science may well need to operate at the highest standard available.

Guideline 15: Situate introspective observations in a nomological net

Introspective observations are of psychological constructs – attributes that are difficult or impossible to define operationally. Those who would use introspective observations should therefore explore the relationships of those observations to other kinds of research results. Cronbach and Meehl (1955) called the "interlocking system" of such relationships the nomological net, and argued that "*unless the network makes contact with observations, and exhibits explicit, public steps of inference, construct validation cannot be claimed*" (Cronbach & Meehl 1955: 291, italics in original).

Some of the elements in that nomological network can be objective laboratory measures, as when Shepard and his colleagues investigated imagery by measuring the reaction times of judgments about the similarity or difference of novel pairs of drawings of objects that were presented in positions that were rotated from each other (e.g., Shepard & Metzler 1971). Other elements in the nomological network can be naturally occurring events, as when Hurlburt (1993, 1997) discussed the "idiographic validity" of the multiple images he reported in the case of Fran, whose case was mentioned in Chapter 3 and will be explored in depth in Chapter 11. Introspective observations can be seductively misleading, so observers should subject those observations to rigorous and explicit construct validation and the examination of inconsistencies: "Triangulate! Correlations between physiology, behaviour and experience can provide us with some clues, but real progress will occur when we investigate, and begin to explain, disparities. We won't understand the mind until we can integrate these seemingly disparate and incommensurable perspectives" (Roepstorff & Jack 2004: xx).

Can introspection be useful?

There are two mistakes that modern psychology might make regarding introspection: (1) to continue to ban all introspective reports even in those situations where they can be accurate; and (2) to begin to allow introspective reports without regard for their dismal historical record. It appears to us that psychology may be heading in both directions. There is, however, a third alternative that we believe to be preferable: that psychology (3) should attempt to bring its history to bear and create better introspective methods.

With respect to mistake (1), we acknowledge the fact that since the time of the introspectionists, people have made vigorous claims about the accuracy of their introspections that turned out to be incorrect. We also acknowledge the reasonableness of the inductive conclusion that since introspection has had remarkable failures and little or no documented success, it is likely that introspection can never be useful. We believe, however, that prior introspections have been substantially flawed, and therefore, despite the reasonableness of the inductive conclusion, it is perhaps an overgeneralization. It is possible that introspection that avoids those flaws (as by employing the guidelines discussed here) may in fact be better than prior introspections. Psychology should, we think, admit that as a possibility and evaluate it.

With respect to mistake (2), we believe that it would require a most substantial historical blindness to begin again to credit introspective reports without taking substantial precautions to ensure that those reports are accurate.

With respect to possibility (3), we have discussed 15 guidelines drawn from the science of psychology that we think should be taken into consideration when planning, implementing, or evaluating introspective reports. Furthermore, we are not claiming that an introspective method that follows all these guidelines would in fact be useful to psychological science. That is a complex empirical issue that can be decided only by making a series of such introspective attempts and subjecting them to the purifying process of science – replication, critique, revision, and so on.

The claim that we are making is a narrow one: It is possible that introspective methods may be useful. We are arguing that introspective methods that follow these guidelines may improve that possibility, but that remains to be seen. We believe it is possible to obtain introspective self-reports in accordance with all these guidelines; Descriptive Experience Sampling is one such method. Other researchers have developed methods that are in accord with many or most of these guidelines, such as the Experience Sampling Method (e.g., Csikszentmihalyi & Larson 1987; Larson & Csikszentmihalyi 1983) and Ecological Momentary Assessment (e.g., Shiffman 2000; Stone & Shiffman 1994; Stone et al. 1998). But unfortunately, psychologists are still using many reports of inner experience that violate many or almost all of these guidelines.

Psychology has much to gain from introspective methods but only if they are done well. Bad new introspections are undoubtedly worse than no new introspections at all. The 15 psychological-science informed guidelines presented here are intended to help those interested in inner experience evaluate and develop introspective methods that are better than those that faltered at the outset of psychology and thus to re-open the realm of inner experience to psychological science.

CHAPTER 5

To beep or not to beep*

We argued in Chapter 3 that there are two mistakes to be made with respect to introspection: (1) believing that introspection is impossible, and (2) believing that introspection is easy. We disagreed with Nisbett and Wilson's (1977) overly general conclusion about the impossibility of introspection. However, we also disagree with Chalmers, who seemed to imply that we can simply observe consciousness: "We know about our own detailed and specific conscious experiences ... we each have access to a rich source of data in our own case" (1996: 215–6). Although it is certainly true that each of us has access to rich data about our own inner experience, as scientists we should recognize that the lack of rigor used in "gathering" these data leaves open the possibility of significant error. In fact, our own explorations have shown that people, including sophisticated psychologists and philosophers, are often substantially mistaken in their "armchair" characterizations of their inner experience and quite surprised by what they observe when they employ a careful and systematic method for observing their inner experience.

We wish to argue strenuously against armchair introspection despite the fact that is a frequently used technique, both historically and recently. As a historical example, the debate over whether imaginal indeterminacy was possible continued for centuries, pitting one armchair against another. Schwitzgebel (2002) summarized:

> An earlier debate, more familiar to most philosophers, also apparently reflecting fundamental disagreement about the experience of imagery, was the debate between Locke and Berkeley about abstract ideas. Locke seems to have felt that he could form an image of a triangle that is 'neither oblique, nor rectangle, neither equilateral, equicrural, nor scalenon; but all and none of these at once' (1689/1975: 596). Berkeley denied that he had the capacity to generate any such images (1710/1965). While Berkeley leaves open the possibility that Locke's imagery is just very different from his own, it is evident that Berkeley felt the more plausible view to be that his own failure to experience abstract images was universal and that Locke simply got it wrong about his own conscious experience. (pp. 37–38)

Thus either Berkeley or Locke got it wrong. Because both were intelligent people trying quite hard to get it right, it follows that observers engaged in armchair observation, even very sophisticated observers, can make substantial mistakes when they draw conclusions about inner experience.

Despite frequent criticism, armchair observation remains common and the faith in it remains unjustifiably strong. For example, there is a "new" tendency to encourage scientists to use retrospective reports alongside brain imaging or other physiological measures (e.g., Jack & Roepstorff 2002). But unless modern researchers can demonstrate that they are more perspicacious than Berkeley or Locke and others who have foundered in similar waters, we should be quite skeptical about their armchair introspections.

The question that modern consciousness studies must answer is whether it is possible to improve on armchair observation, and if so, how. In the previous chapter we reviewed guidelines derived from psychological science that, if followed, should improve the quality and veracity of reports on inner experience. DES follows these guidelines and, we believe, is substantially better than previous introspective methods. In this chapter we focus on the important contribution of using random beeps to trigger observation.

The beeper as navigational aid

At the outset, we wish to acknowledge that there is nothing either magic or unique about a beeper, including the beepers that we employ in our own beeper-based research (e.g. Hurlburt 1990, 1993, 1997; Hurlburt & Heavey 2002). Using a beeper does not guarantee making an accurate observation any more than a sextant or GPS guarantees that you won't run your boat aground. In fact, we think accurate observing requires a high level of skill regardless of whether a beeper is employed. Nonetheless we believe that a beeper is a valuable tool in the journey toward understanding awareness. We divide the potential benefits of using a beeper into three broad categories: time sampling per se, minimizing the reactive disturbance of evanescent phenomena, and phenomenological fidelity. These categories are rather arbitrary – there are other ways of slicing this pie. Some of the categories have been discussed previously, for example by Stone and Shiffman (1994), Stone et al. (1991), Hormuth (1986), Larson and Csikszentmihalyi (1983), Barrett and Barrett (2001), Delespaul (1992), and Hurlburt (1990, 1993). But all these accounts are incomplete, and none focus on the beep as a tool for facilitating phenomenological fidelity.

Time sampling per se

The first two ways in which a beeper can provide navigational aids between supposing that introspection is impossible and that it is easy are the well known features of time sampling.

Aid 1: The beep can provide time samples. Time sampling is not new. Goodenough defined time sampling 75 years ago as "the observation of everyday behavior of an individual or a group of individuals for definite short periods of time and the recording of the occurrence or non-occurrence of certain specified and objectively defined forms of behavior during each of these periods" (1928: 23). Time sampling of inner experience is useful for the same reasons that time-sampling is useful in time-and-motion studies, and need not be further described here. The first use of the time sampling of inner experience was reported by Locke and Jensen (1974), who used a Freon-powered horn to interrupt physical education classes once per day. Students were instructed to write down their thoughts on conveniently placed clipboards. The first use of repeated, random or quasi-random sampling of inner experience began in 1974 independently by Klinger (1978–1979) and by Hurlburt (1976); Hurlburt & Sipprelle (1978).

Aid 2: The beep can come in the subject's own natural environment. A cornerstone of time sampling as practiced throughout behavioral science is that the samples should be taken in the environments that the subject naturally inhabits, rather than in experimental or otherwise artificial situations in order to maximize ecological validity. The Experience Sampling Method (ESM), as practiced by Csikszentmihalyi and his colleagues (e.g., Larson & Csikszentmihalyi 1983) is the largest-scale set of ecologically valid explorations of inner experience.

Altmann (1971) was an early critic of laboratory studies, arguing that relying heavily on laboratory studies risked an inordinate sacrifice of generality and relevance. Pope (1978) showed that longer sequences of thought, and thought content more remote from the participant's immediate circumstances, were obtained when subjects were reclining rather than walking freely, thus demonstrating the importance of ecological validity: if variables such as posture affect thought characteristics, what other variables might have at least as large an effect?

Minimizing the reactive disturbance of evanescent phenomena
Many characteristics that are examined by time-sampling methods are robust, relatively long duration characteristics that are not likely to be immediately disturbed by the sampling method. For example, ESM asks subjects to report whether they are alone or not alone at the time of the beep. By contrast, the characteristics of inner experience are evanescent, transient phenomena of thinking, feeling, sensing. The next five features of the beep can aid in the accurate capture of evanescent phenomena.

Aid 3: The beep can be a quick external signal. A method that pinpoints particular moments has the potential to catch aspects of awareness that may be fleeting and of brief duration. In this respect the beep can be like a flashbulb that slices through the ongoing stream of time at a precise moment to reveal that which might otherwise pass unrecognized. Similarly a beep that marks a precise moment in an ongoing stream of awareness has the potential to reveal aspects of awareness that were previously unrecognized because, like James' (1890/1952) "snowflake caught in the warm hand" of Chapter 4, these aspects existed only for a fleeting moment.

Aid 4: The beep can come at times that are independent of the subject's internal or external states. In armchair observation, you ask yourself, "What am I thinking?" only at particular times, namely whenever motivational and situational conditions are ripe for the formation of that question. Perhaps, for example, you observe only at times where you are in a heightened readiness to observe. If so, then armchair observation will make it seem that you are always in heightened readiness. By contrast, a random or quasi-random beep comes at times unrelated to current motivation and therefore triggers the examination of a wider range of phenomena.

Aid 5: The beep can ask you to pay attention to a contemporaneous (or at least just immediately past) event, thus maximizing the chances that the fullest possible account of the event is still available to awareness. As we saw in Chapter 4, John S. Mill (1882/1961) observed more than 100 years ago that the capturing of immediately past events may be the best procedure for gaining access to awareness. This assertion is consistent with our current understanding of memory processes, which indicates that the more time that intervenes between an event and its recollection, the more likely information will be lost or distorted due to failure to encode in long-term memory, decay, interference, or memory construction processes (e.g., Ericsson & Simon 1980, 1984/1993;

Kahneman & Tversky 1982; Schwarz 1990). Consistent with this, Hurlburt and Melancon (1987) showed in a beeper study that longer-term retrospective reports may contain distortions of frequency of categories of thinking and clarity of inner experience. Similarly Brewer (1988) showed that autobiographical memory decays over time, with ability to recall thoughts decaying fastest.

Schooler, Reichle, and Halpern (2004) studied "zoning out" while reading. They asked participants in an experimental situation to read a passage and press a key whenever they zoned out – lapsed into daydreaming – while reading. They found using a beeper-type probe that people are likely to overlook events such as zoning out even though they have been specifically primed to pay attention to precisely those events. Thus we should have limited confidence in the ability of people to recall accurately moments of awareness as they pass by in the stream of consciousness.

Aid 6: The beep can reduce the reliance on and disturbance by meta-cognition. Self-observation generally begins with a self-directed question such as, "What am I thinking?" But the "What am I thinking?" question *is* the thought process at that time, so the attempt to observe inner experience either results in the constant observation of the "What am I thinking?" question itself, or it requires the difficult if not impossible task of setting that question aside and observing the remainder of the ongoing stream. By contrast, the beep can come to signify "What am I thinking?" in a particularly compact form, and, because it comes from an external source, the question itself does not occupy a central aspect of the subject's inner activity. Of course the beep does disturb the ongoing experience to some extent (it has to be heard and processed), but that disturbance may be less than in other ways of exploring awareness.

Aid 7: The beep can precisely designate the time under examination. Shortly after Michelle Kwan fell during the 2002 Olympic figure skating, a television reporter asked her, "What were you thinking about when you fell during that triple?" Ms. Kwan's answer to the reporter was, "I was thinking, 'Well, that's skating!'" Here we note that, like most armchair observers, the reporter didn't specify precisely which moment she was inquiring about: immediately prior to the fall (in which case the thinking might be the distraction that caused the fall); as the jump was actually happening (in which case the thinking might be about whether to abort the triple into a double); as she hit the ice (perhaps "Oh, pshaw!"); immediately thereafter (perhaps angry at herself or her coach); and so on. Lack of precision in defining "when" must therefore lead to lack of precision in the "what" as well. The beep has the potential of being substantially more explicit about the exact time under consideration.

Phenomenological fidelity

Suppose that your task is to discover the characteristics of inner experience – simply to describe the phenomena that occur. There are six ways that the beep provides assistance in reporting accurately about phenomena. DES, as far as we know, is the only method using beepers that incorporates these six phenomenological fidelity characteristics of the beep.

It should be noted that as DES is focused on describing ongoing awareness, it is fundamentally different from the classic introspection performed by Titchener and others a century ago. For example, Schwitzgebel (2004) presented in our view a fair and accurate account of Titchener's introspective efforts, thus providing the opportunity to compare and contrast DES with Titchenerian introspection.

Whereas both DES and Titchenerian introspection attempt to elicit accurate reports about experience, the two methods are substantially different in their targets. Titchener was primarily interested in what we might call the psychophysical aspects of consciousness, or the fundamental mental processes. Schwitzgebel's paper illustrates this; the examples cited are: comparing the relative brightness of two different colors; discerning a very low tone sensation from a sensation of atonal noise; making the quantitative assessment that two sensations are each an equal distance, in different directions, from a third; distinguishing difference (or combination) tones; reporting the characteristics of the "flight of colors" (complex afterimages); and perceiving non-obvious visual illusions. That is, Titchener was primarily interested in discerning obscure fundamental processes.

By contrast, DES is *not* interested in discerning obscure fundamental processes, but instead is interested in reporting obvious incidental occurrences. If inner speech happens to be present, DES describes that speech; if an image happens to be present, DES describes that image; if a feeling happens to be present to awareness, then DES describes that feeling; and so on. DES does *not* attempt to explore any fundamental processes (perceptual acuity, etc.) that underlie or perhaps create the incidental occurrences caught by the DES beeper. DES is *not* interested in the obscure or the hard to detect. It is interested only in the obvious, the easily apprehendable; that is, it tries to obtain accurate reports about the incidental occurrences themselves.

Thus there is substantial contrast between Titchener's attempts to discern obscure fundamental processes and DES attempts to report obvious incidental occurrences. Titchener had to train his introspectors to *suppress* the very things that DES seeks to discover – whatever happens to be passing through awareness at any given moment. Titchener trained subjects to suspend those incidental awarenesses to be better able to focus on the fundamental processes behind them. DES trains subjects to ignore any interest in fundamental processes and simply pay attention to the details of whatever incidental occurrence happens to be ongoing. The DES task is substantially easier than that of Titchener's introspection, and this accounts for the large differences in training time required. We believe that most subjects can be adequately trained in the DES method in a few sampling days.

Just because the DES targets are obvious doesn't imply that giving accurate reports about them is trivially easy. Just as did Titchener's introspectors, DES subjects have to learn to avoid the "stimulus error," mistaking a characteristic of experience for a feature of the environment. For example, if a DES subject reports seeing an inner image of his living room, he has to learn to avoid letting what he knows about his actual living room influence what he says he sees in the image. Furthermore, DES subjects have to learn to be consistent in the referents of words they use to describe their inner experiences, and DES interviewers have to learn what those referents actually are. For example, as we discussed earlier, DES subjects use the word "thinking" in a variety of ways; for one subject, it means "inner speech"; for another, it means "visual images"; for a third it means "emotional experience."

It is a fact of the human condition that what is obvious at the moment is frequently (for whatever reason) systematically overlooked by retrospection. The DES explorations are perhaps most useful in those situations where the once-immediately-obvious has become the now-retrospectively-forgotten. But that does not change the fact that DES limits itself to exploring the immediately obvious. In so doing, it avoids some of the major pitfalls that plagued Titchener's introspection.

Aid 8: The beep can assist in setting aside preconceptions by asking participants to pay attention to whatever happens to be ongoing at the moment of the beep. By contrast, many if not most formal and informal psychological investigations are in search of something relatively specific, something preconceptually believed to occur. Although there is parsimony in this strategy, there is also great risk of missing what you do not know to look for or substantially disturbing or altering the nature of the awareness you do find. For example, we discussed above the zoning-out-while-reading study by Schooler, Reichle, and Halpern (2004). That study is exemplary in its use of a beep to explore immediately occurring phenomena. Here, however, we observe that that study began with powerful preconceptions that cannot be dispelled within the design of that study. For example, Schooler, Reichle and Halpern believed at the outset that "when one is zoning-out, they are experientially conscious of whatever topic has grabbed their attention, while at the same time lacking meta-consciousness of the fact that they are zoning-out. At some point during the reading episode, they suddenly become meta-conscious that they have been zoning-out and realize that for some time they have been reading without comprehension" (Schooler et al. 2004, quoted by permission). We believe that such meta-conscious awareness is by no means necessary: it is quite possible that a person could read, think about something unrelated to reading, and then return to reading *with no intermediate meta-cognitive awareness.* Whether that happens, or how often that happens, is at central issue in a study of meta-cognition, but the Schooler, Reichle, and Halpern methodology makes it impossible to observe meta-cognition as it naturally occurs or doesn't occur. They explicitly instructed their subjects to take a meta-cognitive stance: subjects were to press a key every time they zoned out. In essence, they instructed their subjects to engage in precisely the behavior that they later "discovered." The beep can provide an alternative that avoids that preconceptual trap. For example, have subjects read in the laboratory and beep them at random intervals. Their task is simply to describe their awareness at the precise moment of the beep, whatever that awareness happens to be. No mention of zoning out or any other phenomena need be made – the study seeks to discover the phenomena that occur while reading, whatever those phenomena are. If at a beep the subject is thinking about something unrelated to the reading, the subject will describe that experience. If not, not. If such unrelated thinking occurs frequently, then we would be justified in concluding that "zoning out" is frequent. If at a beep the subject is thinking about his own mental processes, the subject will describe that experience. If not, not. If such self-observation occurs frequently, then we would be justified in concluding that meta-cognition is frequent and to explore its relatively undisturbed characteristics.

Certainly we do not wish to single out the Schooler, Reichle, and Halpern study as being exceptional in this regard. Many, perhaps nearly all, psychological investigations begin with preconceptions and then attempt to verify them. We do wish to point out that that is a risky, quite possibly extremely misleading, approach to scientific investigation, particularly for sensitive phenomena such as awareness. If our task is to understand consciousness, we must observe the phenomena as closely as possible to the way they naturally occur.

Aid 9: Repeated observations can lessen the importance of any single observation. Repeated observations are of course the cornerstone of time sampling (see Aid 1). But the repeated nature of beep-triggered observations also facilitates the setting aside of preconceptions by lessening the relative importance of any single observation. Suppose the beep occurs and at the moment there is some surprising phenomenon occurring – words seem to be being imagined backwards, for example. The repeated-observation nature of the sampling method can allow the investigator to take a dispassionate, unattached, uninvolved view of the phenomenon. "That seemed like words coming out backward? We don't really have to worry too much about it. If backward words is an important phenomenon, it will reappear at a subsequent beep. If not, not." The phenomenon at any single beep becomes important only if similar phenomena occur at other beeps.

Aid 10: The beep can allow an adequate time to examine and/or describe a particular moment. This is by obvious contrast to think-aloud methods, which presume that the stream of external speaking can "keep up" with the important details of inner experience. However, DES studies (e.g., Hurlburt 1993, 1997) show that inner experience is often much more complex. Multiple simultaneous visual images, for example, occasionally occur, and such experiences could not possibly be adequately characterized by think-aloud methods.

Aid 11: The beep can trigger observation, not manipulation. Most modern psychological studies involve experimental or situational manipulation. For example, Suchan and his colleagues (2002) used fMRI to study visual imagery:

> The subject's task consisted of drawing imagined lines connecting encircled numbers in ascending order and estimating the number of lines crossing. Compared with a control task in which there were no crossed lines, there were significant rCBF increases in the cingulate gyrus, the adjacent superior frontal gyrus and in the left inferior parietal cortex. The rCBF changes of the latter area correlated with task performance time. Since these activation areas are close to those in imagery of movement trajectories, the authors concluded that they appear to be a subsystem for processing mental visuospatial images.
> (Suchan et al. 2002: 163)

Whereas it is certainly plausible to assume that the subjects in this study were engaged in a visual imaging task, there may well be other non-image ways to approach the line-crossing task. This study cannot determine the individual differences of subjects in this regard. Furthermore, imagining line crossings is probably a highly unusual activity for most subjects, quite different from their naturally occurring visual imaging. The beep could be used to collect more natural images as follows: trigger the fMRI data collection and fractions of a second later sound a beep asking the subject to describe his or her experience that was ongoing a fraction of a second earlier. Select for fMRI analysis those samples that happen to include visual imagery and discard the rest. To our knowledge, such an investigation has not been performed.

Aid 12: The beep can identify specific concrete moments on which to test preconceptual general notions. Armchair observation often is based on general notions, sometimes sweeping ("What is my thinking usually like?") and sometimes less sweeping but still general ("What was I thinking while I solved that problem?"). Whatever those general notions are, they are likely to be brought into play any time the armchair observer thinks about his or her inner experience. These types of preconceptions can be quite resistant to change and often exist in the face of considerable contrary evidence. The beeps however, can provide specific, concrete instances against which preconceptions can be repeatedly tested. Because the several moments encountered on the repeated occasions that the beep facilitates are all different from each other at least to some extent, they encourage the observer to pay close attention to those preconceptual general notions as they are highlighted by the differing perspectives of the several moments.

Aid 13: The repeated-occasion nature of the beep allows inductive generalizations. If careful examination of a beeped moment at time 1 reveals characteristic X, and that same characteristic X is also revealed at times 3, 5, 6, 8, and so on, then it is possible to form a truly inductive generalization such as, "Characteristic X is a frequent occurrence for this subject." Armchair observations frequently form the basis of statements that look like inductive generalizations but are actually more reflective of preconceptions than of repeated direct observation.

Criticisms of beeper-based research

Although beeper-based strategies for exploring awareness have existed for decades, they are still relatively rare. Why? At least partially because of the following criticisms. In an attempt to clarify the appropriate limits of beeper-based strategies, we address these criticisms. We use examples from our own DES studies.

Criticism 1: The beep surprises the subject, who is not in a state of readiness to observe. To observe phenomena accurately, it is desirable both (a) to have circumstances favorable for observation (subject immediately prepared and highly trained, known stimuli explicitly presented as in a laboratory, etc.); and (b) to have circumstances favorable for the phenomenon to emerge (subject uninfluenced by any preconceptions transmitted during training, subject in his or her natural environments and engaged in his or her own natural behaviors, etc.). It may be impossible to fully meet both requirements simultaneously. We do note that after a day or two of practice, most of our DES subjects report that it seems to them that they can immediately observe their experience when the beep occurs – that is, that they are not surprised or disturbed by the beep, and they are able to note the experience that was ongoing at the moment of onset of the beep. Such reports of course do not make it so, but it is true that moderately experienced DES subjects seem to be able to respond to the beep quite easily.

Criticism 2: The random nature of the beep makes it likely that infrequent but important characteristics will be missed. This is unquestionably true for some kinds of phenomena. However, many observers of DES have been surprised at how frequently the random darts of the beep actually hit some seemingly rare phenomenon of interest. Our understanding of this is that important but seemingly rare phenomena are actually more frequently occurring than was thought. Clearly more research is necessary on this point, but in the meantime it is wise not to rule out a sampling-based approach until it has been actually established that the phenomenon will not be found using sampling. Stone and Nicolson (1987) recommended combining sampling with continuous recording (diary-type methods) as the most useful strategy.

Criticism 3: Inner experience is a stream, but the beeper approach makes it appear like a series of moments. It is certainly true that most reports of DES subjects make it appear that experience is saltatory, more like a series of beads on a string than a continuous stream. Whether that is an artifact of the method or whether that is the way experience is needs further clarification. It is certainly possible that for some, perhaps most people, awareness jumps from one experience to the next with little or nothing in between. It is also possible that DES is by its nature unable to observe the actual stream-like characteristics of awareness. Further investigation is necessary here.

Criticism 4: There is no way of knowing how much the beep disturbs inner experience. This criticism is undeniably true – the beep does in fact disturb inner experience. DES tries to minimize this disturbance as much as possible by focusing on the moment of awareness immediately prior to the occurrence of the beep (what we call the "last undisturbed moment" prior to the beep). Although this requires a slight "rewinding" of the memory trace of awareness, most participants report little difficulty in doing this, which is consistent with our understanding of short term memory (Atkinson & Schiffrin 1968). Furthermore, there are sometimes external sources against which the claim of validity of inner experience reports can be tested. In Chapter 11 we will discuss the case of Fran, concluding that Fran had no figure/ground phenomenon in her inner (and outer) experience based on five "idiographic validity" reasons. While not definitively ruling out the criticism that the beep disturbs experience, that discussion will limit the extent of that criticism.

Criticism 5: Responding to the beep puts the subject in a reflective stance, and thus beep-triggered introspection does not explore unreflective consciousness. That is absolutely true, and that is a primary reason that we refer to the subject matter of DES investigations to be "inner experience" rather than "consciousness." Theories of consciousness require an extrapolation from reflective observations of awareness; the question here is whether the beeper helps to build a solid foundation from which to extrapolate. It is important to keep this fair criticism separate from a frequent but unfair confound with long-term retrospection and armchair observation.

Criticism 6: Reports about inner experience, whether beeped or not, are private, and therefore unreliable. The extent to which one should credit reports about inner experience is of fundamental importance. In Chapter 11 we will discuss the reliability of DES and show that its reliability coefficients are extremely high.

Measuring reliability, as we will do in Chapter 11, does not measure the extent to which the reports about inner experience actually reflect the contents of awareness. That is a limitation of sampling-based and all other means of exploring inner experience. The fundamental question thus remains: To what degree should we believe the report of a subject? There is always a degree of doubt, and conviction is therefore always short of 100%, whether the reports are about inner experience or outer experience. Why does New York physicist Mary credit Pennsylvania physicist William's voltmeter reading? It is not because the reading was public – in fact, neither Mary nor anyone else was present when William made the reading. Mary credits William because he demonstrates knowledge, care, and skill regarding voltmeters. When William says, "I replaced the voltmeter wires with new ones and obtained the same reading," or "I used two different voltmeters and obtained the same reading," Mary's conviction rises because she sees that William is demonstrating that he knows the frequent causes for voltmeter-reading failure, and has exercised appropriate care to rule out those possibilities.

Certainly included in Mary's crediting of William is the fact that voltmeter readings *can* be public: Mary might know that in certain specified situations (such as in university physics classes) William obtained the same voltmeter readings as did a qualified instructor. That is an important consideration, but it does not override all other considerations.

The question then becomes, how does one demonstrate knowledge, care, and skill when giving reports about inner experience? There is no definitive answer to that question, any more than there is a definitive answer to the question about how to demonstrate knowledge, care, and skill when using voltmeters. But it seems reasonable that the demonstration of interrater reliability is a first step, along with demonstrated sensitivity to other issues surrounding sampling.

Characteristics of a good signal

Suppose that in a particular situation a researcher believes that the reasons to beep outweigh the criticisms. What should the characteristics of the beeping signal be? We do not believe that the signal must necessarily be an audible beep. We discuss now six desirable characteristics of a good signal.

Characteristic 1: Unambiguity. Whatever is used for the signal must be unambiguous in the sense that the signal must mean "Pay attention to your awareness now!" and nothing else. Thus it is not adequate to use, for example, a telephone ring to cue self-observation. At the moment of the telephone ring, the subject must in some way decide *not* to engage in the usual telephone-ring behavior and *instead* pay attention to inner experience. That decision process substantially complicates the attentional task.

Characteristic 2: Easy detectability. The subject must not have to struggle to discern whether the signal exists or not. For example, if the beep is too soft, the subject must engage in a task that is something like, "Is that the beep? Is that the beep? Yes that's the beep!" but by now the evanescent characteristics of the experience have disappeared. If the signal is too loud, a startle response can obliterate ongoing experience.

Characteristic 3: Rapid onset. As suggested above, it is desirable to define with as much precision as possible the exact moment under investigation. That requires the signal to have a clearly defined rapid onset. That makes the kind of vibrator typically used in pagers not desirable, for example. The subject's ability to discern precisely the onset of the vibration is not adequate.

Characteristic 4: Privacy. The subject's task at the moment of the beep is to pay attention to his or her ongoing awareness as undisturbed as possible. Thus that paying attention is a solitary, private task. If the signal occurs in a public way, for example, a beep audible to all people in the vicinity, then the response to the beep is complicated by the social implications: "What will I tell George when he asks me what that beep caught?" DES solves this issue by delivering the signal through a transistor-radio-type earphone.

Characteristic 5: Portability. If the object is to understand experience as it naturally occurs, then the signal must be able to follow the subject easily to wherever that experience takes place.

Characteristic 6: Require a response. We use a beep that continues uninterrupted until the subject pushes a button to terminate it. This forces the subject to take some action in response to each beep. We have used beeps of short duration (half a second), but have found that self-terminating beeps make it easier for the subject to ignore the beep and continue on with whatever activity was ongoing. Certainly that is possible also with a beep that must be stopped by the subject, but the probability of adequate response is greater if the subject has to make at least some response.

Discussion

We have identified 13 ways that beeping can aid in the introspective enterprise. We wish to emphasize that that does *not* imply that anyone who uses a beeper has direct access to the truth about inner experience. In this respect, the beeper is like the laser as a surgical tool: the laser is quite effective, allowing surgeries to be performed that were impossible without it. But you still want it to be operated by a skilled practitioner. The exploration of inner phenomena is in fact difficult: events are private, evanescent, and sensitive; people (subjects and investigators) hold strong but untrue preconceptions about inner experience;

and so on. The beeper is a useful tool in the exploration toolbox, but it does not necessarily solve every problem, nor does it guarantee the fidelity of the results.

Note

* This chapter is an edited version of Hurlburt, R. T. & Heavey, C. K. (2004). To beep or not to beep: Obtaining accurate reports about awareness. *Journal of Consciousness Studies, 11,* 113–128. Used with permission.

CHAPTER 6

The Descriptive Experience Sampling procedure

We have seen that science (Chapter 4) and technology (Chapter 5) provide many guidelines for the exploration of inner experience. Distilled to their essence, those guidelines show that there is only one legitimate question about the facts of inner experience: "What are the details of your inner experience at this very moment?" Of course, there is nothing uniquely magical about the particular words used to express that question; "What's going on with you right now?" or "What's happenin'?" would be just as good as long as it is understood that those locutions mean precisely the same thing as "What are the details of your inner experience at this very moment?"

The Descriptive Experience Sampling (DES) method for exploring inner experience, to which we now turn, is a simple yet sophisticated method that asks that one legitimate question about randomly selected moments of experience. As a way of introducing DES, we present a lightly edited transcript of an initial meeting. We invite you to imagine yourself in the role of Annette, a prospective subject in a DES study.

Russ: Hi! I'm not sure what my associates have told you about our project. Shall I start at the beginning, or do you have a good sense of what we're about?

Annette: (not her real name) Please start at the beginning.

Russ: OK. I'm interested in inner experience, what people are like from the inside, so to speak. To be interested in such things is not new, of course – people have been interested in what other people are really like since the dawn of recorded history or before – in fact, what inner experience is like is one of the world's most interesting questions. However, it turns out...

> We'd like you to be genuinely interested in discovering your experience.

Annette: (interrupting) What do you mean by "inner experience"?

Russ: For the moment I'd like to be a bit vague about this, if you don't mind, because I'm more interested in exploring *your* notion of "inner experience" than in defining it my way. But in general I mean thoughts, feelings, perceptions, sensations, observations of the world, tickles, urges, itches, pains – anything that appears "in the footlights of consciousness," so to speak. Clear enough for the moment? [Annette nods.] Good.

We'd like you to tell us what inner experience is, rather than us to tell you.

Anyway, as I was saying, it turns out that for a variety of reasons it has been remarkably difficult to explore inner experience adequately because there are a number of pitfalls that can make the exploration difficult or inaccurate. The major pitfall is that most methods of exploring inner experience over the last thousands of years have been *retrospective*: the investigator would ask you to think back over the last day (or over the last week or over your entire lifetime) and describe what your inner experience is *usually* like. You'd probably scratch your head and do your best to answer that question, but it turns out your answer might not correspond with the truth – not because you were lying, but because many people don't know the characteristics of their inner experience.

However, I've been using a method for the last twenty or so years that avoids many of those pitfalls and may do a better job of describing inner experience than has ever been possible.

Should you agree to participate, I'll give you a beeper like this. [At this point Russ displays a small, shirt-pocket-sized random interval generator.] It has a standard transistor radio type earphone that you wear like this [Russ demonstrates]. Once you turn it on, the device will do nothing for a while, and then it beeps. These beeps occur at random times – nothing that I or you do affects when the next beep might occur.

At each beep, your task is to pay attention to the inner experience that was ongoing at the moment of the beep – to "freeze" it, as it were – and then to jot down some notes about it in this notebook [Russ displays a small spiral-bound notebook].

I'd ask you to wear the beeper into your everyday environment and to engage in whateever activities you would usually do (short of swimming, which would be hard on the electronics!). When the beep

We want this to be about the natural you, not you in some contrived situation.

occurs, I ask that you "freeze" your experience, interrupt your activity (whatever it is), and jot down a few notes about it in the notebook. After you've collected six beeps, which is likely to take three or four hours, we will get together and discuss each beep in detail.

Annette: What am I supposed to write?

Russ: Well, I'd like you to write in the notebook whatever it takes for you to recall in detail what the experience was like at the moment it was occurring. Here again, I'm being a bit vague because I don't want to tell you what to write. I want you to convey the features of your experience as they occur to you – in your words, your way – and what you choose to write is up to you. It may develop, as we get more experience together, that I'll ask you to pay particular attention to some kind of detail and make some notes about that particular detail, but that is fairly unusual.

> You're a co-investigator. Write what *you* need.

By the way, if you prefer, we can arrange other ways of taking notes about what was going on at the moment of the beep. For example, I could give you a small tape recorder if you would prefer to record your notes rather than write them in the notebook.

Annette: No, thanks, I'd just as soon write them down.

Russ: Fine. So you'll wear the beeper until you get six beeps, and then we'll discuss those beeps in detail. That discussion is likely to take about an hour, and I'd like it to take place within 24 hours of the beeps, either later that same day or the next day. We like to have "fresh beeps," as we say. I don't particularly care when you wear the beeper, although I do request that you wear it at times that you are engaged in different activities. If you always wear it when you're watching TV, for example, the results are likely to be somewhat one-sided.

> We'd like to match the variety of your experience.

Annette: How long would I have to do this?

Russ: That's a bit hard to specify in advance, but typically somewhere between four and eight sampling days. The days themselves can be scheduled at your convenience – they do not have to be consecutive, but I'd like to have them reasonably close together if possible.

Each sampling day thus requires a commitment of somewhat over an hour of your time: You wear the beeper for about three hours while you perform whatever activities you typically would at that time. Responding to each beep usually takes just a minute or two, so you've invested six or eight minutes in the sampling process itself. Then there is the hour-or-so discussion of the details of the samples.

Annette: I should be honest with you – I don't think I'd be very good at this. Over the last few days (since I made this appointment with you) I've tried to pay attention to my inner experience, and I found that I just couldn't do it.

Russ: That's very common, and you're pointing to one of the reasons that earlier studies of inner experience have failed. As you have observed, it *is* usually difficult to pay attention to inner experience. Here's why: When you decide to pay attention to your inner experience, you ask yourself, "What's my inner experience like right now?" Of course, you rule out the "What's my inner experience like right now?" question itself, because that isn't the inner experience you intended to observe. When you rule out that question, there's nothing left in inner experience to observe because that "What's my inner experience like right now?" question *is* the content of inner experience at that moment.

However, using the beeper allows most people to sidestep that difficulty quite easily. It's as if the beep itself gives the "pay attention to my inner experience right now" instruction, freeing you to pay attention to the ongoing experience without having to interrupt it by issuing the "pay attention" instruction yourself.

But let me emphasize that just because other people find it easy does *not* mean that you will find it easy (or even possible) to respond to the beep. If it proves difficult or impossible, please tell me. It would be important to know that it is difficult or impossible (perhaps we can figure out why – or perhaps this beeping technology simply doesn't work for you, and that would be important to know).

So that's the project in a nutshell. If you're still interested, I'll continue with some more details, but if you have heard enough to know that you would rather not participate, that's fine too.

Annette: I'm still interested.

Co-investigators

Russ: OK. Before we go any farther I'd like us to be absolutely clear that I view us as co-investigators in this project, and I hope you will adopt the same stance. You have something I need in order for this project to advance – your inner experience. You are the expert about that, and I am totally lost without your participation. On the other hand, I have a method and expertise in exploring that inner experience, so I can help you understand the details of your experience. Together, we have a good shot at learning something interesting, but neither of us can do it alone.

> We call equality the "one legitimate relationship," encouraging participants to help us shape the investigation by, for example, suggesting particular lines of questioning, etc. We have found that any hint of superiority serves in a subtle or not-so-subtle way to shape participants' reports or foster their resistance.

You are *not* my "subject," and I will not manipulate you or place covert requirements on you, and so on. I hope we can share a common goal – understanding your inner experience – and that we can work together to achieve that goal as fully as possible. I have an idea about how to proceed (after all, I've been doing this for 30 years), but I have never tried to understand *your* experience, and we may have to invent a brand new way of exploration in your case. So if what I say or ask doesn't seem right or seems off the track, by all means tell me about it.

> What you see is what you get. There is nothing hidden in this investigation.

Furthermore, I'd like to be perfectly clear that you have total control over this project. If you agree to participate today, you can change your mind tomorrow. If we do conclude our study, I'll likely write a description of your inner experience. I will want you to critique it, and I'll modify it if possible so that it reflects accurately what both you and I have found. I'll ask you whether I can publish portions of that account in journal articles or books (I'll change the names to protect your privacy), and you should feel free to give or to decline to give permission at that time. You have no obligation to anything at any time.

I fully recognize that we would be exploring something that is by its very nature absolutely private, and that I have no right to view your experience unless you invite me to do so.

It may happen that the beep occurs when you are doing something or thinking something that you would prefer not to discuss. In that case you should feel free to tell me that something occurred that is none of my business, and I'll respect that. I have things that are none of your business, and I presume that you have things that are none of mine.

The topic of our investigation is fundamentally your private property. We'll take pains to protect your privacy.

If a particular beep is none of my business, please tell me that explicitly rather than simply trying to omit talking about the sensitive portion of that experience. I make this request for practical reasons. When we discuss a sample, I will keep questioning until I feel that I have a clear understanding of your experience. If you are holding something back, I'm likely to feel that my understanding is somehow incomplete, so I'll keep questioning and questioning, trying to understand it fully. It's just easier if you say right off, "This beep is none of your business."

I'd like you to be absolutely comfortable, with no reluctance, in saying, "That's none of your business." If I can trust you to tell me that something is none of my business when that is the case, then I can feel free to ask whatever I might wish to ask in order to understand some aspect of your experience.

Actually, I might say, it's fairly rare that people invoke this none-of-your-business privilege, because it turns out that most experiences are fairly mundane or prosaic (as judged by the people themselves, not by me). But I want you to fully appreciate the privilege so that our conversations can be candid and complete. Still with me?

Annette: Sure.

We believe that there is one and only "one legitimate contract" between subject and investigator in this situation: Feel free to tell us *nothing* about your experience – it's your private property. But if you tell us anything, tell us the truth, the whole truth, and nothing but the truth.

We convey as forthrightly and repeatedly as possible that our subjects should feel perfectly free to give the none-of-your-business response. It is only on that basis that we can feel free to ask for the details of an experience. We can feel free to ask anything we want only if we believe that our subject will tell us that something is none of our business.

The other side of the coin is that if the subject elects not to say none-of-your-business, then we ask that the subjects tell us the truth, the whole truth, and nothing but the truth about their experience. We mean that request in its deep, real meaning, *not* as the shibboleth of modern jurisprudence.

The Court Clerk, in the United States, administers the oath: "Do you swear to tell the truth, the whole truth, and nothing but the truth, so help you God?" Nearly identical oaths are administered in most other countries' legal systems. Despite the fact that this is stated as a sacred oath, its interpretation in the legal system is often as if the swearer had said, "I swear to tell the truth in as narrow a way as seems advantageous. I will feel free to withhold as much of the truth as the attorneys will let me get away with. I will feel free to say things that are deliberately misleading as long as there is some technical sense in which they are not entirely false." It is beyond the scope of this book to speculate about why judicial systems continue to administer the "truth, whole truth, nothing but the truth" oath when its shallow hypocrisy is so patently clear, but we note in passing that this hypocrisy has a long history: Henry Garnet, the Jesuit martyr of the 1500s, is believed to have written the "Treatise of Equivocation" as a way of instructing Catholics how to equivocate in Protestant courts.

When we desire that our subjects tell us the truth, the whole truth, and nothing but the truth, we mean that to be taken in its deepest sense. We wish our subjects to make their experience transparently available to us. We wish them to adopt the strategy that is the *opposite* of the hostile witness. We want them *not* to mislead us, but to take us as directly as possible to the heart of their experience. We want them *not* to hide behind our failure to ask the important question – we want them to help us learn to ask the important questions if we haven't figured it out on our own. We want our relationship to be cooperative, not adversarial.

Sampling mechanics

Russ: Good. Here's how the beeper works. The beeper creates beeps on a random schedule. It decides when the next beep will come, although it should never be more than about an hour between beeps. I haven't programmed in the beeps, and the beeps aren't linked to any characteristic of your behavior. They're simply random.

This button is an on/off switch and volume control for the beep. Getting the volume right may take a little practice. If it's too loud, it will startle you, and you'll likely forget what was in your inner experience. If it's too soft, you'll find yourself asking yourself, "Is that the beep?" and when you discover that it is in fact the beep, what will be in your experience at that moment is merely the question "Is that the beep?" which is not our real concern. How loud the beep must be depends on where you are: if you're in church or in the library, it can be quite soft, but if you're driving it will have to be quite loud.

It is *always* OK to say that you couldn't respond to the beep – because it was too loud, or you were engaged in an activity that you didn't want to interrupt, etc.

Don't try to make something up just to answer a question. It may well be that I ask questions that are impossible to answer, that don't apply to you, or that you don't understand. Simply say "I don't know" or something like that. Our task is to describe accurately your inner experience, and we'll accomplish that most efficiently if we're honest with each other about what was happening at the moment of the beep and how well we understand it. If a question is impossible to answer, then it's impossible, and that's OK.

"The moment of the beep" is the last undisturbed moment before the beep begins.

When the beep comes, I'd like you to focus on the very moment that the beep occurred, that microsecond just before your awareness was disturbed by the beep. I'm not interested in what your reaction to the beep was – I'm interested in your experience just at that instant that the beep began. It's rather like a flash photograph. The very beginning of the beep is the flash. I'm interested in what was ongoing right at the moment of the flash. The flash very often makes you blink, but the photo records your face immediately prior to the blink. Just like the flash photo, I wish our research to record the experience that was ongoing immediately *prior* to your reaction to the beep.

We want to know your experience at the moment of the beep. Not more, not less.

I'm not particularly interested in why your experience was the way it was. Sometimes you'll need to give such an explanation so that we can have effective communication about your experience, but I'm primarily interested in *what* the experience was like, *not* in *why* it had the content or features it had. Furthermore, I'm not interested in whether a particular sample is typical or unusual. The random method will tell us whether something is usual or unusual. If a kind of experience is typical, then we'll see many of them, and if not, not.

I'll be interested in the content of the experience – what you were thinking about or how you were feeling, for example. But I will also be interested (actually, probably more interested) in the phenomenon of the experience itself – how this particular thought or feeling was experienced.

Annette: You're losing me here. Once again, I'm not sure I will be able to do what you want.

Russ: Maybe you will, maybe you won't – either is OK. Let me reassure you a little. Prior to sampling, most people think sampling will be difficult, but yet most people have no difficulty whatsoever once sampling begins.

Furthermore, the method will evolve as we do it – that's part of the reason we meet repeatedly over several or many days. During the first few days you will come to understand the kinds of questions I ask, and as a result you will become better able to answer them. At the same time, I will come to an understanding of the kinds of experiences you have, and as a result I will become better at asking good questions.

> We won't be perfect at it at first, but we'll learn how to do it together.

I'd actually prefer that our first few sessions seem like something of a struggle. We will be struggling in parallel to find the best way to explore and describe something that I have never seen before and you have probably never tried to describe before.

> We want to evolve a way of talking about your experience that is natural for *your* experience. We don't want to impose our way of talking.

I could, of course, give you a list of the kinds of questions I sometimes ask, but I'd rather not do that. I want us to approach your experience in whatever way seems most natural for you. I want to color your expectations as little as possible. That may lead to some challenging moments in the first few sessions, but that's just part of the game.

I hope I've allayed your misgivings, because while such misgivings are common initially, they generally evaporate as sampling progresses. The beep is "magic" in that regard – for most people most of the time, the beep makes simple what seems like it might be difficult. And I hope you will forgive my evasiveness – I simply don't want to shape your expectations any more than is necessary. I promise to answer whatever questions you might have about any aspect of this study or your experience as fully and candidly as I can, or to explicitly request, as now, to delay giving an explanation until a later time.

So are you ready to give it a shot? Remember, any commitment you make is just one day at a time – you can change your mind at any time.

Annette: Sure. What the heck.

The expositional interview

Annette agrees to sample. We choose a sampling day, and she wears the beeper for perhaps three hours – long enough to get six random beeps. Then, either later that day or the next day (we want to talk about "fresh beeps"), we meet for the "expositional interview," where I interview her about those six samples. The purpose of this in-depth interview is to help her describe in substantial detail the features/characteristics of each of the experiences, one beeped moment at a time, that were ongoing at the beeped moments. We call it the expositional interview to indicate that our intent is to expose (to make known, bring to light) what is hidden from us but present to the subject (though not necessarily, at first, clearly known to the subject either).

Our task in the expositional interview is to discover what's there, to reveal the details of a phenomenon that is readily available to the subject but about which he or she has probably not directly communicated. We "roll up our phenomenological sleeves" (thanks to Eric Schwitzgebel for that phrase) and try to expose the phenomenon that was ongoing at the moment of the beep. We approach this task much like an archeologist approaches a bone: the bone is there – it's not a figment of the archeologist's imagination. The task is to brush away the silt, allowing the bone to be seen more clearly than it was originally, but it is still the same bone. We try not to alter the bone in any way, but instead to remove anything that is not the bone until the bone is clearly in view.

Once we have exposed/discovered/described the experience at one particular sample, we move on to the next. We try to treat this next exposition/discovery/description as a new event, independent of previous events. That is, we try to "cleanse our phenomenological palate," and not fall into the trap of being unduly influenced by what we've said or heard before. For example, it is frequently the case that at the end of the discussion of one sample, we say something like, "Well, as best we could figure for that sample, the experience was like talking to yourself, but let's make explicitly sure that we understand that this is early in sampling, and perhaps we were mistaken. I'm not saying we're wrong in our description; I'm merely saying that let's not presume that we were right. If talking to yourself is something that you do frequently, we'll see it down the road, and we can describe it again then. And if we were mistaken about what we said about this sample, then we won't see similar phenomena later. So we don't need nor want to be particularly attached to what we've just said or observed."

And so sampling proceeds. Annette wears the beeper and obtains a half dozen samples (there's nothing magic about six, except that it generally takes us about an hour to discuss five or six samples); we meet shortly thereafter and discuss those samples; the next day or a few days later she wears the beeper again and gets another six samples; we meet again to discuss them; and so on. During this entire procedure I view this as a partnership: Annette has something I don't have (access to her experience) and I have something she doesn't have (a sophisticated method for exploring experience). Together, we may be able to do something interesting/worthwhile that neither of us can do alone. Annette is likely to believe me, and to take the role of co-investigator seriously. For example, she may say something like, "Y'know, I'm a runner, and I sometimes get into the runner's high. Should I wear the beeper while I'm running?" I'll respond something like, "Sure. But let's not assume that there is in fact a runner's high. Let's also not assume that there is in fact *no* runner's high. Maybe there is, maybe there's not. Either way is fine. So wear the beeper while you're running, and maybe we'll find out something about your runner's high. Maybe we won't. We will find out something about you as you run, and that may well be interesting regardless of whether a runner's high is involved."

There may well come a time when we believe it is to science's advantage to explicitly prescribe when and where a subject samples. We have no objection in principle to such specification. However, at this stage of relative ignorance about inner experience, it seems more profitable to explore, and to allow subjects to help us plan the exploration. They do, of course, know more about themselves than we do. Our task is to help them not to get caught up in their preconceptual understandings. So we do *not* explore the runner's high – that would assume what is at issue, whether or how such a thing exists. But we *will* explore the experience while running, and if we find out something about the runner's high, fine. If not, fine as well.

The understanding/description produced in the expositional interview is clearly not a complete account of everything that was ongoing at the moment of the beep. That would be impossible. At the physiological level, there are billions of neurons and trillions of patterns of neurons that are firing in some sequence, and our task is not to describe those patterns/sequences. At the sensation level, there are thousands of square centimeters of skin, each responding to its environment separately and in patterns, as well as all of the sense organs sending their neurological sequences. Our task is not to describe all those patterns/sequences. Our task is to pay attention to the main characteristics that occurred in experience at the moment of the beep. Despite the fact that many commentators, and most subjects prior to sampling, believe that that is a difficult if not impossible task, it turns out that most subjects find it quite easy if the signal (the beep) is structured appropriately (unambiguous, fast rise time, neither too loud nor too soft, and so on) and the task is understood appropriately (we'll ask the one fundamental question and no others).

Does that mean that DES reports *all* things that were ongoing in awareness at the moment of the beep? No. We do believe that subjects can report the main things. In fact, most people, most of the time, are engaged in creating a relatively simple awareness. Imagine yourself at a football game, for example. There is a blooming plethora of perceptual possibilities: the sound of the peanut vendor in the aisle, the smell of the beer spilled beside you, the impact of the argument the fellow in the row in front of you is having with his neighbor, the coldness in your feet, and so on. But despite of all these events happening nearby, you are easily able to focus on Jerry Rice, a hundred yards away, as he catches a pass and heads out of bounds. Most people most of the time are extracting something (or some things) out of the welter to form inner experience (thoughts, feelings, perceptions, or whatever). DES simply asks you to report the main features of that experience at the moment of the beep.

So if the beep occurs, you report that you were watching Jerry Rice catch a pass and sprint out of bounds. Does that mean that the peanut vender, the beer smell, the argument, and so on, are simply not in your experience at the moment of the beep? No. It means that either they weren't in your experience, or they weren't sufficiently main features at the moment of the beep to be recalled when you reflect on your experience. DES does not try to sort out that difference. Could it if required? Perhaps. We don't know. Is it interesting/scientifically useful simply to pay attention to the main characteristics? We think so for the reasons described in this book, but the history of science will be the final judge.

Extracting the salient characteristics

Once we have, beep by beep, discovered/exposed/described the main features of each sampled experience, we engage in a pattern-recognition task that we call "extracting the salient characteristics." Actually, much of this work has probably already been done as part of the expositional interviews. It is quite natural for a subject to say at some point, "This experience is quite similar to the one where I. . .." Our response is likely to be, "Well, let's make sure we don't commit ourselves to the similarity now. . .." But often the similarities become simply too strong to ignore, and the subject will say, in a way that is convincing, "This sample is just like the one. . .." When the subject talks like that, we have identified a salient characteristic.

Some salient characteristics pass unnoticed by the subject, for whatever reason. Regardless of whether or not the subject has identified salient characteristics of their inner experience during the sampling process, we painstakingly review all the samples, looking for any patterns or features of their inner experience. After this review we typically write an idiographic description of the subject, which we then show to the subject for comment. Once this process is completed, we have a high-fidelity characterization of the person's inner experience. Is it possible that we miss salient characteristics of the person? Yes. However, our experience has shown that with an adequate number of sampling days and varied sampling situations, we can create descriptions that subjects themselves consider accurate portrayals of important features in their inner worlds.

Between-group characteristics

Sometimes the particular subject may have some external characteristic in common with other subjects. Perhaps a group of subjects have been diagnosed as depressed, for example. It will then be of interest to extract salient characteristics across subjects within the group, as a way of attempting to learn something about, for example, the experience of depression. Will we find all the important characteristics of the experience of depression? No, but the more subjects sampled in the more situations, the better. Is it necessarily the case that the experience of depression is the same or similar across people? No – that is precisely the issue. Is it true that some biological aspects of depression are causally related to the experience of depression? Probably, but we don't really know. We do believe that appropriately designed DES studies could bring some light to bear on this issue.

Questions and answers

Q: You observe that experience is evanescent, and yet you allow 24 hours between the beep and your conversation about it. Isn't the subject likely to forget or confabulate details over that interval?

A: Probably some, but we don't think very much. We have performed DES in a variety of ways, ranging from following the subject into his natural environment and interviewing him immediately after the beep occurs to allowing a week or so to elapse between the beep and the interview. Although we have no systematic data, our impression is that once a subject becomes experienced, there is not much change between immediately after the beep and overnight, but that if we allow two nights to intervene, the ability to focus on the beeps declines. We and others have examined the issue of delay in reporting in thought sampling (Hurlburt & Melancon 1987), finding that a delay is likely to exaggerate the vividness of reports. But it is questionable the extent to which that research applies to DES.

Without question, sooner is better than later, but too soon is disruptive to the subject's natural environment (the interviewer is inserted into the environment, the subject must interrupt his ongoing activity, etc.) and therefore disturbs natural experience. Our sense is that within 24 hours is a reasonable compromise, although certainly further research on this point would be desirable.

Q: Why six beeps and not seven or five?

A: Six is a practical response to many factors. First, we can rarely discuss more than six beeps in an hour-long expositional interview. That is an intensive interview, and an hour is a pretty long time for all involved, so we don't like to extend it. Second, our subjects (and we ourselves) generally seem to be able to keep six samples distinctly in mind without becoming confused about the similarities and differences between them. Third, early in sampling, subjects make a variety of mistakes – not understanding what is the moment of the beep, responding to presuppositions, and so on – and we don't want to demoralize the subject by having to correct the same mistake too often. Fourth, we often run out of time in an hour interview after discussing only three or four samples. We have to discard any beeps that we don't discuss. We don't want to demoralize the subject by discarding too many beeps. Fifth, some subjects have simple, straightforward experiences, and we could discuss more than six such samples in an hour. However, those subjects' experiences are usually quite uniform, and discussing six quite similar beeps is generally enough. Sixth, once the subject has become experienced, it is often possible to discuss more than six samples in an hour. At that point, we might increase the number of samples above six.

Q: Do subjects confuse the details of one beep with another – perhaps something that happened at beep 2 is reported as being part of beep 3?

A: Rarely do experienced subjects confuse the details of one beep with another, as best we can tell. The nature of DES is to focus on brief, specific, clearly defined moments. The concrete nature of those moments makes it easy for subjects to be unambiguously focused on one instant at a time, and confusion between them is rare.

Q: Why do you inquire about the insignificant details of the samples?

A: Because inquiring about details is a way (perhaps the only way) to encourage the subject to focus on the actually occurring experience. Here's an example:

At the beep, Julie was at the kitchen sink, washing magic marker off her hands. She's a 3rd grade teacher and she's cleaning up, just home from school. As she washes, she recreates in her imagination two scenes, one right after the other, from a dream she had had two nights before: She sees herself slitting her two-year-old daughter Tanya's throat with a kitchen knife; and then she sees Tanya hooked up to heart monitors and brain scan equipment in a hospital. The monitors reveal that the brain is dead but the heart is still beating. Julie takes the knife and plunges it into her daughter's heart. The beep came during the first scene, but the beep did not interrupt the sequence.

We asked the kinds of questions that the method requires: "In the first scene, what part of your daughter do you see?" Body and head. "What's she wearing?" Blue dress. "What hand do you have the knife in?" Right hand. "What exactly does the knife look like?" Stainless steel, serrated, brown handle, maybe six inches long, like one she actually has in her kitchen.

We don't actually care what Tanya was wearing or what color the knife was. We have no theoretical or practical position that implies that brown is better or worse than black, serrated is better or worse than straight, or that either is related to any personality or behavioral characteristic. We ask what color it is because we want Julie to pay attention to her experience at the moment of the beep.

The alternative to asking those questions is, of course, not to ask those questions. But not to ask is to encourage Julie to avoid paying attention to experience when the going gets rough. To ask detailed questions about easy experiences and to fail to ask the same kinds of questions about difficult experiences is to convey as forcefully as possible, "I agree with you. This is too hard. Let's avoid this and talk about something else."

Q: It seems cruel to ask for such details.

A: It might seem that exploring such characteristics in such detail would intensify the horrible feelings, but in fact the opposite was true. Julie struggled to spit the details out, but once out in sampling's supportive and nonjudgmental atmosphere, Julie was visibly relieved.

Q: It's hard to believe you can learn anything important from only 20 or 30 randomly chosen samples.

A: Yes, it is hard to believe. However, it turns out that when you examine moments in detail, even single moments, you learn a surprising amount about a person. Consider this single sample, from Les Hutchins' thesis:

> Racquel was at Wal-Mart looking at a "vegetable doll" at the moment of the beep. She was visually examining and attending to the eyes of the doll and thinking to herself how funny they looked. At the same time she was looking at other shoppers in her periphery. Furthermore, she felt a scared feeling which manifested itself as shaking in her body and a mental alertness at the possibility that the people around her may be looking at, and making judgments about, her. Visually examining the eyes of the doll, looking at other shoppers in her periphery, and feeling her body quiver were all aspects of Racquel's sensory awareness at the moment of the beep. (Hutchins 2003:60)

One gets to know a lot about Racquel from this single sample. Take 30 such samples and examine them for similarities, and important patterns do emerge.

Conclusion

DES is a simple method: Ask what was going on at the moment of the beep and keep out of the way of the answers. That is in fact all there is to it. However, that is something like saying that violin playing is a simple thing – play the right notes and avoid the wrong ones. There is a substantial delicacy required to perform the DES method well, and that delicacy is not naturally inborn in all potential DES practitioners, and it certainly is not fostered by modern psychology (quite the contrary). We believe that DES can be learned, perhaps not by everyone but by many, in the same sense that violin playing can be learned: it requires commitment, substantial practice, and probably the advice and support of someone with a good ear.

CHAPTER 7

Transcript of a DES expositional interview

In Chapter 6 we set the stage by showing how sampling subjects are invited to participate. In this chapter we present a transcript of a DES interview to illustrate how the sampling process actually works.

The following is a complete, unedited, annotated transcript of an interview and the ensuing interviewer-written description. The intent is to allow the reader to judge first hand the ways in which the methodological concerns have been dealt with – to take the methodological discussion out of the theoretical realm into the phenomenological one.

Sandy (not her own name) was an 18-year-old female college freshman who agreed to participate in a sampling study that would fulfill her Introductory Psychology research participation requirement. This particular study involved four meetings: the first to explain the procedure and then three sampling meetings scheduled a few days apart. The following transcript is the verbatim account of the interview regarding the last sample of her last sampling day. We have inserted comments throughout.

The interview

Russ.1: Then let's go on to [sample] number 15.

Sandy.1: (Looks at sampling notebook) At 8:25 [yesterday evening] – this is going back to all the other samples. I was reading – I was staring at the word "life" in the book – in the Primus book – and I had an image in my head – it was a black and white image, by the way – of . . . OK, I was staring at the word "life" and I had said "life" to myself in my own tone of voice, so. . .

> At this point in her sampling experience, Sandy knows that Russ would like to hear a general description of her sample, so she is prepared to begin with little prompting from him. "Going back to all the other samples" refers to several earlier samples where an image and inner speech had accompanied reading.

> "Said to myself in my own tone of voice" is Sandy's term (as she had used it in discussions of previous samples) for the phenomenon we call inner speech. We generally adopt the participant's own terminology in sampling interviews, rather than require them to adopt ours. The implication is that Sandy said the word "life" in her head in a voice that was experienced as being just like herself speaking aloud – same timbre, intonation, pitch, etc.

Russ.2: (Interrupts) and that was just before the beep or at the beep also?

Sandy.2: At the beep...

> Sandy's description at Sandy.1 was "and I *had said* 'life,'" so Russ asks Sandy to clarify whether that word was being said before the beep (in which case it would not be considered part of this sample) or at the moment the beep began (in which case it would be part of the sample and we would call it inner speech). She says it was at the beep, implying that her choice of verb "had said" should have been "was saying." Most people, including Sandy usually, are quite accurate in choosing the proper tense of verbs when they discuss a sample.

Russ.3: OK.

Sandy.3: . . .and immediately an im. . .a black and white image came in my head and it was like the word "life" because it was . . . the background was black and the word "life" was white and it was right here (gestures with left thumb and forefinger about a foot in front of her eyes and perhaps 8 inches to the left) and then I had . . . uh . . . I don't know whether it was my hand or somebody else's hand but it was a hand like this (gestures with right hand, palm directly up about a foot to the right of where she had indicated the word "life") with the brown soft sand right there (uses fingers of left hand as if touching something on the right palm) and then it was trickling down like somebody was pouring it.

> Sandy's left thumb and forefinger are held as if making the letter "C," approximately two inches from the bottom of the "C" to the top. This gesture occurs repeatedly during her description of this sample. Clearly she meant it to be indicating the size and the location of the letters in the word "life."

> Her right-hand gesture is with the palm directly up, in precisely the position one would use if actually holding a small pile of sand. When she refers to the sand trickling down, she tips this hand to her left as if dumping out the pile of sand.
>
> Note the care with which Sandy describes the hand: "I don't know whether it was my hand or somebody else's hand but it was a hand like this." This is an extremely sophisticated clarification of a subtle issue, and we have not given Sandy any particular training in this regard except to have asked repeatedly for the precise details of her experience. Furthermore, we have no reason to believe that Sandy is extraordinarily sophisticated in this regard – instead, it is the sampling procedure with its insistence on the moment of the beep that fosters this kind of refinement. In sampling interviews in general, not just with Sandy, it is striking how precise people are when describing what was and what was not present in their moments of experience.
>
> Note Sandy's use of the definite article in "with *the* brown soft sand right there." This indicates that the sand existed as a concrete particularity for Sandy. She did not refer to "*some* brown soft sand" or "a pile of brown soft sand," as if it could be a little pile or a large pile, but to "*the* brown soft sand," precisely this pile and no other.

Russ.4: OK. So the, so there's like a black background...

Sandy.4: (Interrupts) Yes.

Russ.5: ... and the word "life" is printed somehow sort of on the left side of this image, and...

Sandy.5: (Interrupts) Yes...yes (gestures again with left thumb and forefinger "C" just as before)

Russ.6: ...and, and, and is it possible to answer the question what kind of letters are these printed in? Is it like written-out letters or printed letters or typewritten letters...

> Note the indeterminacy of Russ' questions in this series (as elsewhere): "So there's *like* a black background"; "and the word 'life' is printed *somehow sort of* on the left side"; "*is it possible* to answer"; and then a series of possible choices: "*like* written out letters or printed letters or typewritten letters." As a general rule we try to undermine our own questions and conclusions as part of the art of not "leading the witness," not accepting anything as established until the participant has established it herself with little doubt.

Sandy.6: (interrupts) Lower case ... lower case typed letters, but they were big, pretty big for ...(trails off but has quizzical look apparently at the incongruity of the typewritten nature and the size of the letters)

Russ.7: And by "typed" do you mean like a sort of an old fashioned typewriter...

Sandy.7: (interrupts) Yes, yes.

> The question at Russ.7 may appear to be a leading question – Sandy had not herself referred to an "old fashioned typewriter." Several comments are in order. First, the intent of this question was to clarify the "written-out letters or printed letters or typewritten letters?" alternatives of Russ.6 – to amplify the distinction between letters produced by a printer and those by a typewriter. Second, had she not interrupted to affirm his first alternative, Russ would have provided some additional alternatives to undermine the possible leading effects, perhaps by saying something like "...like a sort of an old fashioned typewriter or by a computer generating a typewriter font such as Courier?" Third, the line between (a) commentary that indicates that Russ has understood what Sandy has said (both explicitly any nonverbally) and (b) commentary that leads the witness is necessarily fine in its details. Fourth, we should be clear about the magnitude of the possible leading here. Even if we grant that Russ led Sandy to the "old-fashioned typewriter" detail, the main aspects of the experience, that her experience was a visual image with white letters as if typed on a black background, was established without leading.

Russ.8: ... so what we would call a Courier kind of font kind of a deal?

Sandy.8: Um hm.

Russ.9: But bigger than a typewriter would...

Sandy.9: (interrupts) Oh, yeah!

> Note the certainty with which Sandy affirms Russ' description. When people have clear access to a particular inner experience, as apparently Sandy did here, they are extremely confident of the details of that experience. This confidence is just as unshakable as when standing in front of a real stop sign you ask the person what color the sign is. "Red." "Don't you really mean purple?" "Of course not. It may look like purple to you, but it's really red."

Russ.10: . . .and white!?

Sandy.10: Yeah!

Russ.11: ‘cause a typewriter usually types in white . . . er, in black.

Sandy.11: Um hm.

> Part of what makes Sandy’s access and accuracy convincing are her nonverbal responses to these details. The quizzical look at Sandy.6, for example, is easily interpretable as meaning something like, “I know that typewriters print in small letters, and I know I’ve indicated that these letters that I imagined are big, and I know that doesn’t make sense, but I’m just telling you what I saw!” The look is slightly apologetic, as if she is sorry that she is not telling Russ what he wants to hear (which of course is not true).
>
> Qualitative research such as this is often criticized on the ground that subjects are just trying to please the experimenter or trying to be socially acceptable. Sandy’s affect here is incompatible with that view. She is trying to tell the truth, even though she thinks it slightly weird and probably not what Russ wants.

Russ.12: OK. And then there’s the. . .the. . .

Sandy.12: The, the hand, the palm of the hand is like this (gestures palm up with right hand just as before) and there was a pile about this big (gestures with left hand about two inches above right palm) of brown soft sand (moves left hand back and forth as if outlining the pile of sand with fingers) and the hand was going like this (tips right hand to left as if pouring out sand) just like watching the sand pour off the hand.

Russ.13: OK. And so earlier on when you said that the image was black and white that apparently was referring to the “life” portion of the image ‘cause. . .

Sandy.13: (Interrupts) And the hand was white too, but the sand was the only thing that was brown.

> Note that Sandy’s first description of this image, at Sandy.1, was that “it was a black and white image, by the way.” That turns out not to be true. There are some strikingly black and white details in the image (the word “life” and the hand), and these are doubtless what Sandy was referring to when she said the image was black and white. However, the image per se is in color – it includes the brown sand.

> This illustrates the fact that the interview procedure is aimed at discovering what the person means, not at simply categorizing what the person says. What Sandy *meant* is that she had an image in which black-and-white and color were starkly interposed; what she *said* (at first) was that she had a black and white image. Whether that distinction is important depends on your current needs; the point is that Sandy did not initially say what she actually meant, and it required a careful interview to clarify what she meant.

Russ.14: Uh huh.
Sandy.14: The hand was white too.
Russ.15: So, so like this whole display is like a black and white....
Sandy.15: (interrupts) Um hm.
Russ.16: ...or shades, shades of gray. (Sandy nods) Well, is the hand, is the hand pure white or is the hand sort of gray like it would be, like you'd see a hand in a black and white photograph or a black and white movie, which would be sort of shades of gray?
Sandy.16: No, it's like the color of the typed letters, white.
Russ.17: Pure white. (Sandy nods). So the hand, the hand is a pure white hand (Sandy laughs nervously) with no shadows....
Sandy.17: (Interrupts) No, nothing, just...
Russ.18: ...or whatever, but holding on to this what is now a brown...
Sandy.18: (Interrupts) light brown sand. Um hm.

> Note that Sandy here corrects the details of Russ' characterization of her experience – he said "brown" and she refined that to "light brown." This kind of correction is important from the perspective of leading the witness – she certainly was not easily led about this detail. Furthermore, it demonstrates how clear and concrete her recollection of this experience is: "brown" is not as good a characterization as is "light brown."

Russ.19: Um hm. And, and then do you, do you see the sand being, the sand moving...
Sandy.19: (Interrupts) Yes.
Russ.20: ...so this is a moving portion of the...
Sandy.20: Of, of my image, um hm.
Russ.21: OK. And, and, it's, is it a left hand or a right hand?

> Sandy had repeatedly (as at line Sandy.3, Sandy.12, and Sandy.13) referred to "a hand" or "the hand." As she did so, she had repeatedly held up her own right hand, with the clear implication that the image "looked like this." Therefore, it was reasonable for Russ to infer that she meant that the hand she saw was a *right* hand. The question here ("is it a left hand or a right hand?") is another example of Russ' careful undermining of his own interpretation.

Sandy.21: (Shakes head as if bewildered). Like this hand (holds up right hand, palm up, and looks at it quizzically). I don't know.

Russ.22: OK.

Sandy.22: Right hand, yeah, the right hand. But I wasn't aware of that at the beep, I mean, now that I'm, I'm picturing that image again, because I can still have that same image, it was a right hand, but I wasn't aware of that...

> Three comments about the distinction between "a hand" and "a right hand." First, note the care with which Sandy distinguishes between what was part of her awareness at the moment of the beep and what can be inferred after the beep. At the moment of the beep, it was just a hand. When pressed, she can conclude from the geometry of the hand that it was in fact a right hand, but she is adamantly clear that the "rightness" of the hand was not a feature of her awareness at the moment of the beep. Most samplers learn quite easily and naturally to make a clear distinction between what was happening at the moment of the beep and what can be inferred later; this is a typical example. Taken by itself, this example is rather trivial, but the example is impressive when taken as evidence about how careful Sandy (like most samplers) is to distinguish the moment of the beep from any other moment or interpretation.
>
> Second, we should not confuse Sandy's addition of the "rightness" detail with a post hoc filling in of details. The geometry of the hand was present from the very beginning; what occurred post hoc was merely her realization that this geometry implied that the hand was a right hand.
>
> Third, whereas Sandy is not particularly clear about what the meaning or significance this hand has to her (see Sandy.34 in the interview below), she is perfectly clear about some aspects of the

> meaning of this hand. For whatever reason, as this image presents itself to Sandy the essential nature of this image is that it is of "*a* hand holding sand," *not* of a "*right* hand holding sand." The rightness of the hand is simply a true but mostly irrelevant fact of the hand's visual characteristics. This is a sophisticated distinction that Sandy makes easily and confidently, which reflects the power of the method to get to the details of awareness as experienced.

Russ.23: OK. And do you, and do you, so you're sort of going like this, do you see that hand from this perspective or from this perspective (models different angles of his own hand) or from looking...

Sandy.23: (Interrupts) From here (uses left hand to point first to her left eye and then to draw an imaginary line downward toward her right palm). Like from here, like I was...

Russ.24: (Interrupts) So as if it's your own right hand...

Sandy.24: (Interrupts) Yes.

Russ.25: ...looking at it as if you're holding it up (Sandy nods affirmatively) kind of like this. And, and, at the moment of the beep do you know that this is your hand or is this...?

Sandy.25: (Interrupts) I didn't know whose hand it was, no.

> Recall that at Sandy.3 Sandy had said that she did not know whose hand it was: "...and then I had ... uh ... I don't know whether it was my hand or somebody else's hand but it was a hand like this (gestures)...." Russ' question at Russ.25 ("do you know that this is your hand or is this...?") could be seen as a subtle pressure to change her story. She does not succumb to that pressure, and reiterates her original opinion.

Russ.26: So that we're, so when we're saying it's like your hand it's just like yours but it could be somebody else's.

Sandy.26: Yes. It could have been anybody's right hand.

Russ.27: OK. And, and the brown, tan sand. Is this like the real color of real sand, like beach sand, if you went to...

Sandy.27: (interrupts) Beach sand, exactly.

Russ.28: OK. And...

Sandy.28: And I could almost like feel, like experience the, the feeling of the sand, touching the, like the palm of my hand.

Russ.29: And, and when you say you could almost feel, is it, does that mean that in your imagination you were feeling that?

Sandy.29: Yes.

Russ.30: OK. In your hand were you feeling that? As if it was in your hand?

Sandy.30: Yes.

Russ.31: OK. So your hand was...

Sandy.31: (Interrupts) But I was, my hand was on the book. I wasn't, no, I wasn't aware that my hand was on the book at the time. I was just staring at the word "life" and then immediately this image popped in my head where the "life" was typed over here in white (gestures as before with left hand thumb and forefinger), the white hand was over here (gestures as before with right hand palm up), and I can see it and there is the sand about to here (gestures as before with left hand about two inches above right palm) of brown, (Russ: Um hm) tan sand and then the hand was just going like this (rotates right hand as before) and pouring all the sand off the hand.

Russ.32: And, and so it felt like your hand was actually doing that (Sandy: Yes) even though your, your real hand was still up and under the book?

Sandy32: Yes.

> Sandy is quite aware of the real impossibility of what she is describing: Her hand feels like it is pouring sand even though it is in reality holding the book. Her expression indicates that whereas this impossibility seems strange to her, it was in fact what she was experiencing.

Russ.33: Um... Um, and, and just out of curiosity – I don't, don't ask this question usually, but just, just, just because I'm curious – does this have something to do with life as far as you know, or...?

> As we've said, the DES procedure properly applied asks one and only one question, namely "What was going on with you at the moment of the beep?" It asks that question in many different forms, and presses for details in many different ways, but all are variations on that single, simple theme.
>
> A substantial part of the DES technique is to maintain this only-at-the-moment-of-the-beep focus. People in general initially have difficulty constraining themselves that narrowly, and the sampling technique training involves repeatedly exercising that single question as well as discouraging other other-than-the-moment-of-the-beep conversation.

> Here Russ himself violates the only-at-the-moment-of-the-beep focus and asks Sandy to speculate about the meaning or significance of this image. We don't usually ask that kind of question because we are extremely skeptical about people's ability to interpret or generalize about themselves, and statements about meaning require exactly that kind of interpretation. However, at Russ.33 Russ lets his guard down and asked a question that required Sandy to interpret. (In Russ' defense, the present sample was the last in Sandy's series of samples, so the only risk in asking the question was that Russ would believe the answer instead of maintaining a skeptical stance.)
>
> All that being said, we emphasize that from the DES perspective, Russ.33 is a bad question, but Russ asked it anyway.

Sandy.33: I think, uh, at the, I wasn't aware of it at the time, not that I know of now, I mean. I could have been just for that split second that I was imagining this, but that's what I'm gathering from the word "life" being over here, me feeling it from the sand, and then the hand being right there next to the word "life" in my image.

> It is noteworthy that even though Russ had asked a question that required her to interpret, rather than simply to give details of a given moment, Sandy answered his question as if it were about the specific sampled moment. That is, Sandy had apparently misunderstood Russ' question, which in fact was "Does this have something to do with life...?" and answered as if he had asked, "At the moment of the beep, did you know that this image had something to do with life?" answering that she did not have such an awareness at the moment of the beep.
>
> This mishearing of Russ' question indicates that Sandy has fully entered into the nature of the sampling task. Our previous sampling discussions had prepared her to focus only on the factual details of specific moments and to avoid interpretation or generalization. When Russ asked the outlawed interpretation question, she apparently departed from the words he had actually asked in that question to understand it in line with the nature of the sampling task.

> We take that as evidence of the disarmingly simple yet powerful nature of the sampling procedure. In an important way, what Russ actually asked is not as important as Sandy's understanding of the task as she had learned it from her series of sampling interviews.

Russ.34: So somehow the, somehow the sand represents life? In, in what way?

Sandy.34: (Shrugs, shakes head, and laughs nervously as if nonplused)

Russ.35: OK. So, so there's something about this that represents like the origins of life, or the basics of life, or the...?

Sandy.35: (interrupts) Or this is life and throwing it away, I mean, I don't, I have no idea.

> Sandy is clearly doing a better job of participating in the sampling process here than Russ is. Russ forced her to give an explanation/interpretation ("like the origins of life"), in violation of the sampling focus-on-the-moment procedure. She gave it, but she qualified it as strongly as possible: "I mean, I don't, I have no idea."

Russ.36: Um hm. OK. And anything else going on at the moment of this beep?

Sandy.36: Just completely mesmerized, you know, by my image.

Russ.37: So, and by mesmerized do, do you mean...

Sandy.37: (Interrupts) Like shocked that I was feeling it and seeing it and everything. I mean I was, I couldn't do anything! I was just, it took me a while to shut off the beep, even!

Russ.38: OK. So, so you were sort of, in, in your awareness you knew that you were drawn into this image or something like that?

Sandy.38: Um hm (nods affirmatively).

Russ.39: So your, your body is suspended, your emotion is suspended, (Sandy nods affirmatively throughout) and your ability to, your ability to do anything is suspended at the moment, until... I guess you finally did turn off the beep...

Sandy.39: (Sighing) Yeah!

> Six and a half minutes into the interview about this sample, a new feature is introduced for the first time. This kind of facet of the experience might easily be overlooked by any process that did not include a thorough and open-ended interview.

> Note that the interview was not totally clear about whether the mesmerized quality was present at the actual moment of the beep or as a result of the beeping process. Russ' impression is that it was present at the moment of the beep, but that impression comes from the general flavor of the interview, particularly his conviction that Sandy had internalized the distinction between at the beep and later (see discussion after Sandy.33). However that impression was not explicitly verified in the interview and may be incorrect.

Russ.40: Anything else?
Sandy.40: Uh uh (shakes head).
Russ.41: OK, then I think that does it for me.

The result

The second step of the DES procedure is for the investigator to write a description of each sample. Here is that output for Sandy's sample:

> At 8:25 p.m. Sandy was reading a biology book, speaking to herself in inner speech the words she was reading. At the moment of the beep, she was innerly saying the word "life" and simultaneously visualizing an image that included on the left the word "life" as if typed by an old typewriter, except the letters were approximately two inches high and were white against a black background. On the right in this image was a white hand, palm up, holding a small pile of light brown beach-type sand. As Sandy watched, this hand tipped to the left and trickled the sand out. The hand and the word "life" were pure white against a black background; the only color in the image was the light brown sand. This image seemed to mesmerize her, to suspend her motion for a moment.

The question of validity

This interview, just under eight minutes in length, is slightly shorter than the average DES interview. We have tried to make the transcript as accurate as possible, eliminating nothing, to give as realistic a being-there experience to the reader as possible.

The basic question in this situation is whether at 8:25 p.m. Sandy was in fact saying "life" to herself and seeing a black and white and light brown image that seemed to mesmerize her. Clearly we do not have the technology at our disposal to answer that question definitively.

However, science proceeds on the basis of probable answers, not on the basis of definitive answers, so the question is better phrased, How likely is it that at 8:25 p.m. Sandy was in fact saying "life" to herself and seeing a visual image that had a black background, white letters spelling "life" on the left and a white hand with light brown sand on the right, and that she seemed to be mesmerized by this image? We think the answer is: Quite likely.

Certainly it is possible to disagree about some of the details, as we have indicated in comments to the transcript above, but such disagreements do not undermine the general characterization of Sandy's experience at this sample or the efficacy of the method. For example, reconsider the mesmerization detail that was disputed after Sandy.39. The question was whether Sandy was feeling mesmerized at the precise moment of the onset of the beep, before she was disturbed by the beep itself, or whether that mesmerization was the result of responding to the beep. Our first observation is that this disagreement seems to be about a relatively minor point – the overall characterization of the sample (in image of "life" and a hand with brown sand) seems largely satisfactory regardless of whether we accept that Sandy was mesmerized or not.

Our second and more important observation is that the sampling process, spread out as it is over several sampling days, can provide an emerging, evolving, improving view of salient phenomenon. If mesmerization is a frequent characteristic of Sandy's awareness, then subsequent samples will provide new opportunities to explore the mesmerization phenomenon more adequately and to discuss in much more detail precisely how it is apprehended. If mesmerization is not a frequent characteristic of Sandy's samples, then it was perhaps not an important characteristic in the first place and its inadequate exploration in this sample was inconsequential.

The overall question, of course, is whether it is possible to explore awareness accurately, and if so, whether the DES procedure is an effective tool. We think the answers to both questions are Yes. Sandy is not an atypical subject. Some people are less clear about their awarenesses, and a few people are more clear. This sampling interview is not atypical of the DES procedure: some samples are more complex, some more straightforward.

CHAPTER 8

How to do DES

The moment of the beep

As we have emphasized, DES is a simple method: it simply asks the one legitimate question ("What are the details of your inner experience at this very moment?") and listens to the answers. But that description of DES is true at about the same level as the well-known description of sculpting: Have in mind what you want the statue to look like and chip away everything else. Both descriptions are more adequate for an advanced practitioner than for a beginner.

We have been teaching DES for many years, and this chapter aims to describe some of the characteristics of the DES technique that we have found useful to explain to our students. The list is not complete. We think DES is a skill/art that requires individualized training and practice, a situation not that different from, say, violin playing. Individual violinists have their own strengths, deficits, and bad habits, and the good violin teacher tailors the lessons according to that individuality. However, just as there are some elements of violin playing technique common across many or most violin students, there are some elements of DES technique common across many or most DES students.

In the previous two chapters we showed how we set the stage for sampling by providing annotated transcripts of an invitation to sample and of an actual expositional interview. Here we discuss the details of the DES procedure. The question "What are the details of your inner experience at this very moment?" has two parts, the "at this very moment" part and the "details of your inner experience" part. We'll discuss each in turn.

How to define "This very moment"

DES takes as its task to describe moments of awareness that are happening at randomly selected "right nows" and at no other times. Identifying the "right now" may seem like an easy task: get some kind of signal, and pay attention to experience at the onset of that signal. In a sense, it is in fact that simple. But in practice, it turns out that most people need guidance to accomplish this.

There are two parts to the task of identifying the "right now." The easy, but by no means trivial, part of that task is the creation of the signal itself. In Chapter 5 we described six characteristics of a good signal: unambiguity, easy detactability, rapid onset, privacy, portability, and response requirement. Once you have a good signal, you are left with the often challenging task of using that signal to arrive at the "right now."

The phenomena of experience are rapidly changing and evanescent, so the precision of the selection of "this very moment" is of substantial consequence. Let's assume that we are using a beeper or other signaling device that has the desirable characteristics that we just discussed. It is still a substantial skill to help the subject use such a beeper to describe the moment that was occurring at the very onset of the beep. The object is to "catch awareness in flight," so to speak, to apprehend experience before it is substantially disturbed by the process of observation. We recognize that no observational process can occur without altering in some way the experience that is being observed; we are not striving for perfection in this regard. However, we have evidence that we think shows that with sufficient care, it is possible to apprehend experience that is "pretty darn close" to what was actually occurring at the moment of the beep.

At the moment of the beep

By the "experience that was ongoing at the moment of the beep," we mean that experience that was actually occurring the millisecond *before* the beep began. When the subject hears the beep, we want her to "rewind her experience" and report about that experience that was ongoing in that instant *before* the beep occurred. We are *not* interested in any *reaction* that the subject may have to the beep itself, and we are *not* interested in what was occurring a second or a half second *before* the beep.

Several metaphors are useful to convey this notion to the subject. We say it is like a snapshot. When someone takes a flash photo of us, we see the flash and often say, "I blinked!" But the blink is a reaction to the flash itself; the photo reveals that the ongoing behavior did not include the blink. In DES, we are interested in the same thing that the snapshot catches – the behavior before the blink.

Another metaphor is the parallel universe. Suppose that there are two parallel universes, identical in all respects except that one includes the beep and the other does not. In DES, we want to know about what is happening in one universe at the precise moment that the beep begins in the other universe.

It may seem rather easy to employ these metaphors and encourage subjects to describe the moment of the beep. However, aiming exploration at the precise moment of the beep is decidedly difficult for most people who are learning the DES method. We don't entirely understand the reasons for this difficulty, but here are some factors that we categorize as being more a function of the DES practitioners or more a function of the DES subject. Prospective DES practitioners (a) don't always fully accept the importance of limiting discussion to the precise moment of the beep; (b) find that limiting discussion to the precise moment of the beep requires substantial directedness – almost confrontation – that many prospective DES practitioners find unpleasant; (c) think asking variants of the same question ("What are the details of your inner experience at this very moment?") over and over is boring/unimaginative/nonintellectual; (d) get "captured" by the subject's interesting but off-the-target remarks; and (e) have preconceptions about what to look for.

DES subjects (a) want to tell what they take to be an interesting story, and that is often somewhat remote from the beep; (b) want to explain themselves, and explanations are always remote from the beep; (c) want to report the "freshest" experience, and reactions to the beep are always slightly fresher than the experience at the moment of the beep (only a fraction of a second fresher, but that can be enough); (d) want to give accounts of themselves that accord with whatever self-theory they may have; and (e) want to talk about things that they have had practice talking about, which is not the details of some randomly selected experience.

As a result of these and probably many other factors, practitioners and subjects often conspire (without directly discussing it, of course) to talk about things that are *not* occurring precisely at the moment of the beep. Without question, that is the path of least resistance, and most people who are learning to do DES require substantial training and support to break this bad habit.

Whether or not it comes easy, it is essential to DES to discriminate between what happens at the moment of the beep and what happens before or after that moment. DES tries to describe what happens at the moment of the beep and to ignore what happens before or after. We have found in training DES practitioners that they usually need considerable work and practice in identifying those aspects of what the subject says actually are present in experience at the moment of the beep.

Q: Why is randomness important?

A: Delivering the signal at random times is desirable for two reasons beyond that "random" means "at unexpected times." First, we discussed in Chapter 6 the desirability of equality between investigator and subject – we called it the "one legitimate relationship." The random nature of the beep contributes to this relationship. If a beep appears at random times, those times are unexpected *both for the subject and the investigator*. It is not the case that the investigator is manipulating the subject by timing the beep to correspond with some activity or other. The beep comes when it comes, independent of the desires of either participant, and thus each beep underscores the equality of the two participants.

Second, as we sketched in Chapter 4 and will discuss in detail in Chapter 10, it is desirable to "bracket presuppositions," to be open to allowing experience to reveal itself with as little a priori meddling and interference from preexisting beliefs and ideas as possible. The randomness of the beep contributes to this. To allow the beep to come at random times is to indicate in a very powerful way that we (both subject and investigator) *do not* know what are the important features of experience, including when the desirable time to observe it might be. The random nature of the beep allows both participants to roll up their phenomenological sleeves and try to understand whatever comes their way.

Psychologists, both professional and amateur, often believe that they know which events are important and therefore what to pay attention to, and they are sometimes correct. But they are often mistaken, and their methodology (formal or otherwise) blinds them to the possibility of their mistake and to the possibility that other alternatives might exist. The feminist pays particular attention to male domination; the cognitive psychotherapists pays particular attention to what people say to themselves; the behaviorist pays particular attention to the stimuli following some class of events; and so on. All are doubtless right on some occasions and wrong on others, but all are ineffective in deciding which is which.

Depending on randomness to choose the moment/topic is a way of suspending all those preconceptions about *which* moments/topics are important. If male domination is in fact an important issue, then it is likely that it will emerge from a random sample. If what people say to themselves is important, it is likely that will emerge from a random sample. If either of those things does emerge from a random sample, that will be good evidence that it is in fact important – not merely that it is of theoretical interest. On the other hand, if male domination or what people say to themselves are not important issues, they will probably not emerge.

Now there are certainly situations where it would be desirable to sample at specific, non-random times, so as to deliver a beep at particular times of interest. For example, we are presently designing with Yani Dickens a study that will explore the experience of golfers while putting. It would be very inefficient to wait until a random schedule happens to produce an adequate number of during-putting beeps, so we will contrive to deliver beeps at just the proper times. However, we think it is desirable for such targeted beeps to be introduced into the beeping schedule only after an adequate number of random beeps have been explored.

Q: Why is the moment of the beep so important? So what if we describe experiences that are a few seconds before or after the beep? They are still the subject's experiences.

A: Every DES report is a combination of (a) a description of what was actually ongoing at the moment of the beep contaminated with (b) the subject's self-theory and presuppositions and (c) the practitioner's presuppositions. A good DES report contains a lot of (a) and not very much of (b) and (c). We have shown to our satisfaction that it is possible for most subjects to give descriptions about events occurring at the moment of the beep that are pretty darn purely (a). That is true in large measure because, as we just saw, the randomly selected moment helps both subject and practitioner bracket presuppositions.

But that changes dramatically as soon as you allow the report to be about some time (any time) other than the precise moment of the beep. Subjects choose to report about some event that was occurring before or after the beep *not* because it was selected by some dispassionate agent (the random beep) but because it somehow fits the subject's self-theories or presuppositions. Practitioners want to hear about events that occur before or after the beep *not* because it was selected by some dispassionate agent but because it somehow fits the practioner's presuppositions. By allowing talk about events before or after the beep, they sacrifice the bracketing-presupposition help that was provided by the random selection. Worse, they actually amplify the presuppositions by choosing events that favor them.

As a result, reports about moments that are before or after the beep may *not* be pretty darn pure (a), but are perhaps substantially contaminated by (b) or/and (c). To what extent are these reports contaminated? That's hard to tell; certainly neither the practitioner nor the subject are in an advantageous position to be able to evaluate the contamination because presuppositions generally operate prior to conscious considerations. But by systematically sticking to the moment of the beep, you can avoid having to worry about it. It doesn't matter greatly how much before or after the beep the event occurs; you lose the bracketing-presupposition benefit of the random beep whenever you depart from the moment of the beep, by however long, and that is a substantial loss.

We generally find in training DES practitioners that identifying the experience that was actually ongoing at the moment of beep is the fundamental, and necessarily first, skill of DES.

We saw in our example of Amy in Chapter 2 one important example of why developing the skill of getting to the precise moment of the beep and nothing else is important: some subjects have much difficulty grasping the concept of at the moment of the beep. Amy didn't know at the outset that she lacked this ability, because she had nothing with which to compare. But it is reasonable to suppose that our consistent pressure on her to identify what was happening at the precise moment of the beep contributed to her rather dramatic improvement. Amy is not alone in this regard. We have worked with other subjects, some of whom took much longer than Amy (and with much more frustration) to grasp the moment-of-the-beep concept, but who in the end were quite dramatically changed once they did grasp it.

There is, unfortunately, no formulaic way to get to the moment of the beep – you simply have to do whatever it takes to ensure to the highest degree possible that the experience being described actually took place at the moment of the beep. That said, here are some questions that may be useful:

- What was ongoing in your experience at the moment of the beep?
- [After the subject has described a long scenario] Of all that, which was actually ongoing right at the moment of the beep?
- Some of that seemed to be before the beep, some after the beep. Which was actually going on right at the instant the beep began?
- Was that actually ongoing in your experience right at the moment of the beep?
- Was that in reaction to the beep, or was it ongoing at the instant the beep began?
- Was that actually in your experience the millisecond before the beep began?
- Would you have been experiencing that at that moment even if the beep hadn't occurred?

- Is that background or context, or was that actually occurring in your experience at the moment of the beep?
- If we could have taken a flash photograph of your experience just as the beep began, would that have been in the photo? Or would it have been just before the photo or just after?
- If we somehow had a recording of your experience, and we could rewind that recording back to the instant just before the beep began, what would we have found right then – not before, not after, but right then?
- That sounds like it must have been in reaction to the beep. Is that right? We're interested in what was ongoing a microsecond before you had that reaction.
- By "at the moment of the beep" we mean that last undisturbed microsecond before the beep begins. Was that experience ongoing at the moment of the beep?

It is almost always desirable to establish that an experience was actually happening at the moment of the beep before you try to understand the details of the experience. *If the experience wasn't happening at the moment of the beep, no amount of interview about that experience will contribute to grasping the experience that was ongoing at the moment of the beep.* That seems obvious, but it is a difficult concept for many beginners to put into practice.

Experience

We now turn to the "experience" portion of "What are the details of your inner experience at this very moment?" For reasons that we have discussed throughout this book, it is not possible to give an unequivocal definition of experience. We mean whatever is occurring at the moment of the beep; whatever is in awareness at the moment of the beep; your feelings, thoughts, sensations, tickles, urges,...; whatever appears before the footlights of consciousness at the moment of the beep; whatever you are thematically noticing at the moment of the beep; whatever you are paying attention to at the moment of the beep; and so on.

We are interested in what is immediately present to awareness, not what is the result of inference, theory, deduction, and so on. We are interested in what is happening in the subject's experience at the moment of the beep, not in his or her explanation of why it is happening, whether it is typical or atypical, and so on. We are interested in the phenomenon as it presents itself directly and immediately to the subject. We are interested in what *is* taking place in experience, not in some process that the subject believes *must be* taking place or *probably is* taking place in the body. We are interested in the phenomenon as it is, not as the subject believes it is or would like it to be or believes it should be.

Fortunately, with a little practice, most DES subjects know with confidence what is meant by "inner experience" as we use the term. Once the moment of the beep is clearly defined, there is little doubt, for most subjects, about just what is going on at that moment.

It is usually somewhat difficult, at first, to keep the subject focused on what was immediately available at the moment of the beep. Most subjects want to tell about what was happening before the beep, as if to justify what was happening at the actual moment of the beep. Most subjects want to give explanations of *why* something is happening, not merely descriptions of *what* is happening. Most subjects have some theory about the way their inner experience works, and want to explicate that theory. But if the DES interviewer keeps a consistent focus on the exact moment of the beep, and largely ignores those other strands of conversation, eventually the subject will focus more and more consistently on the experiences themselves, whether or not they are typical or interesting or easy to explain.

As throughout DES, there is no formulaic way of inquiring about experience. That said, here are some useful questions:

- What exactly was in your experience at the moment of the beep?
- [If it is established that thinking is part of experience] What exactly were you thinking at the moment of the beep?
- How did that thinking present itself to you?
- What were the characteristics of that thinking?
- [If the subject has difficulty with those questions] Well, some people describe thinking as being in words. Some people say it's in pictures. Some people say it just happens without words or pictures. Some give other descriptions. You may have a similar or different way of experiencing that thinking. What was your thinking like at the moment of the beep?
- [If it is established that seeing was part of experience (whether inner or outer) at the moment of the beep] What exactly were you seeing at the moment of the beep?
- [If it is established that hearing was part of experience (whether inner or outer) at the moment of the beep] What exactly were you hearing at the moment of the beep?
- [If it is established that tasting was part of experience] What exactly were you tasting at the moment of the beep?

- [If it is established that feeling was part of the experience at the moment of the beep] How did you experience that?
- [If the subject has difficulty (which is common) describing ongoing feelings] Well, did this feeling seem to be in your body or in your head, or both, or neither?
- [If in the body, but still with difficulty] Is it possible to say which part or parts of the body were in your experience at the moment of the beep? It is also fine if you're not sure or if you don't remember.
- [If in the head] You said a bit ago that a thought was experienced in your head. What are the similarities and differences between that, which you called a thought, and this, which you are calling a feeling? Or do those two words refer to roughly the same kind of experience?

A good general question, applicable when an experience is to some degree similar to something that has already been discussed, is "How is this experience similar to or different from that experience (at some particular previous beep)?" That question focuses the subject directly on his or her experiences with a minimum of verbal intermediation. The result of such a question is that the descriptions of both the current and the previous experiences become clarified.

Here are some *risky/inadvisable* questions:

- What were you thinking about? [Asked before it has been established that some sort of thinking was actually ongoing.]
- What were you feeling? [Asked before it has been established that some sort of feeling was actually ongoing.]
- What is your thinking (feeling, etc.) like? [That asks about thinking in general, rather than the particular thinking that was ongoing at the moment of the beep.]
- Why do you suppose you were thinking (feeling, etc.) that? [People don't generally have access to the "why."]
- Did your thinking cause your feeling, or vice versa? [Unless there is a direct experience of causation, people are not good judges of causation.]
- When I'm in that situation, I usually feel (think, etc.).... Did you...?

The subjects' language often provides clues about what they are talking about. When they use simple declarative sentences in the simple past tense ("I saw an image of a soldier") they are usually describing the experience we are interested in – the experience that was ongoing at the moment of the beep. When they use verbs in the past-perfect tense ("I had been reading"), they are usually describing what happened before the beep. When they use terms such as "because," "since," "on account of," or "due to," they are usually describing what they take to be the cause of their experience. When they use terms such as "must be" or "probably is," they are usually describing the features of some self-theory. When they use terms such as "usually," "often," "generally," or "ordinarily," they are usually describing what they frequently do, rather than the experience that was ongoing at the moment of the beep.

In an important sense, then, it is desirable when subjects speak in simple, declarative, simple-past-tense sentences. However, there is nothing ironclad about this rule. Language is a flexible tool, and it is possible to use language in a variety of ways different from those described in the previous paragraph. For example, subjects can say "I saw an image at the moment of the beep" when there was no visual experience whatsoever ongoing at the moment of the beep.

When subjects indicate by words ("You won't believe this but...," "I don't know what to make of this, but here goes...," "I'm willing to tell you this if you promise....," etc.) or expression (squirming, blushing, hem/hawing, etc.) that what they are saying is weird or embarrassing, we take that as evidence that they are talking about a specific experience. Penny said she was seeing an image of a photograph of her dog, just seeing the photograph, not her thumbs and fingers holding it, or a table on which it might be sitting, and so on. That seemed surprising/weird to her, as if she expected that her fingers should be there but they weren't. We asked her where the image seemed to be, if that question made sense, and with a quizzical, surprised expression said that it seemed to be out in front of her, in the position where she would hold it to look at it. That, too, seemed strange to her – she apparently assumed that an image would be in her head.

Both these visceral surprises are indicators that she was trying to report accurately what she experienced, not "cleaning it up" for our (or her own) consumption. It doesn't matter what her presuppositions about the nature of images were; the fact that she was reporting contrary to those presuppositions gives us confidence in her report. For example, *we* were not surprised at all that thumbs are not part of the image – images frequently don't correspond to reality, so the fact that you could see thumbs while holding a real photograph doesn't at all imply that you would see thumbs while looking at an image of a photograph. But Penny had presuppositions about images, and her report caused her to contradict her own presuppositions. That self-presupposition contradiction contributes to our confidence.

We have found that subjects give frequent and substantial verbal hints when they are not confidently describing moments of experience. We call such hints "subjunctifiers," because one frequent such hint is the use of subjunctive mood when speaking. The subjunctive mood is a verb form that represents an act or state as being contrary to fact, possible, or doubtful. When DES subjects use the subjunctive mood, they are communicating with their grammar that they don't fully believe what they are saying. Here's a transcript from a DES training seminar co-led by both of us. Tim, a student in the seminar, is being interviewed by Chris. We've italicized and counted the words or phrases that we take to be subjunctifiers. You might quibble with a few of them, or think that we've slightly over- or undercounted, but it is evident that Tim did in fact indicate clearly by his explicit words that he was not simply describing his awareness. This is not a matter of reading Tim's mind – it's simply a matter of listening carefully to his words.

Chris: Uh, so should we go on to beep number 2, unless anyone has another comment? OK. Beep 2.

Tim: This is kind of funny. Um. I was sitting on my upstairs porch having, *I guess*[1] *like*[2] a hypothetical conversation in my mind with Russ. Um, which *I think*[3] the comment was in the beginning about transferring my thesis and then it went to sampling, and I had an image and was thinking verbally at the same time, but I was more aware of, *I guess*[4], the content and the specific words that were going on in the conversation, but I was aware that the beep came right at a point where I said in my hypothetical conversation the word "sampling."

Chris: OK.

Tim: So.

Chris: OK, so you were saying a sentence?

Tim: Yeah. I. . . .

Chris: Do you know what the sentence was?

Tim: No. I just said that the word came. *I don't know*[5] . . . *if*[6] even, *like*[7], all the words were there, they were *like*[8] implied *to some extent*[9]. I knew that there were some words there. *I guess*[10] the conversation was faster than it would have taken place because there were just implied words, *I guess*[11], in my hypothetical little conversation.

Chris: OK.

Tim: *I suppose*[12].

Chris: And so you said some words were there. What do you mean by "there"?

Tim: *Like*[13] *I guess*[14] in consciousness. *I suppose*[15]. (Laughs) Um, *I guess*[16] *like*[17] ....

Tim has said 172 words so far, and 30 of those words are parts of the 17 separate subjunctifiers. He is telling us in a fundamental way that what he's saying is *not* to be taken at face value.

If you want to understand whether someone is simply describing experience, develop a taste for listening for subjunctifiers. People who are simply describing what they experienced use the simple past tense and do not lapse into the subjunctive mood verb form or use any of the other qualifiers that indicate doubt or contrary to fact.

This is strikingly true for both sophisticated and unsophisticated speakers. People with whom we've sampled who wouldn't know the subjunctive mood from a pineapple are very accurate users of the subjunctive. If they are seeing an image, and if that image is clear and in color, and you ask them the color on the shirt the person in the image was wearing, subjects are (confidently) declarative: "It was red, like fire-engine red but with a bit more blue in it." But if the image or the shirt was something that they were not directly experiencing, a typical response is unconfident and has multiple levels of undermining "subjunctivity": "*Well*[1], *uh*[2], it's *like*[3] *as if*[4] I *should be able*[5] to really see it, but, *y'know*[6], *maybe*[7] *I'll say*[8] it was red, *I guess*[9], but *I'm not really sure*[10]." That's 10 subjunctive underminings by our count, and that's not a particularly extreme example of DES subjects' subjunctivizing. DES subjects who are not sure about the details of their experience use multiple ways of communicating that unsureness, of undermining the clarity of their own reports.

> When subjects undermine their own reports, as by subjunctifying, we should *gain* confidence in them as accurate reporters. It may seem counterintuitive, but the *less* confident the report, the *more* confidence in the reporter. The particular report that they are actively subjunctifying should not, of course, be believed – the subject is trying to tell us that by subjunctifying. However, that very fact also tells us that the subject cares enough about the truth of reports in general to be undermining this particular report. Subjunctification means that the subject has some kind of access to the truth; if we can unlock that access, then reports will become simply declarative without need for the subjunctive mood.

Keeping subjects from straying away from their experience can be challenging, but here are some tips. It is usually good practice to tell someone what *to* do rather than what *not to* do. Following that general principle, it is desirable to ask people to report what was happening at the moment of the beep; if they stray (e.g., into the past or into theory), it is desirable to bring them back to the moment of the beep with a comment such as, "Yes, but what was happening *right at* the moment of the beep?" There, we are simply ignoring the strayed topic and returning to the moment at hand. We typically *don't* recommend informing subjects about how they have strayed; that is, we *don't* say things such as, "When you say 'generally', it usually means you're not talking about the moment of the beep." To say such things would be to focus on the "general" and the way of speaking about them, when we prefer to say focused on the experience at the moment of the beep. Therefore we usually simply say, "Yes, but what was happening at the moment of the beep?"

For the same reason, we think it desirable *not* to refute or argue about whether something is or is not experienced at the moment of the beep. We *do* try to clarify the issue, but if we determine that what the subject says is about something other than the experience at the moment of the beep, we recommend simply ignoring it. A metaphor that might be useful is that the subjects' responses are like a mixture of wheat and chaff coming out of the chute of a threshing machine. The more you pay attention to the wheat, ask about the wheat, seek to clarify the wheat, and simultaneously to ignore the chaff, the more wheat will appear in subsequent threshings. Eventually, most of what the subject says will be wheat.

Questions and answers

Q: How do you communicate that you want an honest report?

A: First, we ourselves strive to be scrupulously candid. Our intention is to communicate as straightforwardly transparently as possible to the subject. We tell our subjects exactly what we are doing and why, without holding back on any details. On those rare occasions where we are not entirely transparent, we explain why. For example, occasionally subjects ask in the middle of sampling how they are similar to and different from other subjects. We explain that whereas we'll be happy to answer that question at the conclusion of sampling (and we do so), we'd rather focus exclusively on their own experience while we're in the midst of sampling so that they "don't go looking" for things that characterize other people.

Second, we frankly communicate explicitly and implicitly the sense of incompleteness and inadequacy of our definition of "experience," of what we wish the subject to report. "We don't know the characteristics of your experience," we might say, "and if you don't mind we would like to be a little vague on this point. We are reluctant to give you a list of what we might expect because many or most things on that list may not apply to you. You may well have phenomena in your experience that we have never before encountered, and if that is the case, we would like to hear about it. On the other hand, your experience might be similar to many others, and if so, we would like to hear about that. Either way is fine with us. Our task as we see it is to try to understand your awareness at the moment of the beep, as if we were on the inside experiencing it for ourselves. That is of course impossible, but it is our goal."

Third, we recognize that our understanding of the subject is imperfect. We communicate that we're trying to do the best we can, but if we can't get it just right, then that's OK. In particular, we don't want the subject to give the impression that things are clearer or easier to describe than they really are. If unclarity is part of the experience, then we want that same unclarity to be part of the description.

Fourth, we recognize the importance of privacy to the willingness to give accurate reports. Toward that end, we encourage subjects to tell us that something is none of our business (on the rationale that we have things that are none of their business as well). Only if subjects feel free to say something is none of our business can we feel free to ask for the details of their experience.

Fifth, we stress the equality between investigator and subject. We do not manipulate or place covert requirements on subjects. We ask the subject for guidance. We do, of course, have some ideas about how to proceed, but we have never before tried to understand *this particular subject's* experience, and so we may have to invent a brand new way of exploration in this instance. So we ask the subject to tell us if something doesn't seem right or seems off the track. Together, we have a good shot at learning something interesting, but neither of us could do it alone.

Sixth, we give total control over all aspects of the project to the subject. Any agreement to participate that we make today can be rescinded tomorrow – subjects have no obligation to do anything at any time.

Seventh, we are patient. DES is much like fishing. It's a matter of casting the hook into perhaps-auspicious waters and then waiting. Perhaps something interesting will happen; perhaps not. If not today, perhaps tomorrow.

Eighth, and perhaps most important, we are pretty darn sincerely, honestly, wholeheartedly interested in the truth, not in ratifying some theory or favorite position. We think that comes through to the subject.

Q: How do you not "lead the witness"?

A: We'll return to this topic in Chapter 10, where we will discuss how the investigator might try to acquire a taste for not leading the witness. Here, we'll give a few procedural tips.

First, try to ask open-ended questions. Subjects then have to examine their own experience and describe it, rather than merely assent or decline to assent to the investigator's question. Open-ended: "What were the characteristics of your inner speaking at the moment of the beep?" Closed-ended: "Was your inner speaking in your own voice?" It turns out that there is all manner of variation in the details of "your own voice," and honestly open-ended questions are necessary to elicit those details

Second, try to keep questions open-beginninged as well. "What were the characteristics of your inner speaking?" is an open-*ended* question, or at least it could be construed that way, as if you had said, "Tell me about any speech-related perceptions you may have been having at the time of the beep." But the *beginning* of the answer to that question is firmly fixed: the question compels you to talk about inner speech whether or not it existed, or was salient, or was subtle, or whatever. By contrast, an example of an open-*beginninged* question is, "Tell me about whatever was going on in your experience, and if nothing is going on, that's OK too." This question does not presuppose what we're going to talk about – could be inner speech, or tactile sensations, or images, or possibly it will be nothing. A closed-beginninged question presumes the existence of the thing it is asked about – in our example, it presumes that inner speech was ongoing at the moment of the beep. That may be true, but it may not be true as well.

"Open-beginninged" is a term of our own coining, as far as we know, and it is an essential characteristic of DES. One of the biggest mistakes of psychological science is to believe it knows the characteristics of experience. One psychologist believes that inner speech is always ongoing and therefore focuses on inner speech; another believes that emotions are always ongoing and therefore focuses on emotions; another believes that images are always ongoing and therefore focuses on images; and so on. Our DES studies show that those beliefs simply aren't true. It therefore is a mistake to *assume* that inner speech, or emotions, or images, or anything else is ongoing at the moment of the beep.

Therefore, the art of DES is to ask about *whatever* is ongoing; that's what we mean by an "open-beginninged" question.

The more the investigator has shed his or her preconceptions, the more open-beginninged questions naturally become, and the more skeptical you become of closed-beginninged questions.

Third, undermine almost all questions. Here are some examples:

- From what perspective do you see the image, *if that makes sense*?
- What, *if anything*, was ongoing in your experience?
- *I can ask questions that don't have answers,* but do you…?
- Which of these, *if any*, was most central to your awareness?
- What is…*if you can say?*
- Was that…*or doesn't that apply here?*
- Tell me about whatever was going on in your experience, *and if nothing is going on, that's OK too.*"

It is desirable to have, and to convey, a *lack* of confidence in DES interviews:

- We're not really sure that DES will work with you. It would be just as useful to us – perhaps more useful – to try to understand why it doesn't work as to understand your experience.
- Don't tell us anything more than you know…
- If you're not sure or don't know, say so…
- No one particular sample is particularly important, so don't go beyond what you can faithfully report. If the phenomenon is frequent, we'll see it again, and perhaps (or perhaps not) you'll then be in a better position to report…
- "I don't know" is always a good answer if that's the way it is.…

We recommend saying such things over and over and over and over. To the extent that subjects buy into our own undermining/indifferent stance, they can themselves feel OK about themselves being unconfident. Then if they are confident, that becomes stronger and stronger evidence of credibility.

Undermine everything until you hit solid rock.

Fourth, sometimes purposefully lead in the wrong direction. For example, if we suspect that a subject is describing unsymbolized thinking, we may say, "So are you saying that you are experiencing words?" We will candidly "admit" to this misleading device, explaining that this is not meant as a manipulation but that it is simply a necessary way of undermining *all* our questions. If we always ask questions where we expect the answer to be "Yes," we might give some pressure in that direction. We honestly don't want ever to imply that the best answer to a question is simply to agree with what we say.

We wish to emphasize that these are not merely linguistic devices; they honestly reflect what we honestly think. We ask open-ended questions because we honestly think subjects know more about their experience than we do, and we want to hear from them. We ask open-beginninged questions because we honestly don't presume to know what the features of their experience are. We undermine our questions because we honestly know that we can ask questions that don't have answers, and it's not fair to a subject to ask impossible questions without providing an out.

Q: Do you use your arcane terminology ("unsymbolized thinking," "subjunctification") with your subjects?

A: No. It is generally a good idea to refer to a phenomenon using the words that are natural to the subject, rather than requiring the subject to learn the DES vocabulary. There are at least four reasons for this. First, it's easier for the subject. Second, there is a substantial probability that we are mistaken, early in sampling, about what the subject is saying. The longer we can resist the temptation to classify it into one of our own categories, the more likely we will discover this kind of mistake. Third, there is a substantial possibility that the phenomenon the subject is describing is similar to, but not identical to, the DES prototype. If we stay in the subject's vernacular, such nuances have a better chance of appearing. Fourth, we do not want to give the impression that the DES task is simply to classify experience into one of our predefined categories. That is not in fact the case, and we don't want the subject mistakenly to believe it.

This puts a bit of a burden on the investigator, but it's an honest burden in the sense that it is our task to understand what the subject is saying, regardless of the words he or she uses. That means we have to discern how the subject intends the words that are used. There is some attention and effort involved, but it is necessary.

For example, when referring to the phenomenon we call unsymbolized thinking, one subject will call it "pure thought," another will call it "just thinking," another will call it "that weird deal where I know I'm thinking something but not really thinking it," another will call it, "that kind of no-word thinking that we talked about a few samples ago." We would typically not mention the term "unsymbolized thinking," even when it becomes clear that that's what a subject is describing. Likewise, when a subject says "I was just thinking" or "I was having a 'pure thought'," we don't jump to the conclusion that just because other subjects have used this locution to refer to unsymbolized thinking, this must also be an instance of unsymbolized thinking.

The object is to get the subject to focus on what's happening with them, not to get them to master a new vocabulary. Our job is to understand their vocabulary. (As a humorous example of the perils of expecting the subject to learn our vocabulary, our term "unsymbolized thinking" was once understood by a listener in a large lecture to be "uncivilized thinking.") So we often use the subject's own words, rather than our own.

Q: So does that mean that we're safe if we stick to the subject's words?

A: No. DES asks subjects to perform a task that they have never done before, and therefore you should presume that the subjects won't be very good at it. That includes the subjects' choice of words. Subjects very often don't have at their disposal the precise word to reflect what they want to say, so they do the best they can, using words that are somehow close to but not exactly on the target.

Therefore you can't blindly use the subject's own words. Suppose a subject says, "I was worried." It's a mistake to presume that the subject is actually trying to say that she was worried, and it's a further mistake to assume, even if she was worried, that you know what are the characteristics of "worry" as the subject used the term. Therefore it is a mistake to respond, "What were you worried about?" because it is entirely possible that the subject used the word "worried" to refer to some state that doesn't have an "aboutness" characteristic. The fact that when you use the term "worry" you usually are "worried about" something does not in any way imply that your subject uses the term in the same way. Better, you might ask, "What do you mean when you say you were worried?" or, more simply, "Worried?" That gives the subject the opportunity to refine her locution on her own terms, perhaps to say she wasn't really worrying but was just feeling blue and tense.

Q: Do you focus on what is meant or what is said?

A: Neither. The task is to extract the truth about the person's experience, and that may be distinct both from what the person says and from what the person means.

Communication is always imperfect. Sometimes even well intentioned communication is substantially misleading. The fact is that people often, especially early in sampling, say things about their experience that are simply not true. Frequent examples are: "I was saying to myself that I..." when in fact there were no words present in experience nor any experience of speaking; and "I was seeing an image of..." when in fact there was no visual experience. These subjects are not trying to mislead – on the contrary, they are trying hard to tell the truth. But because they are not practiced at observing their experience accurately, much less reporting it accurately, their reports are often inaccurate, sometimes wildly inaccurate or diametrically opposed to reality.

The focus of DES is on what the person *should have meant to say* if she were actually focusing on what was actually ongoing at the moment of the beep and actually trying to describe that moment. That often requires some training.

Q: It's difficult to know how accurately people are reporting their experience. There seems no way to discern whether people do or do not have experience and to what extent. So wouldn't it be wise to steer clear of the whole hornets' nest and just report what people *say*? Suppose I am assessing someone for substance abuse, and they report that they drink three times a week. I would feel very good saying, "The client reported that he drinks 3 times a week." I would not be comfortable saying "The client drinks 3 times a week." It seems to me that this is the same situation we are in when we try to speculate on the actual characteristics of inner experience.

A: We agree with your metaphor, but it seems you need to follow that metaphor to its end. The fact of the matter is that if you are doing an "assessment of substance abuse," at the end of the day you or someone is going to have to draw some kind of conclusion about the substance abuse itself – that's what "assessment" means. If you insist on merely reporting just what people said, then you're merely shoving the decision about the actual substance abuse on to someone else. *Somebody* has to decide whether there is substance abuse or not.

More accurately, somebody has to decide something like whether the probability that the benefits of some particular substance abuse treatment outweigh the costs of that treatment is sufficiently high to justify imposing that treatment. So in this scenario we're not technically assessing substance abuse itself, but assessing the probability that some treatment will be beneficial to a person.

We have to stay within what we can know, but we have to do as good a job of that as is possible. It is simply not good enough to remain at the "he said" level; if that's all you do, there's no reason to distinguish between a good method and a bad method.

So both of your suggested alternatives are not good. "The client *reported* that he drinks 3 times a week" is not good because it says too little. "The client *drinks* 3 times a week" is not good because it says something that is probably not true. The target is somewhere between your two poles. We want to try to get at how much the subject *actually* drinks.

The reason that psychology has trained practitioners to use the "client reported" pole is because it knows about the invalidity of those reports, and it hasn't figured out how to improve that validity substantially. But we think that DES is a substantial improvement in the validity of reports about inner experience. We think that there is a "pretty darn right" answer to the question, "What was ongoing in your experience at the moment of the beep?" We think that DES can get "pretty darn close" to that experience. That allows us to do more than simply say "He *reported* his experience. . .." We examine inner experience carefully, helping the subject learn to distinguish the truth from the untruth, and then can say something like, "His inner experience is probably, from the standpoint of simple description,. . ."

Certainly the science of inner experience needs additional refinement, so that we can more adequately specify what "probably" and "simple description" mean.

Q: But it's still a matter of "he reported." We don't have direct access to his experience.

A: You are both 100% correct and very misleading. DES subjects say many things about their experiences that are simply not true, as judged by us and by subjects themselves given time to reflect. The phrase "he reported" doesn't distinguish at all between reports that are true and reports that are false. You could modify the phrase to, "He reported and we subsequently verified. . ." or "He reported but we subsequently disconfirmed. . .." which is much better. The only disadvantage of that is that it gives primary emphasis to the reports, which may or may not be the central basis for the understanding of the experience which is developed.

We think that in many cases the use of "he reported" is an irresponsible dodge, which if unpacked means something like, "I'm going to say something that is irrefutably true, so that I cannot be personally faulted. But without really saying so, I'm going to push the important decisions on to someone else; and I'm not going to go to the trouble of finding/using a more valid method." That is, of course, a confrontational version of "he reported," but if it serves to make you a bit uncomfortable every time you write "he reported," it will have been worth it.

Q: How do you avoid making assumptions that are implied by the context?

A: Sooner or later, if you stay working with DES and carefully listen to what people say, you will discover that *nothing* about inner experience is *ever*

> implied by the context. So eventually, avoiding making assumptions that are implied by the context gets to be very easy. But if you're just learning to do DES, you probably have to practice, over and over, fighting against the notion that other people have the same kinds of experience that you do if you're both in a similar situation. Similar-contexts-implies-similar-experiences is simply not true, and you have to work at ridding yourself of that preconception.

Here's an example. Melissa was in the grocery store at the moment of the beep, and her written report of her experience was, "I'm in the grocery store in the cereal aisle, and I was thinking cereal – what would [daughter] Shannon like?" What does that report tell us about Melissa's actual inner experience? Not much. Here are some possibilities: 1: There was no actual thought process available to awareness – she was just looking at the cereal boxes, and eventually one would appear to be satisfactory; 2: She was remembering that she had been mean to Shannon earlier that morning and now was resolving to be nicer to Shannon. She happened to be in the cereal aisle, so she wrote down something about cereal, but actually she was thinking about making up, and wasn't really thinking about cereal at all; 3: She herself really wanted Cheerios, but she knows Shannon doesn't like Cheerios – she was sort of pouting/mad because she always gives her what she wants. And so on and so on.

Those are all consistent with what Melissa wrote; they're all quite different from each other; and they're probably quite different from what you or I would be experiencing if we were in the cereal aisle, and, for that matter, likely to be quite different from what Melissa herself might be experiencing in the same aisle the next day.

Here's what Melissa was actually experiencing at that moment as revealed by the expositional interview. She was repeating the word "cereal…cereal… cereal" several times in her own inner voice while she was heading toward the cereal boxes. At the same time she was trying to figure out, in unsymbolized thinking, what Shannon would like. It was as if a brand of cereal would somehow appear, and she would somehow respond No; and another brand of cereal would appear, and she would respond No; and so on, except the cereal brand didn't appear in any visual or auditory way and the word No didn't actually have any formal characteristics (it wasn't spoken, heard, or seen). Nonetheless, there was something sequential and cognitively known about this mental sequence of presentations/negations.

The point here is that you can *never* be confident that you know from an initial report or the context what the inner experience is actually like – you have to inquire in detail. Believing that you know is the operation of a preconception that needs to be bracketed, and is one of the more pervasive difficulties those new to DES face.

Q: Does that mean we shouldn't ask for context?

A: Basically, yes. Sometimes you have to know the context to understand what a person is saying, and if you have to know the context, then you have to know the context. But in general it's not a good idea to inquire about the context for three reasons:

1. It dilutes the focus on the experience by requiring the person to describe two things (context and experience), not just one.
2. It raises the likelihood that the subject will give causative explanations, jumping from the context to explain the experience.
3. It may give us the impression that we know what he's talking about just because we have been in similar situations.

Q: I still think knowing the context is helpful.

A: It may be important; the art is not to be captured by it. The aim is to apprehend experience, and you must distinguish as clearly as possible between what was happening (as a fact of the universe) and what was actually being experienced. For example, suppose the subject says, "I was watching TV and wondering what the announcer meant?" If you ask, "What were you seeing on the TV?" you presume that the TV was part of the subject's experience. It is quite possible that the subject was entirely engrossed in the wondering, without any experience of the TU at all.

Q: Can't you just give a list of good DES questions and let us ask those?

A: Not really, because the questions have to be tailored to the experience. Certainly the one legitimate question ("What are the details of your inner experience at this very moment?") and its variants ("What was going on?" "What was in your experience?" and so on) are always good questions. Sometimes students of DES are reluctant to ask the same question over and over, as if that showed lack of creativity. But the fact is that you can ask the one legitimate question hundreds of times before it becomes boring.

If we're not clear about a phenomenon, we find it useful to ask, "How is this sample similar to or different from that other (previous) sample?" That has the virtue of being not leading, and provides a secure point of reference (the sample already discussed). It also allows the first sample to be revisited, which gives the opportunity for a reliability check.

The good news is that sampling is renewable – we can get as many beeps as we want. We do not have to be overly concerned about whether we completely grasp a phenomenon as it is presented as one beep. If the phenomenon is important for the person, we'll see it again and can clarify it as we go.

Penny, in her role of graduate student, had viewed many hours of videotape of sampling interviews, and had transcribed many of those interviews (a concentrated, laborious task), but had never sampled herself. When she sampled, she had some unsymbolized thinking moments, and when she described those moments for the first time, she sounded just like most other subjects when they describe unsymbolized thinking for the first time: she was hesitant, unsure. Maybe it was a feeling. Maybe it was a thought. But if it was a feeling it had no bodily referent. No – it wasn't a feeling, it was definitely a thought. All this was with an apologetic delivery that she should be able to do better. That's just how typical naïve subjects describe unsymbolized thinking for the first time.

Penny was not naïve, and yet her descriptions were the same as that of naïve subjects. That leads to the conclusion that the attempt to describe a moment is robust, and is *not* particularly influenced by the past. If the intent is clearly laid out, that we wish to get to the particular moment as it is actually experienced, then that intent will override other experience. It is difficult to lead the witness once that intent is implanted, just as difficult as if you were holding a can of Coke and someone said, "Look at that green can." No amount of such leading would cause you to see the can as green. You might *say* it was green (you might acquiesce), but you wouldn't see a green can.

Q: But can't you provide some general rules for how to do it?

A: We have tried to do some of that earlier in this chapter, but here are a few additional suggestions. They are probably not as specific as you would like, but that's the way it is.

- Cultivate a sincere preference for the truth – don't be distracted by the fascinating or the plausible.
- Don't assume you're good at DES.
- Don't assume you can learn DES any faster than you can learn to play the violin.
- Be particularly wary in situations where you feel self-righteous.
- Recognize that your basic understandings are at risk.
- The aim is transparency.

- In learning DES, you probably need to pass through stupidity many times.
- If you have an expectation about what you will find, it will screw you up.
- If you're in a hurry, it will screw you up.
- Old habits die hard.
- Undermine yourself.
- Be even-handed, and convey evenhandedness.
- Make sure you know what is and what is not in experience at the moment of the beep.
- Nail down the specific before the general. You can go from the bottom up, but you can't go from the top down.
- Collect a heap of specifics before any analysis.
- Let the first analysis be simply the creation of sub-heaps. Save the characterization of those sub-heaps for after the sub-heaps are created. Don't let the characterization drive the creation of sub-heaps. That requires a new set of bracketings, and that is too hard work.
- Make the first heap and the sub-heaps for you yourself, privately.
- Make the first characterization of the sub-heaps for you yourself, privately.
- Make the public characterization merely a clean-up (Bowdlerization) of your own private sub-heap characterizations.
- You don't have to be perfect because you'll always get another chance.
- Fatal mistakes are rare. You usually have the opportunity later to counterbalance.
- Embarrassment is the most sensitive compass you have. Don't run from it – walk toward it.
- Patience!
- Practice speaking the detailed truth about personal things.
- Talk about specifics.
- Undermine everything until you hit solid rock.
- Be alert for subjunctification.
- Determine the degree of metaphoricity.
- DES is hard until you get the knack. Then it's easy.
- Probably no one has ever taught you observational skills.
- It's politically correct to think that your opinion is as good as someone else's opinion. That's simply not true.
- Our society is actually politically diametrically opposed to bracketing. We applaud people for having the women's point of view, or the black point of view, or the Republican point of view. But when it comes to in-

ner experience, there is no women's, black, or Republican point of view. There are simply individuals with experiences.

- Our society values passion, but passion is usually downstream of presuppositions.
- Our society doesn't care about inner experience.
- Our society overvalues unconscious explanations.
- Our society overvalues plausible explanations.
- Our society overvalues psychological explanations.
- Our society overvalues explanations.
- See also near the end of Chapter 10.

Q: Is the aim of DES to take what is sometimes called a "thin slice" of experience?

A: There is considerable ambiguity in what is meant by a "thin slice," because there are at least two distinctly different ways to slice experience. We might call those the temporal slice and the experiential slice. If what you mean by "thin slice" is temporal, then the answer is clearly Yes!!! We wish to know what is ongoing in experience at precisely the moment of the beep, not a second before, and not a second after. The metaphor of the photographic flash fits well. The flash catches the walker in mid stride, the talker in mid sentence, and so on. That is the aim of DES, and we try to approximate that pretty well.

However, once we have identified ("sliced") the moment with adequate precision, then we wish to take as *thick* a slice of experience as is actually present at the moment of the beep. We are interested in all the complex layers of experience that actually exist, not just the thinnest, "topmost" layer. It happens, as an empirical fact, that many people have only one or two "layers of experience" ongoing at the moment of most beeps, and in those cases we discover and report only one or two aspects of each experience. For them, the experiential slice is thin as well. But that thinness is driven by the characteristics of the subject's experience, not our intention. We wish to discover all that is present to experience, whether that be one thing or twenty.

Q: I'd like to go back to the undermine-everything facet of DES. When you undermine yourself, isn't that a sign of weakness? And aren't you therefore likely to be pushed around at worst or at least not taken seriously by your subjects?

A: It's a striking paradox that there's strength and confidence within the undermining/lack of confidence activity. We agree that in everyday (non-

DES) interactions, self-undermining is resorted to out of weakness and/or insecurity. For example, people say things like "but maybe that's not true for you" or "maybe I'm reading it wrong" even if they really believe in what they're proposing. That undermining is *backpedaling to avoid confrontation*, which has a very different flavor and yields very different results from the DES undermining, which is *frontpedaling to provide space for the truth to emerge*. The DES frontpedal undermining provides subjects with freedom and autonomy that is necessary if they are to be co-investigators, to be accurate about their experience, to find the truth. It lets them know that they are not constrained by the interviewer's presuppositions and opens up the possibility that they need not be constrained by their own presuppositions either, all the while training them to be detailed and precise.

The DES combo of curiosity (a strong desire to want to know/ask the questions) and freedom (undermining the words/expressing a lack of confidence) creates a fertile environment in which the truth can germinate.

CHAPTER 9

A sampling journal

Learning about DES

Sarah A. Akhter & RTH

Russ: Sarah Akhter was a new graduate student at the University of Nevada, Las Vegas. She had a long and substantial interest in consciousness and meditation prior to her arrival at UNLV, and had been a student of the Diamond Approach (the spiritual teaching, path, and method of the Ridhwan Foundation) for six years. She knew very little about DES, but a few months after arriving at UNLV she expressed interest in learning more. This led to a series of conversations which included her wearing the beeper as a DES participant, her observing the sampling of a fellow graduate student, and our jointly conducting a series of DES interviews with an undergraduate volunteer.

Early in this series of conversations, I asked Sarah to keep a journal of her experiences as she learned more about DES, on the possibility that such a journal might prove useful to others who are considering becoming involved with DES. I suggested the following "rules": she should write for herself alone, not for me or for some possible other audience; she should write as if to a private diary; like all diaries, I would not ask to see what she had written, but if at some point she wanted to show me, I would likely be interested; if it came to pass that she wanted to show me, she should feel free to edit out any aspect for any reason; that she should try to "get stuff down," not to polish it – that could come later if she desired; that she was the owner and had complete control over what would or would not be done with it. Sarah did keep a journal during these conversations, and a few months later showed it to me.

Sarah has a high standard of personal conviction – she's not likely to believe something just because someone (me, for instance) says so. She holds many beliefs about consciousness that I disagree with or think misleading, and I suspect she feels the same about mine. Perhaps especially for that reason, I think she has something important to say to people who are embarking on, or considering embarking on, a DES journey, so I asked her if we could make portions of this journal public. She assented, and here it is, with some of the editing described above and my commentary.

Sarah: I first encountered Descriptive Experience Sampling while preparing for an admissions interview to the clinical psychology PhD program at the University of Nevada, Las Vegas. While reviewing faculty research online, I found an audio file of a lecture Dr. Hurlburt had given at the Tucson Consciousness Conference a few years earlier.

To my surprise, the lecture was quite different from other talks I'd heard on consciousness. Instead of discussing theories of human potential or modes of insight-oriented practice, Dr. Hurlburt presented a specific methodology for collecting data on individuals' inner experiences, along with some of his recent findings. I was intrigued by the proposition that inner experience data could be collected with such a rigorous method; I'd never heard of anything like it before and I wanted to learn more.

As luck would have it, I got into the program at UNLV – and got a chance to explore DES. I started off by sitting in on DES lab meetings with Dr. Hurlburt, Dr. Heavey, and their students but soon I was invited to serve as a DES subject, and then as an interviewer/investigator. The following "story" outlines my trajectory of learning about DES. Though it does not cover everything I thought about and learned during this period, it does document some of my initial questions, impressions, struggles, and insights. It has been edited in favor of clarity and relevance to the reader who might be contemplating DES as a subject or an investigator.

Being a sampling subject myself

Sarah: A few months into my DES exploration, Dr. Hurlburt invited me to serve as a subject for his lab, which meant wearing the beeper to collect "samples" and then being interviewed jointly by Dr. Hurlburt, Dr. Heavey, and their students about those samples. I happily agreed, yet as the time drew near I became anxious about the endeavor. I worried that my thoughts would be read, that the beeps would expose parts of me I wouldn't want exposed. What if my thoughts were too private to share? What if I was thinking about sex or having rude thoughts about someone? Or, just as bad, what if I didn't have any interesting thoughts or experiences at all? What if the way I did things was stupid or awful or somehow worse than how other people do things? What if I turned out to be weird or absolutely nuts? Did I really want that information exposed to my professors and fellow students, or anyone at all?

Though Dr. Hurlburt made it abundantly clear that I was in complete control of how much to share during the sampling interview, I realized that for DES to reveal the most accurate picture of me as possible, I'd have to try to be completely honest and forthright about my experience. To do this would require letting go of the way I customarily present who I am to others. I'd have to get over the impetus to portray myself in favor of just discovering myself. The difficulty was that I didn't know what the discovered me might look like, and I'd just signed up to find out in public. As I took the task quite seriously, being a DES subject was a pretty scary proposition. Yet my curiosity to know more about myself, and about DES methodology, compelled me to take the plunge.

Russ: Sarah's concerns about revealing herself are very frequent among new DES subjects, and we routinely (as we did with Sarah) try to allay those concerns by repeatedly emphasizing that the subject is in total control, and that the concerns are almost always worse than the reality. Subjects often equate "tell me the truth about particular moments of experience" with "reveal your most personal secrets," but that's not what it usually turns out to be.

Being sampled day 1

Sarah: The first day I sampled was physically awkward and somewhat stressful. As I was not used to wearing the beeper and earpiece, it felt strange and restrictive to go about my day wired up. I attached the beeper to a belt loop on the back of my jeans and tried to secure the earpiece in my right ear. I ran the wire connecting the beeper to the earpiece along my back but it was loose and easily caught on things (i.e. my shoulder, the doorknob to my office, my dog's head). Each time this happened the tension of the pulled wire popped the earpiece out of my ear, and this got irritating after a while. The worst part about wearing the beeper that day, though, was my awareness of the beeper itself. Not being able to forget I was sampling made me hypervigilant for the beep, and continuously anxious about the fact that the next day I'd have to report my thoughts.

As requested, I sampled for several hours. Despite what seemed like my obsessive anticipation, the beep startled me each time it actually came. I'd feel dazed and dumbfounded for a few seconds before fumbling around to press the button to stop the sound. Luckily, some of my anxiety about overexposure was reduced after collecting a few beeps. My experiences seemed benign and, quite frankly, mundane. I realized it was unlikely that I'd get beeped during a thought or an action that would be too embarrassing to share. I relaxed a little.

The instructions were to jot down a few notes about what I was aware of in my experience at the moment of each beep. Though I understood the assignment theoretically, in trying actually to do it I struggled with what to look for and report in my experience. Certainly, I knew what I'd been *doing* at the moment of each beep (looking at my calendar, having a conversation, petting my dog, watching *Oprah*), but I wasn't sure this was the same thing as what I'd been *aware of in my experience* at the moment of the beep. My solution was to record what I'd been doing.

Being interviewed about those samples by the DES students and professors was anxiety provoking and confusing. I felt like I was on the hot seat. I'd assumed the interviewers would want a mini-story about each beep and maybe even an explanation about why I was doing what I was doing at a particular moment. But as it turned out, my narrative was only important to the extent that it conveyed the elements of my experience at the moment of the beep; the interviewers were completely disinterested in any interpretation or explanation of why I was doing what I was doing. For example, I reported that at the moment of the first beep I was looking at a page of my day planner, focused on a notation I'd made to myself about an upcoming exam. My inclination was to explain *why* I was looking at the planner and what that notation *meant* to me in general. Instead they wanted to know exactly *what* I was aware of at the moment of the beep and *how* I was aware of that experience.

They asked incredibly specific questions about seemingly anatomical details of my experience that I simply couldn't answer. How much of the page did I see? How did I see the notation? Where did I see the notation? What characteristics of the notation did I see? What I was able to report seemed gross compared to the precise and refined details they were after. Furthermore, the more questions they asked, the more confused I became about my experience. I thought I remembered certain things, but when pressed for specifics, I wasn't so sure those things were true. Was the notation made in black or blue ink? Was it straight on or at an angle? I was tempted to claim details of my experience based on plausibility, but the nature of the questioning – the reliance on detail and discrimination – made me stick to what details I could remember. It was clearly imperative to report only what was true; in fact, the questioners conveyed that it was preferable to say "I don't know" than to report a deduction or hypothesis about a detail of experience.

I felt pretty inadequate after that interview. The types of questions asked had surprised me, and although I now had a better understanding of what the interviewers were after, I doubted that I'd be able to capture the level of detail and accuracy necessary to be a good subject. I wondered if other people struggled with this task as much as I did. If not, did my professors and the other students interpret my difficulty as a sign of mental deficiency or some kind of craziness? I hated the idea that they might know something about me that I didn't know.

Russ: In some ways, Sarah's first sampling experience was more difficult than that of the typical subject: she was being interviewed by her own professors and her own fellow graduate students, whereas most subjects have a more distant relationship with the investigator. However, I think Sarah's reactions are pretty typical: most subjects are somewhat concerned about being judged and about being seen to be adjusted or nuts.

It's not at all unusual for subjects at the end of the first sampling day to feel inadequate or unable to perform the sampling task. We don't tell subjects prior to sampling what kind of questions we will ask because we don't want to "prime" or influence them to expect any particular kinds of experience. Consequently, our first-day questions are nearly always surprising and to some degree disconcerting to subjects. We try to reassure subjects that their felt inadequacy is a characteristic of the early part of the method and shouldn't be taken personally, but despite that, many subjects feel personally inadequate until they get the hang of our questions.

Sarah continued to express an interest in serving as a subject as a way of exploring what DES was all about, and we therefore continued for three more sampling days. The DES lab was occupied with other issues, so Sarah's subsequent sampling experiences did not involve the students or Dr. Heavey; I was the investigator and Sarah was the subject. Those samplings were fairly atypical in the sense that the conversations involved some sampling interview and some related, more theoretical conversations.

I also note that despite Sarah's thinking that she would be "obsessively anticipating" the beep, the beep always surprised her. That is typical of DES subjects, and it is an example of the difficulty people have of characterizing their own experience.

Being sampled day 2

Sarah: My second sampling day was technically easier. I was more comfortable with the rhythm and mechanics of the sampling procedure and I'd habituated to wearing the beeper and the earpiece. Dr. Hurlburt had suggested that I run the earphone-beeper wire inside my shirt and this new arrangement secured the earphone and solved most of my wire issues. The earpiece still fell out of my ear from time to time, but it was far less distracting than it had been the previous day.

Though I was less anxious about the basics of the process, I now felt unsure of how to capture the kind of information that I knew would be asked of me during the next sampling interview. A big problem for me was not truly understanding what was meant by the central phrases of the sampling instructions: "aware of" and "in your experience." I struggled with the parameters of awareness in this context: Did this mean awareness in general or awareness in the moment? Was this referring to mental awareness, bodily awareness, or some other kind of awareness? Furthermore, how aware of something does one need to be? Is it possible to be partially aware of something, or to be aware of two things at once?

The word "experience" caused similar confusion for me. Does experience include everything happening within a human being, conscious and unconscious? Is experience only reportable if one is aware of it? What about things you know you are experiencing but that you might not be aware of just at the moment of the beep?

My clues from the previous interview session were that the context of my experience at the moment of a beep wasn't centrally important and, furthermore, the story about *why* I was doing something wasn't important either. But the details of *exactly what* and *how* I was experiencing seemed important.

Without much clarity on these issues, I went ahead and collected several beeps. I used a microcasette recorder to record my "notes" instead of writing them down as I thought I might be able to be more accurate in this way. But other than that, I couldn't think of anything else to do to increase my ability to notice and report the details of my experience. Wouldn't I just notice what I noticed, nothing more, nothing less? How could I make myself notice more? Was it possible to grow my capacity to notice? If so, then wouldn't I be fundamentally changing who and how I am, effectively becoming a different person over the course of sampling?

Even in the absence of an audience and multiple investigators, the second interview was pretty frustrating. I felt anxious, thin-skinned, and somewhat defensive when reporting my experiences. I still worried that my reports were strange and abnormal, and that Dr. Hurlburt might think I was nuts or consider my reports invalid because they were so bizarre. Here's an example:

> I was scanning a research report, feeling "energy," an active movement inside my head, as if things were moving around in my brain. I understood this to be a manifestation of a mental or cognitive searching, but there were no mental or cognitive features directly in my awareness at the moment of the beep.

I was particularly sensitive about my description of the head "energy," not because I myself thought energy was strange but because I was convinced it sounded way too "new agey" and weird to be considered accurate description. This train of thought led me to question the validity of my experience and to wonder how to discriminate what was *real* within my experience. Maybe I just *thought* I'd felt the head energy, but it wasn't really there. Isn't that what happens in persons suffering from delusional disorders?

I proceeded to work my way into feeling pretty uncomfortable about my ability to capture and communicate my experience, but Dr. Hurlburt reassured me that that my reports were on track with the task. I still felt I was missing the big picture and I was mentally drained from trying to understand.

Russ: In fact I had a sense that Sarah's reports were pretty good, and I said so, probably repeatedly. I was led to that conclusion for several reasons. First, she was quite obviously trying to do a good job, and she was clearly distressed by the difficulty of it. I take those as visceral signs that she was substantially engaged in the sampling task. She was not merely going through the motions, but was trying to give accurate reports. That's a good thing. I certainly didn't set out to cause Sarah distress, but I myself saw Sarah's distress positively – as a clear sign of the effort and care with which she was approaching this task. Of course it is true that merely trying to give accurate reports, even trying *hard* to give accurate reports, does not guarantee that the reports are accurate. But at this early stage of sampling, I'm more concerned with the subject's being engaged in the task than with her having mastered it.

Second, she did in fact give clear descriptions of phenomena, including her head energy sensation. The fact that she was distressed about what seems to be a clear description indicates to me that the phenomenon under consideration is a real phenomenon, not merely a figment of her imagination (as was apparently her worry). Sarah was clearly distressed but stuck to her description of head energy. That's evidence (not conclusive, to be sure, but evidence nonetheless) that she has pretty direct access to her head-energy phenomenon. It would have been easier for her (distress-wise) to have abandoned the phenomenon and told me something that she thought I would find more plausible, but apparently that would have been denying palpable experience.

By the way, I do think that much of the new-age discussion of energy is probably misguided, but that is not at all what Sarah is describing here. Sarah is describing a phenomenon – a sensation in her head that feels like energy. That's very different from talking about the actual existence of some kind of energy and the function or value that that energy might have. Sarah seemed to be sticking to describing the phenomenon despite its new-agey connotations, and that's what we're after.

We will see below (on the third sampling day) that Sarah's characterization of herself as "feeling pretty uncomfortable about my ability to capture and report my experience" is actually a substantial misunderstanding of what was happening to her.

Being sampled day 3

Sarah: By the third sampling day I was completely comfortable with the beeper and description procedure, and I noticed a change in the quality and content of my descriptions. During the interview I was more easily able to articulate my experience in detail and I felt more definitive about what was and was not part of my experience at the moment of each beep. It began to dawn on me that I *was* able to observe my experience but that I was simply not used to looking at the *form* of my experience. Furthermore, I thought my experience at each beep would be dramatic, personal, and clearly singular but instead it was often rather ordinary, nothing "secret," and multi-dimensional. For example,

> I was going out to get the newspaper early in the morning and stopped on the front porch. At the moment of the beep I was looking at the tree in the neighbor's yard, noting the dappled soft lighting, the "funky" hues, the graphic presentation of the tree in its space. At the same time I was aware of other sensations – the raw coldness of the air on my skin, the colors of the early morning. I was not engrossed in any of these sensations, but I was paying more attention to the presentation of the tree than to the other sensations.

The details of this and other beeps were becoming clearer to me, and I spent a lot less time worrying about getting it right or questioning the reality or validity of my experiences. I also found that I was no longer giving much thought to the possibility that my experiences were too weird for Dr. Hurlburt. Once I realized that I wasn't being judged or analyzed – that it was perfectly fine for my experiences to be exactly what they were – my confidence grew and our communication became clearer and more in sync.

Russ: Above, on the second sampling day, Sarah had expressed substantial distress at not being a good subject, at not being able to apprehend her experiences, at the impossibility of the DES task. Now she reports that it's becoming easier, giving three explanations: that she now "*was* able to observe [her] experience"; that she came to realize that instead of being "dramatic and singular" her experience was "often rather ordinary and multidimensional"; and that she "realized that [she] wasn't being judged or analyzed." I think all three are important, but the first is of primary importance.

Sarah's earlier distress had been primarily caused *not by an inability to apprehend her experiences* (as it had seemed to her) but by the fact that the experiences discovered by DES were *not the way she had expected them to be.* Discovering this discrepancy is an exceedingly common occurrence among DES samplers, often happening (as here) on the third sampling day. Sarah apparently had conceptualized herself (prior to sampling) as having inner experience that was populated by thoughts; recall that before her first sampling day she had written, "What if my thoughts were too private to share? ... I worried that my thoughts would be read, that the beeps would expose parts of me I wouldn't want exposed [like] thinking about sex or having rude thoughts about someone." As it turned out, her inner experience did *not* include many thoughts. Instead, her central experiences involved frequent sensory awarenesses (for example the head energy, the dappled lighting, and the raw coldness). Early in sampling, Sarah did *not* conceptualize herself as having such sensory awarenesses.

Thus, early in sampling, there had been a substantial discrepancy between what was *actually* occurring in her experience (sensory awarenesses) and what she presupposed *would be* happening in her experience (thoughts). Early in sampling, her mistaken expectations caused her distress: when the beep occurred, she was looking for some thought process, and if the beep happened in the midst of a sensory awareness, she couldn't find the experience of thinking (because it wasn't there) and also couldn't accept the fact of sensory awareness. As a result, she (incorrectly) understood herself to be unable to perform the sampling task.

Much of this book is about bracketing presuppositions, and this serves as an example of the importance of bracketing for the subject as well as for the investigator. It took Sarah a few days to bracket her incorrect presupposition that she would always or at least frequently have the experience of thinking. Once that bracketing was in place, her distress subsided and the observation of her actual experience became much easier.

By the way, Sarah is noting here our communication became clearer and more in sync. I agree, but being in sync was as much about being in sync with herself (experiencing the phenomena that were actually there to be experienced) as about being in sync with me.

Being sampled day 3, continued

Sarah: After completing the sampling interview, we reviewed all of my samples from the past three sessions. Dr. Hurlburt noted that most of my beeped experiences had been sensory and emotional, while relatively few involved traditional cognition or thinking. He "lifted" this pattern of experience directly from the data, he did not interpret or try to make meaning out of it, nor did he make any judgment about it.

DES seemed to have an importance that I hadn't been able to grasp until this point. It was getting at information about my experience that I'd never before accessed – or even known was available for accessing – and revealing a kind of inner experience thumbprint when looked at collectively. It was strange and surprising to learn that my pattern of experience was actually quite different from what I'd originally thought it would be. At the outset of sampling I had assumed I would be thinking all the time. But instead, my sampling data – data I stood behind because I'd collected it and struggled to be accurate about it – revealed that I spend most of my moments attending to sensations and emotions. Stranger still, I could see that my pattern of inner experience fit with many idiosyncratic things I knew to be true about myself but that I'd never been able to see clearly or articulate objectively. I was surprised at how quickly DES had revealed this previously "hidden" pattern that now seemed so obviously true.

Russ: I would observe how remarkable it is that deeply hidden patterns can be made obvious by simply talking honestly about 10 randomly selected moments of existence. These were *not* special moments, moments of significance, moments of deep reflection or revelation. They were mostly mundane everydaynesses. Sticking to the truth and avoiding the contaminations of interpretation and explanation is rare, and Sarah felt its power.

Being sampled day 4

Sarah: On day four I sampled after an emotional interchange with a loved one and I was convinced that my rotten mood would interfere with my ability to collect robust data, and that it would pervade the data. But during the interview we found that I was able to provide descriptions of my experience on par with my other reports, and that only one out of five beeps was directly related to my emotional state. This surprised me. Did this mean that my assumption that I was in a bad mood was incorrect? Or was I in a bad mood but DES didn't capture it? Could this mean that patterns of inner experience are stable regardless of affective state?

Russ: Sarah's comment illustrates a fundamental, repeated observation in DES: People are not necessarily good judges of the general characteristics of their own inner experience. This is true even when they, like Sarah, are bright, sensitive individuals who are seriously interested in consciousness.

Observing a sampling interview (of Jack)

Sarah: Soon after I'd finished this stint as a subject, the DES lab (including me) conducted a sampling interview with "Jack" as a training exercise. So far, I had been a DES subject, and had had several in-depth discussions about DES with Dr. Hurlburt. Now I had an opportunity to view sampling from the role of interviewer, to listen to someone else try to get clear on what had happened at the moment of the beep. Dr. Hurlburt interviewed Jack about his first sample, and then the other students jumped in to ask about other samples.

I was relieved to see that being a DES interviewee was apparently as hard for Jack as it had been for me – prior to that I had nothing against which to measure my own process. Jack's reports of his beeps were not clear and singular, but instead were amalgams of narrative and interpretation laced with clues about his experience. It was the interviewer's job to ask questions in the service of untangling that mess and zeroing in on the details of his experience. I noticed Jack struggle with not being able to answer the interviewers' detailed questions and I remembered how that had felt for me.

I also noticed that the interviewers asked a mix of more-or-less effective questions. The most effective questions guided Jack in discriminating the elements of his experience present at the beep without pushing a personal agenda or leading the subject. They invited Jack to come forth and show himself, and Jack did so willingly and with focus and little hesitation. Conversely, poorly phrased or agenda-driven questions seemed to force him to abandon his effort to know his own experience in order to please the interviewer, and he seemed to become hesitant, shallow, unfocused, unconvinced and unconvincing. I wasn't sure I myself would know how to ask good questions, or how to avoid asking bad ones, but I could certainly see the difference between the two types of questions in the quality of Jack's responses.

Russ: Sarah is right, I think, to observe that there are good and bad questions about experience, and that good and bad questions have substantially different effect on Jack. We have provided, in this book, a thorough discussion of what we take to be the characteristics of good questions, but in the final analysis, the way you discern whether a question was good or bad is to observe its effect on the subject. If the subject is led to report, or at least to focusedly try to report, the details of his experience, then you asked a good question. If the subject is led to generalize, or to subjunctify, or to theorize, then you asked a bad question. It really is as simple as that.

Conducting sampling interviews (of Kelly)

Sarah: After the Jack interview, new questions and curiosities cropped up for me about DES, this time from the investigator perspective. To get at these questions directly, Dr. Hurlburt suggested I take the role of DES investigator and conduct a series of DES interviews. He agreed to be a co-investigator and found Kelly, a student from an introductory psychology class, who would volunteer to wear the beeper.

During our first meeting with Kelly, Dr. Hurlburt briefly explained DES theory and then got into the nuts and bolts of how the beeper works, what we needed her to do, etc. She seemed to understand her task, at least as well as one can before one actually does it.

Interviewing Kelly day 1

Sarah: Dr. Hurlburt served as the primary interviewer on the first day, which was more of a training day for Kelly than anything else. As in my own sampling and in the Jack interview, Dr. Hurlburt's questions didn't probe the story or context of Kelly's experience. Instead he helped her slice away superfluous information to arrive at the details of her experience at the precise moment of each beep. Kelly blushed red at times, sort of blotchy, and seemed almost unfairly confronted with a task that she was not equipped to do. Dr. Hurlburt wasn't at all thrown by her discomfort, though it was obvious he was sensitively aware of her struggle. He reassured Kelly that initial stress was perfectly normal, yet he continued to ask detailed questions as a way of training her to know what to pay attention to next time she collected samples. She seemed to understand that the task wasn't going to change but that her skills would likely improve.

I could see that Kelly is obviously very smart; I was struck by the fact that the sampling task is hard even for a very smart person. I began to realize that being a good subject (or interviewer, for that matter) isn't about being smart (although I guess that helps) but that it's about catapulting yourself out of your habitual way of encountering yourself and others. That's probably hard for everyone, no matter where you fall on the smart continuum.

Had I been the interviewer I wouldn't have known what questions to ask of Kelly, so one of my goals that day was to figure out how Dr. Hurlburt knew what to ask. I came to see that the questioning and answering were inextricably linked: the information that Kelly was giving in her answers provided clues about what questions Dr. Hurlburt would ask next. It was difficult to pay close attention both to his questions and her answers, so I missed out on a good deal of the art of the interchange. I did manage to figure out that DES interviewing requires continuous and rapt attention to the subject and all aspects of her communication (body language, tone of voice, pauses etc.).

There were some small successes in getting at Kelly's experience at the moment of the beep, but for the most part I thought the interview was somewhat jagged, uncomfortable, and not particularly believable. I had a lot of doubt about her reports. How could she possibly know her experience at this point? Based on my own experience of being a samplee, I supposed that Kelly wasn't prepared for Dr. Hurlburt's discriminating questions about her experience. I guessed that the information she needed to answer Dr. Hurlburt's questions had long since departed from her memory, if in fact it was ever actually stored. How could she possibly have known it would be salient?

I also continued to be impressed by Dr. Hurlburt's lack of interest in the "story" aspect of what subjects say. I, conversely, was magnetically drawn into her story and felt inclined to ask questions about her narrative.

Russ: Sarah comments that "for the most part I thought the interview was somewhat jagged, uncomfortable, and not particularly believable," and I agree with that. This was Kelly's first sampling day, and first-day interviews are often uncomfortable and not particularly believable.

Sarah is correct, I do usually avoid the story aspect of a person's report. I regard stories as being at least partially, and usually largely, a public mask, as practiced attempts at explaining part of one's world while simultaneously hiding other parts. It's usually impossible to tell how much of a story is explaining and how much is hiding, and it's usually impossible to tell which part is which. As a result, I find story accounts nearly always to be unsatisfying – I can never figure out which part is real, which part is misleading, which part is public, which part is personal. By contrast, I think sampled experiences are largely true and only in minor ways the result of public masking. (Certainly there are exceptions – occasionally people lie, for example.) But for the most part, sampled experiences are far more satisfying to me than are the accompanying stories. I therefore listen to the experiences and avoid the stories.

Interviewing Kelly day 2

Sarah: At my request, Dr. Hurlburt was the primary interviewer again. I noticed Kelly was able to report and discriminate her sampling data more comfortably, confidently, and accurately than she had the previous day. I found this day's reports substantially more believable as they were now detailed and confidently asserted; she could not be talked into things that had not been in her experience, nor could she be talked out of the things that she had experienced. She seemed more steadfast in her reporting.

I continued to have trouble following the question-answer interplay. I was pretty nervous about stepping into the interviewer role and I was still trying to get a handle on how to ask good questions. Apparently Dr. Hurlburt's questions made sense to Kelly and her answers made sense to him, but I couldn't figure out how they'd gotten there. I listened and attempted a rough outline of Dr. Hurlburt's questioning process for each beep:

1. He asked what was in Kelly's awareness at the moment of the beep.
2. He listened to the entire beep report, perhaps asking for a clarification here and there, but letting Kelly give her complete description.
3. He asked again what was in Kelly's awareness at the (exact) moment of the beep.
4. He listened again.
5. He broke down the components of what she had said ("So, it seems to me there were three things happening…").
6. He then proceeded to go after one thing at a time. Clarification is a process of honing in, sometimes backing out to make sure, and then honing further in. He also occasionally went back to examples from previous beeps to juxtapose them with the current experience to see if they are the same or different.
7. At the end of the process, he verbalized the refined version. He seemed to make sure Kelly freely endorsed that version, and doubled back to clarify anything about which she was hesitant.
8. He asked if there is anything else to be discussed about that beep, and if not, proceeded to the next one.

Russ: Kelly was typical of DES subjects in the sense that the second sampling day is usually much easier than the first. I agree with Sarah's characterization of the DES questioning technique.

Interviewing Kelly day 3

Sarah: I attempted to interview Kelly on the third day, but one or two questions into each beep I'd reach an impasse and need to turn to Dr. Hurlburt for help. I'd begin by asking about her experience at the moment of the beep. She'd give me her report and then I'd be absolutely stumped. I felt inadequate, frustrated, and stressed out about faltering in front of Dr. Hurlburt and Kelly. Why was

DES interviewing so difficult compared to asking questions in the course of a normal getting-to-know-you conversation?

If I did ask a second question, often it turned out to be a bad one. I'd know immediately from her reaction that I'd trapped her or forced her down my own path instead of trying to discover what her experience was for her. Though I could easily identify when I'd made this mistake, I didn't know how to recover from it. Yet when I'd turn the reins over to Dr. Hurlburt he'd have a stream of open yet specific questions for her; suddenly there seemed to be a million opportunities to recover accurate information about her experience. I began to realize that DES interviewing was a much tougher skill to acquire than I'd thought.

Russ: DES interviewing is in fact a quite particular skill in that it centrally involves setting aside one's own presuppositions. That may seem like an easy thing to do, but it decidedly is not, and it is only the very rare individual who comes to that skill without substantial effort. I'm actually quite happy with Sarah's progress as an interviewer because she can see the effect of her presuppositions on Kelly. That's an essential part of learning DES. Sarah doesn't yet know what to do about it, but because she can see the difference in impact on Kelly between a good and a bad question, I'm confident that she will, with practice, eventually be able to learn how to ask good questions. The fact is that many other people *can't* see the effect on the subject of their own presuppositions; those people are hard to train.

Interviewing Kelly day 4

Sarah: On the final interview day with Kelly, I attempted the role of lead investigator again. I made nearly all the same mistakes I'd made the previous day and continued to struggle with two central challenges: *what* to ask and *how* to ask. I managed to make some progress that day though; when I'd ask a good question, I'd immediately see that I'd get more information about Kelly's experience. When I'd ask a bad question, I'd get a confusing answer. The feedback on my questions was in Kelly's answers themselves and this was getting easier for me to read now that I knew what to look for.

During that final interview I realized that learning the art of the DES interview was a tedious process of trying, screwing up, falling down, getting up, and trying again. I wasn't going to just wake up good at it the following morning. Though I could now identify many salient elements of Kelly's experience, forming well-articulated questions and asking them in a useful order was another story. Strange as it may sound, I began to enjoy the challenge despite the fact that it was difficult for me.

Russ: Sarah was actually better at asking questions than she gives herself credit for, just as she had been better at reporting her own experience than she had given herself credit for.

Conclusion

Sarah: My original – albeit selfish – motivation to explore DES was to see if I could learn something new about myself, to discover information that I'd never seen before. I did. In fact, I found it pretty remarkable that I'd spent years practicing meditation but until sampling had no idea that I spend most of my moments involved in sensory and emotional experience and relatively fewer moments experiencing anything like thinking. As far as I'm concerned that's very significant and basic (in the fundamental sense) information that I'd otherwise not have known. Furthermore, this view of myself is both personal and factual at the same time. It isn't based on interpretation or theory or norms, it's based on rich, hard-earned, straightforward facts about how *I* spend *my* moments that I directly observed about myself.

The core DES instruction for subjects and interviewers alike is to discover what's in the subject's experience at the moment of the beep. At the outset of my DES training, I thought I understood this instruction clearly, but it turned out that my assumptions were wrong. In my everyday life I was used to – even good at – telling people stories about what I thought about my experiences and asking people to tell me stories about what they thought about their experiences. Instead, DES asked me to identify and talk about the *facts* of experience, something I did not know how to do.

It was a rather radical shift for me to consider the facts of inner experience instead of the story about what I assumed those facts were. DES wasn't after *why* I was looking at a tree or what looking at a tree *meant* to me but, instead, *that* I was looking at the tree, *how* I was looking at the tree, *my experience* of looking at the tree. It was frustrating at first, and I felt inadequate for a while. But once I got oriented and focused on the target of experience rather than narrative, I was able to begin learning how to move toward it, both as a samplee and as an interviewer.

Russ: Because Sarah's reactions were in some ways not unusual, here's a summary of what she experienced that might be of interest to someone contemplating involvement with DES:

- She was originally nervous about being sampled but found that her fears were not realized.
- During her stint as subject, she at first thought she could not do the task, that she could not apprehend her experience with fidelity. Later she became quite confident that her reports were largely accurate.
- It doesn't take long for subjects to become confident reporters – a couple of days for both Sarah and Kelly.
- She found that DES revealed several important features of her inner experience that were previously unknown to her despite her substantial interest in consciousness and spiritual practice.
- She came to see that the investigator's presuppositions can have a direct effect on how questions are asked, and thence an immediate effect on how the subject answers.
- Even though she could see the effect of bad questions, she couldn't (at least at first) see how to stop asking them.

CHAPTER 10

Bracketing presuppositions

Insensibly one begins to twist facts to suit theories instead of theories to fit facts.

Sherlock Holmes instructing Dr. Watson

In the previous chapters, we have discussed how to do DES. But in those chapters, we have discussed only briefly one of the most important aspects of DES: the bracketing of presuppositions.

A presupposition is a preconception, something that is taken for granted. It is a notion about the world that is so fundamental that it exists prior to critical examination. It is something accepted without controversy as being true, something that shapes perception, behavior, and affect without the fact of that shaping being noticed or recognized. It is an unquestioned manner of relating to the world that chooses what is seen and what is not seen, what is experienced and how it is experienced, so invisibly that what is seen and experienced seems to be the world itself, not aspects of the world selected, shaped, and distorted by the presuppositional process.

Your presuppositions impose themselves unseen, cause you to distort the world, to overemphasize the importance of some aspects of the world, to fail to see some aspects of the world, to twist or alter your perceptions of your environment and the people in it. The actions of those presuppositions are so taken for granted that it wouldn't occur to you to question that the world could be any other way; the possibility wouldn't occur to you that your perceptions are twisted by your own characteristics.

To "bracket" a presupposition (a concept borrowed from the phenomenologists) is to take the presupposition out of play, to act as if it didn't exist, to accept that its way of seeing may or may not be accurate, to recognize that its conclusions may or may not be true, to allow it to be examined and supported or examined and denied with equal acceptance, to suspend the effect of a presupposition. In a perfect world, it would be desirable to eliminate presuppositions completely, to see the world unencumbered by biases and distortions. Such a sublime state is likely to be beyond the reach of most mortals, however;

to bracket a presupposition is to acknowledge that presuppositions exist but to put their distorting effects out of play.

Presuppositions can have seriously distorting effects both for the DES investigator and the subject. For example, Donald (Chapter 1) had presuppositions of himself as free of anger and blessed with total acceptance, and as a result he failed to see himself as frequently angry at his children, even though sampling showed that his anger was frequent. Donald's case illustrates how blind people can be to the contents of their own inner experience; recall that Donald had transcribed all the contents of his beeps and even in so doing failed to see himself as angry with his children. Thus Donald's general (presuppositional) view of himself as accepting of his children was not merely a failure to see, but instead involved a self-theorizing or self-construing that led to a motivated selective forgetting of his own characteristics. The operation of this presupposition may thus be considered a kind of motivated avoidance.

However, recall also that when we examined each individual beep, Donald could easily recognize himself as being angry at that particular moment. The difference was striking: no awareness of anger when viewing himself in general vs. easy awareness of anger when pointed out moment by moment. Why this difference? Because the DES procedure helped Donald to bracket his presuppositions – to put them out of play, render them ineffective. At the outset, of course, we had no idea what presuppositions were present and in need of bracketing; the DES moment-by-moment attempt to view himself accurately helped the accepting-of-his-children presupposition to emerge and then to be suspended. DES is effective in this regard because the random sampling procedure produces an experience at each beep that can be viewed merely as a single particular occurrence, perhaps typical of Donald or perhaps atypical. The "perhaps typical, perhaps not" nature of the beeped samples facilitates the bracketing of presuppositions: because each single sample is so tiny and apparently insignificant, most subjects feel freed of the presuppositional requirement to present themselves (even to themselves!) in a particular way. Therefore it was relatively easy for Donald, beep by particular beep, to see that he was indeed angry at those particular instances. Once enough of those instances had accumulated, then Donald could, with a bit of outside help, develop a more accurate view of himself as frequently angry.

Presuppositions distort the accurate view of reality, and are substantial impediments to the advance of science in general, not merely the science of inner experience. For one historical example, the astronomer Copernicus (1473–1543) came into the world believing (that is, "presupposing") that the earth is the center of the universe, and in particular that the sun revolves around the earth. Those beliefs were presuppositions accepted without question by everyone of his time. Copernicus' genius was his willingness to suspend his acceptance of (that is, to "bracket") those presuppositions, and thence to consider other possibilities of the relation of the sun and earth. Once he opened himself to those other possibilities, he was able to develop a theory of the earth rotating around the sun that was consistent with his astronomical observations.

To bracket a presupposition, then, is *not* to presume it to be false – that would be creating a new but opposing presupposition. To bracket a presupposition is simply to suspend both belief and disbelief, imperturbably to allow for the possibility that what is taken for granted may be either true or false. Copernicus at the outset did not believe that the earth revolved around the sun; he merely suspended the belief that the sun revolved around the earth. That allowed him to consider other theories and ultimately to discover that the sun, not the earth, was the center of the system.

Let's look at a concrete example of how the bracketing of preconceptions actually occurs in a typical sampling situation. Many sampling subjects report that at the moment of the beep, they were thinking about some specific thing, but that thinking was not in words or images or any other symbols. We call this phenomenon unsymbolized thinking. Most sampling subjects, even those who in fact frequently engage in such thinking themselves, presuppose that such thinking is impossible, presuppose that thinking must be in words or images.

What follows is a fictitious but prototypical expositional interview of "Sam" on his first sampling day's encounter with unsymbolized thinking. We join the expositional conversation after about 40 minutes, during which time we had discussed the first five of Sam's samples.

The sampling discussion	**Commentary**
One of us:[1] What was going on at sample 1.6?	
Sam:[2] I was at home, and I was wondering what to have for lunch.	
Us:[3] Exactly what was this wondering like?	At Us[3], we try, as is our usual procedure, to understand as completely as possible what his experience is like from his own perspective. Here we simply ask for clarification about Sam's "wondering,"

Sam:[4] I was saying to myself that I should make a ham sandwich. Then I changed my mind and decided to go out to get a cheeseburger.	using his own word to reduce the intrusion of any presupposition we might have about what wondering might be like for him. This attempt not to intrude is part of our bracketing process: we try to suspend any hunches we may have about what "wondering" is like and simply ask for clarification.
Us:[5] This "saying to yourself" – what exactly did you say to yourself?	At Us[5], we continue to bracket our presuppositions about his experience. Sam now refers to "saying to himself," rather than "wondering," and we do not contest his new usage, but ask him to elaborate it.
Sam:[6] Well, I was hungry and I wanted something to eat, but I didn't want to go to the trouble to make it, so I thought I'd go out. **Us:**[7] I understand that, but I'm particularly interested in what was going on right at the moment of that beep. **Sam:**[8] I was thinking that I should make a ham sandwich, and then I was thinking that I'll go get a cheeseburger. **Us:**[9] This "thinking" – what was it like?	At Sam[6], Sam gives a general description of his state at the time of the beep, even though we had asked for specific details ("what *exactly* did you say to yourself?"). One of the primary arts of the sampling method is continually to urge Sam to report specific details, even though most people most of the time (as here) retreat to generalities. We continue to try to keep our conversation focused on the specific details of his experience at Us[7] and Us[9].
Sam:[10] [a bit confused] What do you mean, "What was it like?"	At Sam[10], Sam seems a bit confused, even though our question had made perfect sense in previous samples. We have seen this kind of confusion before, and we know from sampling with many previous people that such confusion often signals a subject's first brush with "unsymbolized thinking" – thinking that takes place with no experience of words

Us:[11] Well, at your third sample you said you were thinking in words, like you were talking to yourself, and at your fourth sample you said you were seeing a visual image. Was this lunch thought similar to those or different? By the way, this thought doesn't have to be the same or have to be different – any variation is OK with me. I simply want to know how it appeared to you.

Sam:[12] I'm not sure. I thought I'd make a ham sandwich.... [Sam appears more confused.] I don't know. I can't say for sure.

Us:[13] Don't worry about it. If this kind of experience is common for you, we'll see it again and we'll have the opportunity then to try to clarify our description of that experience. If this kind of experience is not common, then it won't matter that we didn't get the details of this one. But now you have some idea of the kinds of questions that I'm likely to ask, so perhaps it will be easier to pay attention to the details of your experience.

It may turn out that it becomes easier to pay attention to the details, or it may turn out that it is impossible to pay attention to the details. Either way is very valuable to me. So

or images. One might say that we "suspect" that Sam might be describing unsymbolized thinking here, and that is true. However, we bracket that suspicion. Thus at Us[11], rather than lead Sam *toward* reporting unsymbolized thinking, we suggest a few alternatives that actually lead him slightly *away* from it: we mildly suggest the presence of words or images (features incompatible with unsymbolized thinking) but also explicitly allowing for the possibility that this thought has characteristics that are either similar or different from any of the previous ones. It is this even-handed, level-playing-field acceptance of either the presence or absence of unsymbolized thinking that is the hallmark of the bracketing process.

At Us[13] we encourage Sam to give descriptions that faithfully reflect the experience that was present at the moment of the beep. We explicitly do *not* force Sam to commit to a description that he is not completely comfortable with. Sampling will proceed at his pace and at the level of his own confidence in the details of his descriptions. This again is a part of the bracketing process: Sam may be describing unsymbolized thinking, he may not be describing unsymbolized thinking, and he may be describing something that is some combination of the two or some

I don't want you to make up details. At future beeps, if you have access to details, please make note of them. If not, please make note of that also.

You wear the beeper this afternoon, and we'll meet again tomorrow. OK?

altogether new phenomenon. We try to keep ourselves – and Sam – unprejudicially open to any possibility.

One of the delicacies of the descriptive sampling method is that the intent is to arrive at what Sam's inner experience *actually is*, and not what he *says it is*. Very often, sampling subjects say things that are not true, even by those subjects' own standards of truth. For example, here Sam said "I was saying to myself...," but when we encouraged him to provide the details of that saying-to-himself, he withdrew his confidence in that description. It is the sampler's art to give subjects the opportunity to affirm, expand, narrow, modify, or withdraw from statements so as eventually to arrive at straightforward descriptions that they judge to be accurate reflections of their experience at the moment of the beep. That is, we wish to bracket the presupposition that what Sam said about his sample is true – we wish to bracket the presupposition (in Sam and in us) that at the moment of this beep Sam was saying something to himself.

"I was saying to myself" may of course be an accurate description of Sam's experience – bracketing does not mean that we simply do not believe our subject's report. But if the phrase "I was saying to myself..." was a straightforward description of his inner experience, Sam probably could have responded quite easily to our Us[5] question ("This 'saying to yourself' – what exactly did you say to yourself?") by saying something like, "I was saying to myself, 'No, let's have McDonalds.' It was my own voice, just like I was saying it out loud, except there was no real sound and no real movements of my mouth." And Sam probably would have said that with confidence, with very little doubt about the details of this experience.

What happened instead, however, was that Sam *lost* confidence; he apparently wasn't sure about the details of his experience. It is precisely in such cases that the bracketing of presuppositions is of most importance. If we are to allow/assist Sam to come into contact with his own experience, then we have to suspend our own presuppositions, and help Sam to suspend his presuppositions, about the features of his experience. To bracket or suspend presuppositions is to be equally willing to accept an outcome that is in line with the presupposition as one that is contrary to it. If Sam's experience at the moment of beep 1.6 turns out to be in words, fine. But if it doesn't turn out to be in words, fine too. If the experience was clear when it occurred (but he didn't pay adequate attention at the moment of the beep or his memory blurred in the interim), fine – we'll do better next time. If Sam's experience wasn't clear at all, fine. We'll try again, perhaps with more success, perhaps not. If Sam has an adequate grasp of the beeped phenomenon but difficulty translating it into descriptive words, fine (we'll try to help him to describe that experience in words that rest lightly on the experience, characterizing it accurately and not distorting it in one direction or another). If Sam does not have an adequate apprehension of the original beeped phenomenon, fine. To bracket presuppositions is to hold all these possibilities (in words, not in words, clear, not clear, adequate apprehension but descriptive difficulty, inadequate apprehension, etc.) at bay, to be indifferent to which of these possibilities turns out to be the accurate description of Sam's experience. Suspending the presuppositions gives the best possible chance to apprehend the phenomenon (or some subsequent phenomenon) as it actually presents itself.

Thus we must suspend our own presuppositions and also help the subject learn to suspend his. Bracketing presuppositions is a skill, and like any skill requires practice and repetition. Skill building was our intent at Us[13], for example, when we said, "It may turn out that it becomes easier to pay attention to the details, or it may turn out that it is impossible to pay attention to the details. Either way is very valuable to me. So I don't want you to make up details." Emphasizing that "either way is very valuable" is intended to encourage the subject in the future to apprehend phenomena as they are, not according to presuppositions about the way they should be.

When we met again the next day, Sam initiated the sampling conversation something like this:

Sam:[14] I'm very sorry, but I cannot continue to participate in your sampling study. Here's your beeper back.

Us:[15] That's fine – our original agreement was to proceed day by day, and I respect your decision to discontinue. But if you wouldn't mind telling me, I would like to know as candidly as possible why you would like to stop.

At Sam[14] and Sam[16], Sam exhibits what we have come to recognize as the common emotional consequence of personally confronting the results of a presupposition about ones own inner characteristics. "I'm just not very good at it" at Sam[16] is probably best interpreted as a response to an inchoate, vague, inarticulate impression, which if it were possible for him to articulate clearly (which is

Sam:[16] I just don't think I can do what you ask, and I don't want to waste your time. I'm just not very good at it, and you should get someone who is better at it than I am.

not possible for him at this point) might be expressed something like, "I have a presupposition (which I have never examined but which I accept without question as being fundamentally, unalterably true) about the characteristics of my inner experience – that my thinking (everyone's thinking, for that matter) takes place in words or images. However, when I actually look carefully at my own experience, as your beeper is requiring me to do, I find myself to be thinking but I am not aware of words or images. Thus I experience myself as doing something that I fundamentally hold to be impossible. To give up my fundamental thinking-is-in-words-or-images presupposition is totally unthinkable, unimaginable, impossible. In fact it wouldn't even occur to me to suspect that there is a presupposition at work here, so it's impossible for me to imagine that there is even a remote possibility of the existence of such a presupposition – words or images is just the way thinking is. Therefore I conclude that I'm no good at the sampling method."

Us:[17] We can certainly stop sampling whenever you like. But if you're requesting to stop so as not to waste *my* time, then my preference is that we give it another chance. Here's why. I'm still exploring this method, and it may well be that the method doesn't make it easy for some people to describe their experience. But that in itself is just as important to me – maybe more important – than the descriptions of people for whom the method is easy. So I'd like to continue. If we can't get anywhere, fine. But that would be a problem of the method, not your problem. Have you brought samples with you today?
Sam:[18] Yes.

We've sampled with a lot of people, and we've seen this presupposition-dilemma response many times, but that does not necessarily imply that Sam's particular reluctance to continue sampling at this particular time is an example of the presupposition confrontation. It may

Us:[19] Can we have a look at those samples, and then discuss at the end of today's conversation whether we should continue?
Sam:[20] OK, but I'm still afraid I'll be wasting your time.
Us:[21] I'm willing to take that chance, if you're willing to give me the opportunity.
Sam:[22] OK.
Us:[23] Good. Then let's have a go at today's first sample.
Sam:[24] I put on the beeper right after our sampling meeting yesterday, and I was driving home. At the moment of the beep, I was thinking that I needed to go to the dry cleaner to pick up my suit.
Us:[25] What was this thinking like?
Sam:[26] I knew you were going to ask that! And I don't know what to say to you! That's just why I should quit! This beep occurred less than an hour after we talked about yesterday's samples, and I tried to pay particular attention to the features of my experience, 'cause I knew you'd ask. But I couldn't.
Us:[27] You said you were thinking that you should go to the cleaners. Was this a thought? Or would it have been just as accurate to say that you had a feeling that you should go to the cleaners?
Sam:[28] No, it wasn't a feeling. It was a thought.
Us:[29] You're sure?

or may not be – this is in fact another presupposition that we ourselves must bracket.

Therefore Sam's request to discontinue puts us in a slight dilemma at Us[15]. The solution is again, as we have discussed, to try to understand what Sam's experience *actually* was, not what *he said* it was. Does he really want to stop? Is he afraid of wasting my time? Is he facing the presupposition confrontation? All those possibilities have to be bracketed: We are in fact perfectly willing to discontinue sampling, but we have often (in fact, usually) found that that is not the true intent of such communication.

Sam[26] again exemplifies the intense personal distress engendered by the attempt to confront one's own presuppositions.

Us[27] illustrates a useful tool of the bracketing art. By leading in the direction of an alternative – this time a feeling – we make it clear that we are not interested in any particular feature – we'll accept anything that tries to accurately describe the phenomenon. Often such transparent even-handedness helps the subject

Sam:[30] Well, it was a mental thing – it was in my mind that I should go to the cleaners. It definitely was mental – definitely not a feeling.
Us:[31] OK. What can you tell me about the features of this mental thing?
Sam:[32] (exasperatedly) Nothing. I tell you I tried to look, but there were none there. I was just thinking I should go to the cleaners.
Us:[33] I gather that the word "cleaners" was not there?
Sam:[34] Correct.
Us:[35] Was an image of the cleaners there?
Sam:[36] No.
Us:[37] How then did you know that this was a thought about the cleaners?
Sam:[38] I tell you, I'm not very good at this!
Us:[39] The purpose of this study is simply to report what you actually experienced. If your experience was in words, then I'd like you to report words. If it was in images, then I'd like you to report images. If your experience had any other features, I'd like you to report them. But it is perfectly OK with me for you to say that you were thinking but you couldn't observe any words or images. Maybe as you get more experience with the sampling procedure, words or images or other features will become clearer. Or maybe it won't become clearer.

bring the target phenomenon more clearly into focus. The art of bracketing is even-handedly to encourage the phenomenon to clarify itself.
At Sam[30], he gives a definitive response that this is a thought, not a feeling. The confidence with which he gives this response is part of the evidence that he is actually trying to describe a mental event.

At Us[39], as we had done earlier at Us[17], we try to reassure Sam by restating the simple philosophy of the method: Our aim is to describe what is there, nothing more, nothing less."
We reemphasize the bracketing instructions, because repetition is necessary in such difficult skills: images or not images is OK with us. Words or not words is OK with us. All we ask is the honest attempt to observe accurately. If there is any leading in Us[39], it is in the direction of words or images ("maybe. . .words or images. . .will become clearer"); that is, we again undermine our suspicion that

Either way is fine with me. What I want is for you to tell me what you experience, without making things up. As for your not being very good at this, I beg to differ. It would appear that you are doing exactly what I would like you to do: you're struggling to give accurate reports even when that is difficult. I can't ask for anything more than that.	Sam's difficulty may be that he is discovering the existence of unsymbolized thinking.

Let's review what happened in this quite typical interchange. At the beginning of sampling, Sam shares in common with most people the deep-seated, unquestionably accepted notion that thinking takes place in words or in visual images. He probably hasn't thought much about it, but before sampling he would have accepted this fact as being obvious, so obvious that it doesn't require any examination. This deeply, unquestionably held notion that thinking takes place in words or images is what we call a presupposition.

However, when the discussion of Sam's samples arrives at sample 1.6, he is confronted with a dilemma: when he examines his recollection of sample 1.6, he can find no words, no images, no symbols of any kind in his awareness at the moment of that beep. This rattles him somewhat, but he can rationalize it by holding the view that he wasn't really prepared to look for that kind of detail, so he must have simply forgotten it.

The conversation about beep 1.6 sensitizes Sam to the fact that on subsequent beeps he should pay closer attention to the details of his experience; he resolves to do so and puts on the beeper while this resolve is still fresh. When beep 2.1 occurs less than an hour after our discussion of beep 1.6, he is prepared: he observes immediately his awareness at the moment of the beep, in a state of heightened readiness to note the words or images that were occurring at the moment of the beep. Despite this readiness, however, his increasingly careful examination of his awareness at beep 2.1 identifies no words or images or any other symbols, even though he is clearly aware that he is thinking that he should go to the dry cleaner.

This is truly a collision between Sam's unexamined presupposition (thinking must be in words or images) and his own careful observation that reveals a clear thought but no words or images. The result: Sam loses his nerve, and concludes that he must not be a good subject. Presuppositions don't give way easily.

We reassure Sam, and at the conclusion of that sampling day we ask if he is willing to sample for one more day. If he is a typical subject, he'll agree to this one-more-day request. By the time we have finished our sampling discussions for that (third) day, he will probably have become convinced that he did indeed have inner experiences that are clearly thoughts, but which are not accompanied by words or images or any other symbols. He will probably make up his own label for this phenomenon: "thoughts without words," "pure thoughts," "known thoughts," or perhaps "one of those hard-to-describe thoughts like the dry-cleaner thought." Presuppositions are stubborn, but they can succumb to the onslaught of one's own careful observations, once those observations are actually made directly rather than avoided or twisted.

This phenomenon that we call unsymbolized thinking – inner experience that is clearly a thought, but which is not accompanied by words or images or any other symbols – turns out to be fairly common. For some people, unsymbolized thinking dominates their inner experience, occurring at nearly every sample; for others, unsymbolized thinking occurs occasionally but not always; and for others, unsymbolized thinking apparently occurs only rarely if at all.

It's a striking fact of our sampling experience that many people (like Sam) whose own samples reveal a high frequency of unsymbolized thinking do not, prior to sampling, believe that such thinking can possibly exist. For some people, it is incredibly difficult to admit that they themselves produce such a phenomenon. They may have seen it themselves on a dozen samples, and they still continue to have lingering doubt or skepticism about the possibility that thoughts without words or images can exist. It is common for such people to create their own sampling investigations: they decide, for example, to pay particular attention to their beeped moments, to look as carefully as possible, so to speak, for signs of words or images. Such "free-lancing" is fine with us – it's a benefit of the co-researcher model. Eventually they become convinced that not only is the phenomenon of unsymbolized thinking possible, but they are forced to admit that they themselves produce the phenomenon frequently.

Questions and answers

Q: If I understand Husserl correctly, his epoche' was an attempt to suspend any assumptions about the existence of the represented object. At any moment, I might be seeing my real existing house, or I might be hallucinating.

Husserl's point was that I have no way of knowing at that moment whether my experience is the result of perception or hallucination. Do you mean by bracketing or suspending presuppositions the same thing that Husserl meant by the epoche'?

A: Similar, but not the same. Husserl, if we understand him correctly, was trying to get to the pure phenomenon or essence, a lofty goal. Our own goal is much more pragmatic: to get "pretty darn close" to the subject's experience, to severely minimize (but probably not to eliminate completely) systematic distortions about that experience. We agree that suspending judgment about whether something is real or hallucinated is important in getting to the phenomenon as experienced, but that is not our primary goal.

Q: Is the bracketing of presuppositions the reason that you found the open-beginninged characteristic of questions (Chapter 8) desirable?

A: Yes. An open-beginninged question does not presuppose what the characteristics of the subject's experience are.

Q: I worry that the open-beginninged characteristic of the request to report one's inner experience will bias subjects toward reporting the most salient parts of their experience, and they may forget or disregard the rest, whereas a more directive question such as, "at the time of the beep, were you experiencing any tactile sensations?" might reveal some more subtle aspects of experience.

A: We agree. There is a trade-off here, though. The more directive the question, the more likely that presuppositions will drive the output. We agree that DES "biases subjects toward reporting the most salient parts," although we would prefer the term "encourages" to "biases." The closer you stay to what is salient, the less presuppositions are an issue.

Furthermore, once a subject (and the investigator, for that matter) has been helped to see the advantages of bracketing presuppositions (by, among many other techniques, the use of open-beginninged questions), it is then possible to ask the more directive question with substantially less presuppositional risk.

Q: I also worry that open-beginninged questions allow more room for the experimenter's presuppositions to come subtly into play. That's why experimental psychology has generally adopted standardized (often videotaped) instructions for experiments.

A: We disagree. Experimenter's presuppositions come into play to the extent that experimenters are not effective at suspending their presuppositions, regardless of method. There is just as much (probably more) opportunity for preconceptions to be exercised in the writing of multiple-choice questions or videotaped instructions as in open beginninged questions. Therefore we think it's not the medium but the experimenter that is important to the bracketing task.

Q: I agree that presuppositions lurk as much in multiple-choice as in open-beginninged questioning, and that careful experimenters can, with care, reduce the biasing effect of their preconceptions. Still, the presuppositions and their possible effects may be more easily detectable, by other scientists reading the work, in an explicit, formalized set of questions than in an open-beginninged interview.

A: That would be true only if the reader had a different set of presuppositions than did the multiple-choice-question writer (or had no presuppositions, of course). One of the main features of psychology education, unfortunately, is that everyone is encouraged to have the same presuppositions. For example, suddenly we're into computer analogs for cognition (input, output, cache, parallel processing, etc.). Either those are absolutely true descriptions of cognitive processes (which seems pretty unlikely), or they are metaphors whose preconceptual basis has been forgotten by most cognitive scientists. A shared presupposition is probably worse (more pervasive, more insidious, more stubborn; recall "the world is flat") than an idiosyncratic presupposition.

Q: I accept that in directive questions, the preconceptions have an influence on the subject's response from the start. In open questions, preconceptions have an influence only once investigators start reacting to the subject's response to the question. And in the latter case, if the investigators are cool and very careful, the influence of their reactions on the response as it develops can be muted. But one might legitimately be skeptical about how cool and careful investigators can be. Furthermore, with open questions, preconceptions can be more difficult to detect (the lift of an eyebrow, a greater likelihood of following up on one type of response than on another) and so more insidious; and still further, directive questions can also be crafted so as to minimize the influence of preconceptions. So the issue is tangled.

A: We agree with all that. That's what leads us to say that the issue is more with the investigator than with the type of question. Perhaps the main point is that presuppositions *are* important all the time; but scientists usually *criticize* presuppositions only some of the time. For example, mainstream psychology acts as if its own presuppositions (e.g. those present in multiple-choice questions) don't matter, whereas they complain loudly about presuppositions in descriptive investigations of awareness. We just don't think that's good science. Science should be alert to presuppositions all the time; should seek to bracket preconceptions at all appropriate times; should be particularly on guard when most of the scientific community unquestioningly holds the same presuppositions.

Q: As for the ideal of shedding preconceptions, I feel a similar kind of tangled ambivalence. On the one hand, it sounds like a good idea, since it seems more likely to generate unbiased reports. On the other hand, it sounds impossible – who doesn't have preconceptions?

A: We suspect you would grant that there are some people who are more influenced by their presuppositions than are others. You don't have to be perfect in order to be pretty darn good. But in our view, most psychological scientists don't try hard enough to become better at reducing the impact of presuppositions. How much of graduate training is aimed at reducing presuppositions? Not much. Why not? Obviously we don't know for sure, but we suspect because trainers don't think about presuppositions when applied to themselves, which is probably the most dangerous presupposition.

Q: Preconceptions seem necessary, to help you form hypotheses worth testing, to help you gain a sense of whether you're getting misled or getting accurate descriptions, and to know what responses to follow up on and how to follow up on them.

A: We don't know whether presuppositions are necessary. We suspect that it is *possible* to have no presuppositions, and that it is *possible* to live very intelligently without presuppositions, but we're not sure about that (the adept practitioners of the deepest of the Eastern meditative traditions may have achieved this goal). But the issue among scientists is not perfection, it's "good enough." Certainly presuppositions can have utility in the senses you describe, but the risk of that utility is that the presuppositions will blind you (and your fellow scientists) to "play within the rules" that your scientific community has established. Playing within those rules may or may not be a productive depending on the state of the science at any particular time. We recommend the "Copernicus test": would it have been valuable to let Copernicus use the presuppositions of the day to "help him form hypotheses worth testing, and to help him gain a sense of whether he's getting misled"? Clearly not. Was Copernicus an exception? Probably so. Do we need a Copernican revolution in the science of inner experience? That is an important question; we think the answer is yes.

Q: In the last three questions, the questioner asked about "preconceptions," but you responded about "presuppositions." Why is that?

A: Both terms are used in the phenomenological literature. The difference, as we (but not all phenomenologists) see it, is that the term "preconceptions" implies a cognitive or mental realm of action, whereas "presuppositions" is a broader term, including the cognitive or mental but also allowing the motivational or the bodily. We think the broader/deeper notion of presuppositions more accurately characterizes the forces that shape, precondition, twist, or avoid phenomena. We have, of course, argued throughout this book that words are not particularly important, so we have no difficulty with the term "preconception" per se, as long as you don't assume that the way antecedent proclivities or predilections operate is through some kind of cognitive mechanism. That may be true or partially true, but that is at important issue, and using as neutral a term as possible is part of the bracketing of that important presupposition about the operation of presuppositions.

Q: Is it possible to give concrete instructions about how to bracket presuppositions?

A: We think not. But here are some tips:

- If you feel impatience, there is probably a presupposition in the vicinity.
- If you feel angry, there is probably a presupposition in the vicinity.
- If you feel boredom, there is probably a presupposition in the vicinity.
- If you feel proud, there is probably a presupposition in the vicinity.
- If you feel excited, there is probably a presupposition in the vicinity.
- If you think something is really cool or interesting, there is probably a presupposition in the vicinity.
- Whenever there is any exclamation point, there is probably a presupposition in the vicinity.
- The most pernicious obstacle to clear thinking isn't mistaking the false for the true. It's mistaking the half-true for the true.
- The problem with things that you take for granted is that you take for granted precisely those things that you take for granted. You don't examine them.
- Bracketing presuppositions is easy if you genuinely would just as soon be wrong as right.
- A way of examining your presuppositions is to start with your emotions and work backward. It may be easier to recognize your own emotional reaction and bracket what caused it than to recognize at the outset a perhaps more subtle presupposition. If you catch yourself emotionally reacting to what is being said, and use that to cue the bracketing inten-

tion, you may be able to go back and examine what caused the emotion without being as tempted to get caught up in the moment.
- Recognize that, at the outset of sampling, we do not know what the subject's experience is like. We must try to hear sensitively and accurately what she is saying, and that requires us to "turn down the volume" on our own proclivities, hopes, or fears about the world.
- If you find yourself asking leading questions, you know a presupposition is at work.
- Believing that the way you ask questions is good enough is a major impediment to bracketing presuppositions.
- Believing that the standards you accept for deciding whether something is true are good enough is a major impediment to bracketing presuppositions.
- There are two ways to fail to have the truth: ignorance and delusion. Delusion is by far the harder to overcome. Presuppositions are always (major or minor) delusions.
- Bracketing is partially about cognition, an intellectual exercise. But more importantly it is about courage. Courage not to know, not to know, not to know, not to know, still not to know, before knowing. Courage to be stupid, to be stupid, to be stupid, still to be stupid, before becoming simply ignorant.

Here's a fable about presuppositions. A German Shepherd owner lived next door to a family that had a rabbit as a pet. One day, the German Shepherd came home with a very dirty and very dead rabbit – the neighbor's rabbit – in its teeth. The owner, wishing to avoid confrontation, took the rabbit inside and washed and blow-dried it, surreptitiously went over the wall into the neighbor's yard and placed the rabbit in the hutch.

A bit later a scream came over the wall. The dog owner went to the wall and inquired, "What happened?" The neighbor said, "Our rabbit died, and we buried it. And now it's crawled back into the hutch!"

Q: Can you give us some more examples?

A: Yes. Here's a summary of a beep from an undergraduate woman: Catherine is walking toward her dormitory room. She's feeling scared – she had seen a guy in the hall last night and maybe he is in her room. She's feeling scared about the guy, a butterfly feeling, sort of like having a crush on a guy.

A student learning the DES procedure considered this to be an example of feeling (scared) and unsymbolized thinking. The characterization of this sample as being unsymbolized thinking followed from the notion that the scared feeling must have come as the result of a thought about the guy being in her room. However, that notion is a presupposition that assumes what's at issue. There may or may not have been a thought about this guy prior to the beep, and that thought may or may not have triggered the scared response. But the fact is that at the moment of the beep she was scared, and there is no direct apprehension of a thought at that moment. The presupposition that thoughts lead to feelings caused the student to infer the existence of a thought, to hear a thought in a report about a sample that didn't actually include a thought.

Here's another example. The subject, Ricki, was at a friend's house, in the bathroom, in the dark changing from shorts into jeans. One leg is in, and she's working on the next leg. She is trying to hurry because she doesn't want to get caught. There is a light on in the bedroom, but the bathroom is dark. As she struggles with the jeans, she sees herself and the room around her from a point a couple of feet above and a little behind her; she's looking down on herself.

The student learning DES considered this seeing-from-above to be a visual image of herself. In fact, there was nothing in Ricki's description that indicated that this was an image. Ricki was experiencing herself to be *seeing* a real event, not seeing the *image* of an event. The DES student's argument was, How could this be a seeing since it is viewed from an impossible perspective? The answer is that the experience of seeing is not about optics or retinal images; it's an *experience*, and Ricki's experience was that she was seeing herself, not seeing an image of herself.

It is simply a presupposition that led the student to believe that the only event that could be experienced as seeing would be something seen from the perspective of one's own eyes. Certainly it is possible to have an image of oneself viewed from the above-and-behind perspective, but it is also possible to have the experience of actually seeing oneself from that (impossible) perspective. The distinction between seeing an image of something and actually seeing that something is experientially quite differentiated, but only if you ask and listen carefully. The presupposition stands in the way of that.

As that example shows, experience simply does not always correspond to reality. Recall that in a box in Chapter 3 we described Mort's sample of hearing Tom Brokaw talk about cancer on TV; actually it was Dan Rather talking about canvas. Here are some additional examples of that lack of correspondence, all taken from Mort's same sampling day:

– Words with vocal characteristics can be present in experience without being said or heard: Mort is watching TV and has the words "fucking child molesters!" in his awareness, in his own voice, and with a sneer of disgust. However, these words are not said or heard. Somehow they are present in his own voice without the saidness or heardness of speech. At other samples Mort experiences himself as innerly saying things and hearing things, so this lack of saidness and heardness is not likely to be merely a matter of language.

- Two inner speakings can be said simultaneously. Mort is again watching TV, and is saying "Next!" derisively about Dan Rather and, at the same time, is saying "The school system sucks!" Both are being said in inner speech in his own voice at the same time.
- Two seeings can be seen simultaneously and in the same portion of the visual field. Mort is in the process of switching his gaze from the TV to the computer monitor screen, but at the moment of the beep both the TV and the monitor are seen to be directly in front of him. These were not experienced as images, but as simultaneous seeings.
- You can interact meaningfully with the environment without it being in your awareness. Mort was playing a computer game, moving his little man into the corner with the mouse, and his eyes were aimed at the man on the screen. However, his attention was entirely elsewhere.

Mort is a careful observer of his experience, not a disturbed subject. Experience and reality are simply two different realms, and it is not safe to infer the characteristics of one from the features of the other.

Q: Yes, but when someone is telling us something, we will understand it better if we have been in a similar situation.

A: This is, we think, a ubiquitous but dangerous point of view. It certainly would be true to say: "when someone is telling us something about his experience, we will *think* we understand it better if we have been in a similar situation." Whether we *actually* understand the experience better is a quite different question.

The fact that you take similar-situations-imply-similar-experiences for granted illustrates the pervasive, unexamined nature of presuppositions. Similar-situations-imply-similar-experiences is simply not true: Had you been sitting right next to Mort, you probably wouldn't have heard Tom Brokaw talking about cancer, even though the objective situation was essentially identical for you and Mort.

Q: Can you at least tell us what presuppositions to be on the lookout for?

A: The presuppositions that are the most important for you are very personally yours, and you will have to ferret them out for yourself, possibly with the help of associates whom you trust. That said, we can provide a list of some presuppositions that others have found in themselves. If you find youself believing that a statement is true, then you probably also have this presupposition:

Presuppositions about thinking

- Some kind of thinking is always ongoing
- Thinking is in words
- Thinking always uses symbols (words, images)
- Thinking that takes place without symbols must be vague or fuzzy

Presuppositions about inner speech

- Words are always (or at least almost always) ongoing in inner experience
- Inner speech is always in the person's own voice
- Inner speech always has the same characteristics (timbre, pitch, speech rate) as the person's external speech
- Inner speech never has the same characteristics (timbre, pitch, speech rate) as external speech
- Verbal experience always includes words
- External speech is always preceded by inner speech
- You can't have two different inner speakings at the same time
- You can't have an inner speaking that is different from a simultaneous external speaking
- Mental disorders are the result of what people say to themselves
- To discover important differences between groups (as between alcoholics who recover and those who don't), you should look for differences in what they say to themselves

Presuppositions about feelings

- Feelings are always (or at least almost always) ongoing in inner experience
- Feelings are always in the body
- Feelings are always in the head
- There is always (or at least usually) some cognitive component/accompaniment of feelings
- The experience of feelings is always hard to describe

Presuppositions about metaphors

- "In the back of my mind" is a metaphor, not a description of experience
- "I was seeing red" is a metaphor, not a description of experience
- "She sees the world through rose colored glasses" is a metaphor, not a description of experience
- "I feel blue" is a metaphor, not a description of experience

Presuppositions about images/visual experience

- Images/visual perceptions are always (or at least almost always) ongoing in inner experience
- Visual experience always includes figure-ground phenomenon
- Images are experienced to be "out there" like external perception
- Images are experienced to be inside the head
- The experience of seeing an image is looking forward
- When someone is seeing an image, the image has clear edges like a photograph
- When someone is seeing an image, the part of the image that is not seen is dim or fuzzy, just as the part of a photograph that is not focused on
- If images have unusual features, there is some awareness of the unusual nature of those features
- It is impossible to have an indeterminate image (one must see a particular person, not people in general, for example)
- Images are always in color
- Hallucinations are perceptual (visual, auditory) phenomena
- If images are present, they are clear
- People who have images frequently are good at visual tasks such as image rotation
- Visual experience always includes something seen

Presuppositions about inner experience in general

- Everyone always (or at least almost always) has inner experience of some kind
- Other people's experiences are very much like mine (except in extreme cases)
- There is always (or at least usually) some kind of meta-awareness of inner experience
- Inner experience always contains one main feature
- People can remember what they think about

- "I was thinking..." refers to a cognitive process
- What people tell you about their inner experience is true (assuming they are motivated to tell you the truth)
- People are quite knowledgeable about their inner experience because they engage in it all the time
- People have easy access to their inner experience
- People have no access to their inner experience
- Armchair introspection is adequate if you're careful
- Introspection is never accurate
- If a person is in a situation that is similar to one that I have been in, their experience is likely to be much like mine was
- I will be better able to understand a person's experience if I've been in a situation that is similar to the one he/she is in

Q: Any other suggestions for identifying presuppositions?
A: To the extent that you are a partisan – a feminist, a racist, an environmentalist, a psychologist, and so on – you're likely to have difficulty hearing what the person is saying. The "ister" you are, the more difficulty you are likely to have. There may well be good reasons for being a partisan, but those reasons are political, not derived from accuracy-of-observation.

Also, let DES work for you as a training ground. DES is a tool for the chipping away at presuppositions. Not a foolproof, 100% effective tool, but it is a useful tool nonetheless. There are two reasons that DES is useful: First, it chooses what to talk about randomly. The moments are not chosen because they serve some agenda (feminist, racist, environmentalist, psychologist, etc.); they are chosen independently of all agendas. If some theme actually occurs frequently in many samples, then it is possible to infer that the theme is important. (Certainly an "ist" can force a theme into unsuspecting moments, but it's somewhat more difficult.)

Second, because DES chooses rather precisely some concrete moment, there is typically a concrete, explicit answer to the question, "What was in your experience at that moment?" That is, there is at least an experience against which to compare a statement. There is thus something that is pretty close to a right answer to the question, "What was in your experience at the moment of the beep?" By contrast, there is no such independently existing right answer to questions such as, "How did your parents treat you when you were growing up?" "What is your relationship like with your spouse?" Or "What is your thinking usually like?"

Third, here's one final attempt at describing what is meant by bracketing presuppositions. Suppose you are at a wine tasting party where eight cabernet sauvignon wines are being served, and your task is to rate the overall taste quality of each wine on a rating scale from 1 to 10. Now suppose that the eight bottles are all in sight, and each one has its price tag on it, so that you know the price that was paid for each bottle. Now most people have a (probably correct) presupposition that in general the higher the price of a bottle of wine, the better the taste. To "bracket that presupposition" is to *act as if* you did not have the higher-price-better taste presupposition. You know that this is a $100 bottle of wine, but you want to rate it as if you didn't know its price, or that price actually had no effect on your rating. Most people find that to be a very difficult, if not impossible, task. The price-taste presupposition operates outside of awareness – prior to awareness. The presupposition alters the way the wine actually tastes, not merely your rating of it. You expect the expensive wine to taste good, and that expectancy makes it more likely that the wine actually will taste good. That is, the presupposition (expectancy) actually disturbs the phenomenon (taste), not merely the rating of the phenomenon.

Being a good phenomenologist, you know you should bracket this presupposition, so you decide, "All right, I won't let the expensive wine's price tag dazzle me." Now, however, the tendency (again unconscious) may be to expect the wine to taste less good, and therefore you may be likely to *under*-rate it, as a reaction to the possible potential for over-rating. But that is also a disturbance of the actual phenomenon-in-itself. Try your own wine taste – if you're sensitive to your own processes, you'll probably find that it is quite difficult simply to suspend or bracket the impact of price.

This is a simple, but compelling example. It demonstrates the power of presuppositions. So how do you bracket the price-taste presupposition? Probably the best way is to eliminate all cues as to price – decant the wines into eight identical bottles marked with random numbers. Then the tasting can be done blindly, with all presuppositions suspended automatically by the decanting process. However, arranging things so that the investigator is blind is substantially easier with wine than it is with sampling subjects. The DES interviewer gets to know his or her subject quite intimately, and it is usually impossible to perform truly blind sampling research. Therefore, the DES practitioner is forced into bracketing presuppositions, and the ability to bracket presuppositions successfully becomes a vitally important part of the sampler's skill.

Q: In Chapter 8 you seemed to indicate it was likely that we all had presuppositions. Who are you to judge whether I have presuppositions?

A: We do not have the right, nor the ability, to judge whether you do or do not have presuppositions. That is between you and (probably with substantial difficulty) you, or between you and an omniscient being. We do have the right, we think, to point out the probability of presuppositions.

Q: Well, you have presuppositions too!

A: Yes, we do. We have a head start in the bracketing of presuppositions about inner experience, but that doesn't mean that we have been adequately successful in that regard, much less that we have suspended all presuppositions. The attempt to bracket presuppositions is a lifetime effort, unless one has reached a state of perfection (which we haven't). We do think we have some evidence that we have been at least to some degree successful in bracketing presuppositions: we have discovered things that we ourselves thought impossible (unsymbolized thinking, for example), and we have discovered that people are quite different from each other (and therefore different from our presuppositions, whatever they might be).

By the way, discovery is a *very* important concept – it's at the heart of science (and other human endeavors as well). Discovery happens, paradoxically, out of not knowing. Standard science curricula, from grade school to the Ph.D., teach the knowing skills of science but fail to emphasize the importance of the not knowing skills. Bracketing presuppositions is a technology for not knowing, and we should discipline ourselves in this technology so that we may in fact discover.

Q: Why all this abstract talk about the bracketing of presuppositions. Can't we just get on with sampling?

A: First, the bracketing of presuppositions is not abstract, but instead is intensely personally concrete. To bracket presuppositions is to enter into those areas where your whole life you have believed things to be true that are not true. There is nothing abstract about it – it's I against me in a game made up according to my own personal set of rules that are specifically designed to make it difficult for me to see accurately. Seeing things accurately requires disciplined practice, so No, you can't just get on with it any more that Tiger Woods can expect to play great golf without spending time on the range.

The bracketing of presuppositions is, we think, a fundamental issue facing modern psychology (and modern culture as well). It is not an exaggeration, we think, to say that psychology can advance precisely to the extent that it can successfully tackle that issue. For much of its history, psychology tried to avoid the issue, because it is in fact deeply personal and deeply problematic; that may account for the dominance of objective science. The problem is that objective science cannot deal adequately with inner experience, and inner experience is fundamentally important.

We are guardedly optimistic that science can develop methods of teaching the bracketing of presuppositions and identifying those who can adequately do so and in what areas. It won't be easy because of the political and economic consequences and the ubiquity of human arrogance and delusion. However, if psychological science comes to value it, it can be done.

CHAPTER 11

Reliability and validity of DES

In the previous chapters of this book, we have made several analytic arguments in support of the reliability of DES. For example, in Chapter 4 we discussed psychological science's prescriptions for good methods, and how DES embodies those. In Chapter 5 we discussed how a beeper aids the inner experience examination process. However compelling those analytical arguments might be, basic science requires that we examine the conventional reliability of DES, the extent to which two investigators, independently using the DES procedure, arrive at the same results. If we determine that the method is reliable, then we should turn our attention directly to the problem of whether DES reports actually mirror inner experience.

Interobserver reliability of DES[1]

The natural environment, sampling, and interview features of DES present challenges not found in conventional reliability studies. Because the method is new, there is no immediate context for its reliability measurement. The reliability studies performed on the Structured Clinical Interview for DSM-III and DSM-IV (SCID) provide an analogous context because both DES and SCID involve interviews that can be used to rate the presence or absence of characteristics (psychiatric diagnoses in the case of the SCID). Interobserver reliability of the SCID has been assessed in the following ways: test-retest after a short interval (Dreeson & Arntz 1998; First et al. 1995; Williams et al. 1992); test-retest where the initial interview is live and the retest raters watch a videotape (Riskind, Beck, Berchick, Brown, & Steer 1987) or listen to an audiotape (Renneberg, Chambless, Dowdall, Fauerbach, & Gracely 1992) of the original interview; test-retest where both raters watch the same videotaped interview (Ventura , Liberman, Green, Shaner, & Mintz 1998); and joint interviews (Arntz et al. 1992; Renneberg et al. 1992; Brooks, Baltazar, McDowell,

Munjack, & Bruns 1991; Stanley, Turner, & Borden 1990; Wonderlich, Swift, Slotnick, & Goodman 1990).

Of these, the short-interval test-retest method is the most conservative way of assessing SCID reliability because there are more sources of variance:

> The short-interval test-retest approach is a more thorough examination of reliability. In this approach, two raters separately interview the same patient. In this way, three sources of variance are being tested: (1) rater variance in the elicitation of information, (2) rater variance in the interpretation of information, and (3) patient variance in providing information across interviews. In the joint-interview approach, only rater variance in the interpretation of information is being tested.... Compared to joint-interview reliabilities, short interval test-retest reliabilities are ... more generalizable to the actual practice, in which different raters conduct the interview. (Dreesen & Arntz 1998: 139)

Taped interviews have the same source of variance as joint interviews, namely rater variance in interpretation of information; Dreesen and Arntz conclude that short-interval test-retest is the most thorough and most generalizable way of assessing the reliability of the SCID. Given that this conclusion applies equally to DES, we chose this design for the present study.

To assess the interobserver reliability of DES we had two investigators independently interview and subsequently rate the same series of sampled moments from a group of participants. This design answers two important questions: (1) To what extent do two independent interviewers arrive at the same DES ratings? (2) Can DES be applied by anyone other than its originator (RTH)?

We selected the five most frequently-occurring characteristics of experience on the basis of idiographic observations across many participants: Inner Speech, Images, Unsymbolized Thinking, Feeling, and Sensory Awareness (we will return to a discussion of these characteristics in Chapter 13). For this study we created a codebook that contained descriptions of these characteristics along with discussions of relevant rating considerations. We pretested this codebook with two participants and made modifications accordingly. The complete codebook is available on the World Wide Web (Hurlburt & Heavey 2000).

get this!

The study had two phases. Our aim in Phase I was to obtain a heterogeneous sample of inner experiences that was at least approximately representative of the range of naturally occurring inner experiences. Our aim in Phase II was to have two independent interviewers, including one skeptical non-originator (Chris Heavey; this study was part of his introduction to the method) use the DES procedure and codebook to rate each participant's samples. We then computed reliability coefficients for these two sets of ratings.

Method: Phase I

Participants. All 210 students in attendance at one lecture meeting of an introductory psychology class were participants in Phase I and received course research-participation credit.

Materials and apparatus. The Symptom Checklist–90–Revised (SCL-90-R, Derogatis 1994) was administered to all participants. The SCL-90-R asks respondents to indicate the extent to which they are bothered by each of 90 symptoms on a scale from 0 (*not at all*) to 4 (*extremely*). The Global Severity Index (GSI), used in this study, is the sum of all responses and indicates the overall extent of symptom distress. All participants also filled out a brief demographic questionnaire that asked their age and gender as well as other questions relevant to another study but not used here.

Procedure. The investigators gave a brief description of the present study to the 210 students attending an introductory psychology class and invited them to fill out the SCL-90-R, the demographic questionnaire, and a consent form in exchange for research-participation credit and the opportunity to proceed to Phase II; all students did so.

Method: Phase II

Participants. The 210 participants from Phase I were stratified into 10 equal-sized strata (21 per stratum) on the basis of their SCL-90-R GSI scores. One prospective participant from each stratum was selected at random and invited to participate in Phase II. If a prospective participant declined to participate, he or she was replaced by another randomly chosen participant from the same stratum; this replacement occurred a total of 4 times because of scheduling conflicts (3) and lack of interest (1). Sex of participant was alternated between each stratum. These Phase II participants' ages ranged from 18 to 19 and they received additional course research-participation credit and $30 as described below. The two interviewers participating in this study were this book's two authors (the second author, at the time of this study, was a skeptic).

Materials and apparatus. A portable shirt-pocket-sized beeper was used by each participant in Phase II. The beepers (Hurlburt 2000c) emitted a 700 Hz beep through a transistor-radio-type earphone at random intervals whose mean length was 30 min (maximum 60 min). Participants in Phase II were also supplied with a 3 in X 5 in notebook.

Procedure. Each participant in Phase II participated in four meetings: the explanation meeting and sampling meetings 1, 2, and 3. They received $5 at the end of sampling meetings 1 and 2 and $20 at the end of sampling meeting 3. There were no dropouts and no missing data. The interviewers and participants were kept blind to the participants' SCL-90-R scores and strata information throughout the study.

In the explanation meeting, one of the interviewers (randomly assigned) explained the study and its procedure, obtained informed consent to continue, instructed the participant in the DES method, and scheduled the three sampling meetings (typically spread over one to two weeks). Participants were instructed to wear the beeper in their usual, everyday environments until they had responded to five beeps (which typically required two to three hours) on the day of or the day before the next sampling meeting. They were instructed to "take a mental snapshot" of whatever was occurring in their awareness at the very moment of the onset of each beep – that last microsecond undisturbed by the beep itself – and to jot down enough notes to be able to discuss that particular moment in detail in the sampling interviews. They were told that we were interested simply in a complete, accurate description of their awareness as it happened to exist at the moment of the beep. We defined awareness as broadly as possible, including thoughts, feelings, sensations, perceptions, tickles, and so on. We said we were not interested in whether those awarenesses were typical or atypical, or in potential explanations of the source of those awarenesses. All participants were advised that they should feel free to decline to describe any sampled experience, and that we would maintain their confidentiality. We treated participants as co-researchers and encouraged them to take that role, explaining that while we had a method that enabled us to examine inner experience in detail, they had the inner experience itself. Together we might discover something that neither of us could alone.

Each sampling meeting was divided into two halves, one with each of the interviewers separately. The order of interviewers was counterbalanced and alternating. Each interviewer discussed the samples that the participant had obtained and scored the first three of them according to the presence or absence of each of the five primary characteristics described in the codebook. We had asked the participants to supply five samples so that if they did not comply completely, or if some of the samples were unusable, we would have three samples from each day; in fact, we were able to use the first three samples for each participant. The participant was instructed to answer each interviewer's questions but not to discuss the contents of the other interviewer's interview. The participant was not informed that his or her descriptions would be rated. The first sampling meeting was considered part of the participants' training process; ratings from this meeting were not included in the analyses. Therefore each of the ten participants contributed six samples to the analyses.

Results and discussion

The ten participants included five men and five women with a mean age of 18.3 (range 18–19). The mean SCL-90-R GSI score was 65.10 ($SD = 45.03$). As expected because of the stratification, this closely mirrored the GSI distribution of the entire Phase I group ($M = 69.82$, $SD = 46.45$).

Each interviewer rated each of the $10 \times 6 = 60$ samples as to the presence or absence of the five characteristics (images, inner speech, unsymbolized thinking, feelings, and sensory awareness).

For each characteristic, there are three ways that interobserver reliability can be assessed: A "sample-wise" analysis considers the interobserver agreement on particular samples; a "participant-wise" analysis considers the interobserver agreement on the average frequency of occurrence of the characteristic across all six of the participant's samples; and a "typical" analysis extrapolates the participant-wise 6-sample analysis to a more typical DES study. We will discuss each in turn.

For each of the five characteristics, "sample-wise" reliability considers the extent to which observers agreed when rating the 60 particular samples. The percentages of agreements ranged from 83 to 97% and are shown in the second column of Table 1. Kappa statistics ranged from .52 to .92 and are shown in the third column of Table 1. Thus at the level of single samples, there is substantial agreement between the two interviewers: The two interviewers agreed on 91% of all ratings made for these five characteristics, and the median kappa was .76. These interobserver (sample-wise) reliability coefficients compare quite favorably to the analogous single-item reliabilities generally found in questionnaires and are substantially higher than those generally found in SCID studies.

"Participant-wise" reliability is analogous to a questionnaire's scale reliability. For each characteristic, we computed the participant-wise score for each interviewer by averaging all six of that interviewer's ratings of the participant. We then computed the participant-wise reliability by correlating those six-sample averages between interviewers across the ten participants. Those

Table 1. Frequencies and Reliability Statistics for Five Characteristics

Characteristic	Frequency (%)	Sample-wise Observer agreement (%)	Sample-wise Interobserver reliability (Kappa)	Participant-wise Reliability of 6-sample average (Pearson r)	Typical Reliability[a] of 19-sample average (Pearson r)
Images	32	97	.92	.95	.98
Inner speech	31	95	.88	.84	.94
Unsymbolized thinking	21	90	.69	.95	.98
Feelings	24	92	.76	.93	.98
Sensory awareness	22	83	.52	.78	.91

[a] Spearman-Brown estimates

correlations are shown in the second-to-last column of Table 1. The median of the participant-wise (six-sample average) reliabilities was .93.

Typical DES studies use more than six samples per participant. For example, Hurlburt, Koch, and Heavey (2002) obtained between 16 and 22 samples (M = 19) from each participant in their target group. If for the sake of argument we accept 19 samples as a representative number of samples in a typical DES study, we can apply the Spearman-Brown formula (Anastasi 1988) to estimate the typical 19-sample-average reliability of DES characteristics, as shown in the last column of Table 1. The median of these Spearman-Brown estimates of the reliability of 19-sample averages is .98.

The characteristic with the lowest reliability was Sensory Awareness, primarily reflecting the difficulty in determining whether a bodily awareness was or was not part of a Feeling. For example, if a participant experienced anxiety that was manifested as a pain in his chest, this was scored as a Feeling, not a Sensory Awareness. However, if the participant was particularly noticing the characteristics of a pain in his chest, then this was scored a Sensory Awareness regardless of whether the pain was caused by a Feeling. This kind of discrimination proved somewhat difficult, resulting in a kappa of .52. Even so, the typical 19-sample reliability for Sensory Awareness was .91.

Thus we have seen that the five most frequently occurring DES characteristics can be rated reliably. We investigated the extent to which these characteristics are distinct entities by computing kappas for all possible pairs of the five characteristics for each interviewer across all 60 samples. Table 2 shows these interdependency kappas for interviewer 1 below the main diagonal and for interviewer 2 above the main diagonal. For ease of comparison, the main diagonal of Table 2 redisplays the interobserver reliabilities from the third column

Table 2. Interdependencies (Kappa Statistics) for Each Rater

	Images	Inner speech	Unsymbolized T.	Feelings	Sensory A.
Images	.92	–.27	–.30	–.20	–.17
Inner speech	–.37	.88	–.28	–.08	–.05
Unsymbolized T.	–.26	–.25	.69	–.06	.04
Feelings	–.09	.09	–.08	.76	–.22
Sensory A.	–.19	–.17	–.15	.03	.52

Note: Interdependency kappas for interviewer 1 are given below the diagonal and for interviewer 2 above the diagonal, and interobserver kappas (same as Table 1 column 3) are on the main diagonal for comparison.

in Table 1. Inspection of Table 2 reveals that the (off-diagonal) intercharacteristic kappas are in fact much smaller than the (main diagonal) interobserver reliability kappas, as they should be if the characteristics are distinct.

The establishment of high levels of reliability does not, of course, imply that the participants in this study were necessarily reporting accurately about the characteristics of their inner experience – the same reliability coefficients might have been obtained if all participants had been lying consistently. Although technically true and fundamentally irrefutable, such a claim is emphatically denied by all participants, who during debriefing said they had been accurately reporting their experiences.

This design has the potential weakness of "leakage" from one interview to the next: The participant's reports to the second interviewer may to some extent be influenced by the first interview. However, it should be noted that the participant is asked simply to *describe* his or her own inner experience, not to *rate* it – the rating task is performed independently by the observers. In fact, the participants were unaware that any rating was being performed. Because for leakage to occur in this study the participant must actively transmit the "leak" from one interviewer to the next, this methodological weakness is less problematic here than in joint- or taped-interview methods, where any leak is directly observable by both raters. Leakage is not generally considered problematic in SCID reliability studies, most of which use joint- or taped-interview method.

All methods of evaluating DES reliability contain some methodological limitations. That does not nullify DES as a method but requires that different investigators ascertain reliability in different ways to see if reliability estimates converge.

This study lends strong support to the notion that independent observers can rate reports of inner processes consistently. Furthermore, because one rater (Heavey) was skeptical about the method at the outset of this study, it demonstrates that the method can be applied by someone other than its originator (Hurlburt). Until this study, this technique has been applied only by Hurlburt and his colleagues, so independent investigations by other laboratories are clearly called for.

Idiographic validity

We have now shown that the reliability of DES samples is quite strong. Because DES statements about the characteristics of persons (e.g., in Chapter 2 "Amy did not have clear inner experience") can be built up out of many quite-independent samples, the reliability of such statements is extremely high, higher than nearly all psychological tests currently in use. However, high inter-rater reliability does not indicate that DES descriptions actually faithfully mirror subjects' inner experience: high reliability means that subjects' accounts of their experiences are consistent, not that they are true. Here we face the issue of whether it is reasonable to believe that DES accounts faithfully mirror inner experience.

DES descriptions are fundamentally idiographic accounts of persons, and there is no general method for establishing the validity of idiographic accounts. Therefore the question "Do DES accounts faithfully mirror inner experience?" must be asked one subject at a time: "Does the DES-apprehended inner experience of Allen faithfully mirror his inner experience?" "Does the DES-apprehended inner experience of Beatrice faithfully mirror her inner experience?" "Does the DES-apprehended inner experience of Chuck faithfully mirror his inner experience?" and so on. If the answers to most of those sub-questions are Yes, then we can perform a true inductive generalization and conclude that the DES-apprehended inner experience of (most) subjects mirror their inner experience.

One of us (RTH) gave in 1997 the following analysis of the idiographic validity of the DES reports of Fran, a woman diagnosed as having a borderline personality.

The case of Fran[2]

Hurlburt (1993) described many salient characteristics of Fran's inner experience, three of which are discussed here. First, Hurlburt reported that Fran's inner experience was frequently populated by multiple (as many as five or ten) visual images, all occurring simultaneously and all in the same "visual space" (i.e., these images were not a side-by-side collage, but were instead all viewed straight ahead in a physically impossible overlaying that somehow did not provide any confusion for Fran herself). Fran's case is thus an example of the extreme complexity that inner experience can attain as reported by the Descriptive Experience Sampling method. Such complexity cannot possibly be reported by any method other than sampling. For example, had Fran used a think-aloud technique, the most detailed non-sampling method, she simply could not have had time to report adequately one image, to say nothing of five or ten simultaneous images.

Second, Hurlburt reported that some of Fran's visual images (usually those with extremely negative content) often lasted for hours or days, nonstop, uninterrupted. (By contrast, the Descriptive Experience Sampling method finds that images in healthy participants last for only a moment.) For example, Fran reported a visual and auditory image of her father "telling her off." In this image, Fran was seated at the dining room table. Her father was standing over her, pointing his finger at her, telling her she was "no good – a failure." Her mother was seen at the kitchen sink in the background looking over her shoulder at Fran. This image appeared in several successive samples, with the description being the same at each sample, and apparently continued uninterrupted during the time in between, for a total of at least several hours. This long-duration-image phenomenon might be considered impossible without sampling evidence.

Third, Hurlburt (1993) reported that Fran had no *figure-ground phenomenon* in either her inner image perception or her external perception – she took in an entire visual scene without focusing on any of its aspects. This conclusion was based on the fact that in repeated DES interviews, Fran consistently denied the occurrence of phenomena associated with figure and ground: no part of an image appeared to be "closer" or "in better focus," and when she shifted her gaze from one image (or external object) to another, she had no experience of "zeroing in" or of the previous center of attention "losing focus."

A major issue is of course whether descriptive-experience-sampling reports about Fran accurately reflect Fran's inner experience. Because Fran is clearly the only person in a position to know her experience directly, we must use indirect methods to consider the accuracy of those reports. Furthermore, one cannot apply standard validity-checking procedures (which intrinsically use across-group measures) to the idiographic observations of a single person; instead, one must infer validity idiographically, considering the unique characteristics of the particular description. Five such idiographic validity considerations regarding the case of Fran can be identified.

First, the question of idiographic validity applies not to the DES method per se but to the particular individuals who apply the method. In Fran's case, RTH was the researcher. He might be expected to be a valid applier of the method because his previous descriptions of different people differ dramatically from each other, are sometimes surprising even to himself, and are in agreement with other observers in those cases where more than one observer have sampled jointly (Hurlburt 1993).

Second, the lack of figure-ground phenomenon in inner experience leads to an obvious but risky prediction that if Fran viewed the classical ambiguous figures such as the faces-vase or Jastrow's duck-rabbit, they would not "alternate" in her experience. RTH performed this informal validity experiment and found that Fran did in fact report seeing both aspects of each drawing simultaneously with no alternation. A correct risky prediction can be taken as support for an underlying proposition (Popper 1963) and therefore here as evidence of validity.

Third, RTH ruled out miscommunication, misunderstanding, or language deficit as alternative explanations of her failure to report figure-ground experience as follows. Fran asked to borrow the ambiguous figures to show to her coworkers, believing that RTH was mistaken about the existence of the alternation phenomenon. She telephoned a few hours later to report that to her surprise, her coworkers did in fact report the experience of alternation. In this conversation, she gave an accurate description of her coworkers' alternating experiences but still denied that such alternation occurred for her. Thus, it seemed clear that Fran understood what figure-ground phenomena are and was capable of describing them if they had existed for her.

Fourth, the DES descriptions of Fran's inner experience provided plausible explanations of two characteristics of her external behavior. First, during Fran's discovery of her coworkers' figure-ground phenomenon, the coworkers came to realize, much to their surprise, that Fran could pay attention to many aspects of one thing or many different things simultaneously (e.g., her frequent multiple images), as had been discovered by the descriptive experience sampling. The coworkers observed that this multiple-attention ability explained a trait that angered them all: They worked in a bank, and a frequent task was counting money. Each person would stand at a counter and count his or her own individual stacks of bills. Fran irritated her coworkers by repeatedly initiating conversations while counting, causing them to lose count. The simultaneous tasks of counting and conversing were impossible for her coworkers but simple for Fran. Thus it seemed clear that the multiple-experience characteristic of Fran's inner world had real ramifications in Fran's exterior everyday world.

The second sampling-based plausible explanation of external behavior came from Fran's psychotherapist. Before Fran had become involved in the sampling study, her psychotherapist had responded to her complaints of being preoccupied with negative thoughts by training her in *thought substitution* – a cognitive-therapeutic technique aimed at teaching her to think about something positive, based on the rationale that increasing her frequency of positive thoughts would lower the frequency of negative thoughts. However, that therapeutic intervention had been unsuccessful; sampling provided the plausible explanation that Fran was quite capable of thinking about something positive without ceasing to think about something negative.

Fifth, changes in external behavior were reflected in changes in inner experience. Near the end of sampling Fran experienced a remarkable improvement in her borderline symptoms: her exterior disorganization and chaotic psychological fragility vanished. Samples obtained after this improvement were much less complex and included the experience of figure-ground phenomena.

Taken together, these observations led RTH to conclude that the idiographic descriptions of Fran were indeed valid. If their validity is at least tentatively accepted, they are extremely provocative; for example, to our knowledge, no reports of visual perception without figure-ground phenomenon appear in the perception literature, and no mention is made of the possible connection of the lack of figure-ground to psychopathology.

The case of Amy

In Chapter 2, we concluded that at the outset of sampling, Amy had little access to clear experience, but that she had gained that access by the conclusion of sampling. We considered there some alternative explanations, such as that Amy had merely given in to our questioning, or that she has merely arrived late at an understanding of what our questions actually meant.

We concluded that those alternative explanations were implausible; that is, we accepted the idiographic validity of the not-clear-experience account of Amy's sampling. We reached that conclusion by considering the entire situation: that she went from having no clear feelings to reporting feelings; that she was able for the first time to be more open and honest with her friends and mother; and so on.

Thus, we concluded that the weight of the evidence was in favor, in that single case, of the plausibility of the DES results.

The case of Robert

In 1994 Asperger Syndrome expert Uta Frith, her student at the time Francesca Happe', and RTH reported the DES results for Robert, a 25-year-old man diagnosed as having Asperger's syndrome, a form of Autism where the level of intellectual functioning can be quite normal (Hurlburt, Happe', & Frith 1994).

We reported that Robert's experience included visual images and nothing else – no feelings, no inner speech, no bodily sensations, and so on.

Here, we are asking whether that idiographic report of Robert is valid – whether the visual-experience-only characterization by DES faithfully mirrors his actual experience. Hurlburt, Happe', and Frith (1994) discussed this issue to some degree, but here is one not-reported anecdote. Near the end of sampling with Robert, it was becoming apparent that his experience was exclusively visual. No matter what the situation, Robert experienced visual images and nothing else. This characteristic of himself was somewhat surprising to Robert, but he said it made sense to him as illustrated by these stories. When he was a child and lost his first baby tooth, his parents instructed him to put it under his pillow; the next morning, the tooth was gone, replaced by "a quid left by the tooth fairy." That day, Robert took a pair of pliers and pulled out four more teeth! A few months before our sampling meetings, Robert had been in his apartment kitchen and smelled something burning. Looking around, he discovered it was his own hand, which was accidentally resting on a hotplate!

Those stories, objectively true, dramatically corroborate the DES notion that pain or other bodily sensations do not play a part in Robert's inner experience. That of course is not direct evidence that his experience is entirely visual, but it points in that direction.

Discussion

We could discuss other cases, one at a time, and with few exceptions we would arrive at the same conclusion: we can see many reasons that the descriptions are believable and few that they are not. Thus, in a purely inductive step, we believe we have established idiographic validity to our satisfaction.

As we have now seen throughout this book, the case for the validity of DES rests on the following legs:

- The method has been analytically shown to avoid the pitfalls of earlier introspective attempts (Chapter 3)
- The method has been analytically shown to incorporate the features of good investigations as derived from the psychological literature (Chapter 4)
- The advantages of triggering observation with a well defined beep have been analytically established (Chapter 5)
- The interobserver reliability has been experimentally established (this chapter)

- One idiographic case at a time, it seems that the most plausible understanding is that the DES reports faithfully mirror inner experience (this chapter)

The primary weakness in the argument for DES validity is that it rests on one set of observers, us and our colleagues. It is the aim of this book to encourage others to use the method and to contribute to the reliability and validity science.

Notes

1. This section is an edited version of Hurlburt, R. T. & Heavey, C. L. (2002). Interobserver reliability of Descriptive Experience Sampling. *Cognitive Therapy and Research, 26,* 135–142. Used with permission.

2. This section includes an edited version of pp. 946–947 of Hurlburt, R. T. (1997). Randomly sampling thinking in the natural environment. *Journal of Consulting and Clinical Psychology, 65,* 941–949. Used with permission.

CHAPTER 12

DES compared to other systems

Our purpose in this book is to reveal the characteristics of DES, and toward that end we have described DES and given instructions and examples. Now we wish to take a different tack and highlight DES by juxtaposing it with two other methods that are in some ways similar but in some ways different from DES. This compare / contrast method may allow us to put a finer point on some aspects of DES.

Because both DES and qualitative research rely on interviews as a way of gathering data, we choose qualitative research as our first compare / contrast foil. Because both DES and phenomenological psychology try to get directly to phenomena, we choose phenomenological psychology as our second foil.

DES and the qualitative research interview

There are many different systems of qualitative research, each with its own sensitivities, advantages, and disadvantages; we will choose one of them to be the vantage point for observing DES. Reasonable people might differ about which qualitative research approach should have been selected for this task, but in an important way it doesn't matter. Our task is to reveal DES; every revealing comes from some rather arbitrary viewpoint, and the task is not so much to reveal the viewpoint as the target.

For our qualitative research point of departure we choose Steinar Kvale's 1996 book *InterViews: An introduction to qualitative research and interviewing*, a highly regarded book that we recommend as being a thoughtful discussion of many important issues in the acquisition of interview skills and the conducting of research interviews. Kvale's Chapter 2 provides "12 aspects of the mode of understanding in the qualitative research interview.... They represent an attempt to describe the main structures of the qualitative research interview" (Kvale 1996: 29). The juxtaposition of DES and those 12 aspects will allow us to expose some of the details of DES.

Kvale prefaces his discussion of the 12 aspects of the mode of understanding in the qualitative research interview with this example:

> The following interview passage is taken from the article "An Application of the Phenomenological Method in Psychology" by [Amedeo] Giorgi (1975). The research question guiding the interview was: What constitutes learning in the everyday world? The first half of the interview, conducted by a student, is reproduced here.
>
> **R (Researcher):** Could you describe in as much detail as possible a situation in which learning occurred for you?
> **S (Subject:** E.W., 24 year-old female, housewife and educational researcher): The first thing that comes to mind is what I learned about interior decorating from Myrtis. She was telling me about the way you see things. Her view of looking at different rooms has been altered. She told me that when you come into a room you don't usually notice how many vertical and horizontal lines there are, at least consciously, you don't notice. And yet, if you were to take someone who knows what's going on in the field of interior decorating, they would intuitively feel if there were the right number of vertical and horizontal lines. So, I went home, and I started looking at the lines in our living room, and I counted the number of horizontal and vertical lines, many of which I had never realized were lines before. A beam. . .I had never really thought of that as vertical before, just a protrusion from the wall. (Laughs) I found out what was wrong with our living room design: many, too many, horizontal lines and not enough vertical. So I started trying to move things around and change the way it looked. I did this by moving several pieces of furniture and taking out several knick-knacks, de-emphasizing certain lines, and. . .it really looked differently to me, It's interesting because my husband came home several hours later and I said, "Look at the living room; it's all different." Not knowing this, that I had picked up, he didn't look at it in the same way I did. He saw things were different, he saw things were moved, but he wasn't able to verbalize that there was a de-emphasis on the horizontal lines and more of an emphasis on the vertical. So I felt I had learned something.
> **R:** What part of the experience would you consider learning?
> **S:** The knowledge part that a room is made up of horizontal and vertical lines. The application of that to another room; applying it to something that had been bothering me for quite a long time and I could never put my finger on it. I think the actual learning was what

> was horizontal and vertical about a room. The learning that was left with me was a way of looking at rooms.
> **R:** Are you saying then that the learning was what you learned from Myrtis, what you learned when you tried to apply...?
> **S:** Since I did apply it, I feel that I learned when I did apply it. I would have *thought* that I learned it only by having that knowledge, *but* having gone through the act of application, I really don't feel I would have learned it. I could honestly say, I had learned it at that time. (Giorgi 1975:84–86)

This interview investigated what constitutes learning for a woman in her everyday world. It began with an open request to describe a situation where learning occurred. The woman chose the learning situation she would talk about – interior decorating; she described this freely and extensively in her own words. The answer spontaneously took the form of a story, a narrative of one learning episode. The interviewer's first question introduced learning as the theme of the interview; her remaining questions depart from the subject's answers in order to keep learning in focus and to ask for clarification of the different aspects of the subject's learning story.

This interview gives a good picture of a semistructured research interview focusing on the subject's experience of a theme. The purpose was to investigate the subject's experience of learning ...

I now outline the mode of understanding in the qualitative research interview, of which the above interview on learning is one example. ...Twelve aspects of the mode of understanding in the qualitative research interview...will now be discussed in ...detail, with examples from the interview on learning reported by Giorgi and from my own interviews on grading in high schools. (Kvale 1996:27–29)

Twelve aspects of the mode of understanding in the qualitative research interview

We now discuss each of the 12 aspects by providing for purposes of comparison an analogous statement that could be made about DES.

Qualitative Research Interview aspect:

1. *Life World.* The topic of the qualitative research interview is the lived world of the subjects and their relation to it. The purpose is to de-

> scribe and understand the central themes the subjects experience and live toward. In the interview reported by Giorgi, the topic of learning was [a central theme]. In my own investigation, grades were a central theme in the life world of the high school pupils, and the interviews sought to describe and reflect the meanings that grades had for the pupils.
>
> The qualitative research is theme oriented. Two persons talk together about a theme that is of interest to both. (Kvale 1996: 29)

The DES analog:

1. *Experience.* The topic of DES is the subject's experience at some particular, randomly selected, moments. An important purpose is to describe and understand emergent or salient characteristics of the subjects' experience.

DES takes as its data whatever experiences happen to be "caught in flight" by the random beeps. It does not determine, at the outset, any themes that will be the particular focus of the investigation. Sometimes (usually, in fact) during the course of sampling themes seem to emerge, and those themes are often judged to be important by the subject and by us, but that is the happy ending of the DES procedure, not its intentional beginning. At the beginning we do not prejudge what is important or central.

Consider the interview on learning that Giorgi presented. The interviewer has predetermined before meeting the subject that the "central theme" will be "learning." Similarly, Kvale's own example predetermined that grades will be the students' central theme. In the InterView qualitative method, the determination of the central theme comes prior to the interview.

When an interviewer says, "Could you describe in as much detail as possible a situation in which learning occurred for you?" she presupposes that the subject knows what learning is and when and where it takes place. Whether that is in fact true is precisely at issue, but the opening question makes it extremely difficult, if not impossible, to explore that issue. We think that subjects cannot be expected to know the important aspects of their experience in a situation such as Giorgi's learning interview, because that would require (a) an accurate observation of experience in the original learning situation, (b) an accurate recollection of that experience over a long interval, and (c) an accurate characterization of many other experiences so as to be able to determine which aspects of the target (learning) experience are actually importantly related to learning. There is no reason to believe that any one of those obtains, let alone all of them.

We think the distinction between predetermined and emergent themes is of fundamental importance. For example, RTH and his students Stephanie Doucette and Sharon Jones-Forrester have explored the experience in bulimic subjects. They did *not* ask those subjects to describe their *bingeing experiences*, or to describe their *body dissatisfaction experiences*, and so on. Rather, they simply asked their subjects to describe their *experiences*, whatever they happened to be at the moment of the beep. If bingeing or body dissatisfaction experiences were frequent / salient / central / important, it was likely that they would emerge against the random background of other experiences. However, what emerged in those studies was *not* bingeing or body dissatisfaction experience, but rather the complexity / lack of centrality of experience in general. Our bulimia subjects *had no idea*, prior to sampling, that their experiences were complex / unclear. This discovery of a bulimic's complexity /unclarity comes from simply inquiring about experience, and would never have been possible using a method (such as most qualitative methods) that would ask about *bulimic* experience (Doucette 1992; Jones-Forester 2006).

To recapitulate: in DES there is no predetermined theme. If a theme emerges, it emerges from the data for that particular individual, or across individuals. The Kvale and Giorgi interviews are not designed to allow for the natural emergence of a theme – the theme is predetermined.

Qualitative Research Interview aspect:

2. *Meaning.* The qualitative research interview seeks to describe and understand the meanings of central themes in the life world of the subjects. The main task in interviewing is to understand the meaning of what the interviewees say....

   An everyday conversation often takes place on a factual level. A pupil may state: "I am not as stupid as my grades at the examinations showed, but I have bad study habits." Common reactions could then be on a factual level, "What grades did you get?"... A meaning-oriented reply would, in contrast, be something like, "You feel that the grades are not an adequate measure of your competence? (Kvale 1996:31–32)

There is no easy DES analog. Perhaps the best that can be done:

2. *Direct apprehension.* DES seeks to describe experiences that are directly, immediately apprehended by the subject. It does *not* seek the meanings that may or may not be behind those experiences.

Kvale seems to be using the term "meaning" in two different ways here: (a) understanding what the subject is saying; and (b) how the central themes relate to the subject's life world. DES is not primarily concerned with either.

(a) Of course we try to understand precisely what our subject say, but that is not our main task. Our main task is to apprehend the phenomenon, the experience that was ongoing at the moment of the beep, and we try to get to that phenomenon, *not* primarily to the meaning of the words the subject might have used to try to describe it. We often try to help the subject acquit herself more clearly in the description task, so that the meaning of the words used rest lightly on the experienced phenomenon. We also often try to help the subject retract what she has said, if the interview seems to be revealing that what has been said is leading away from the beeped phenomenon rather than toward it. Thus we aim to help our subject get to the phenomenon. Sometimes (usually) that entails clarifying the meanings of the words that have been said, but sometimes not.

(b) DES tries to describe whatever emerges and avoids speculating about the meanings of those emergent themes. If a DES subject were to say something like, "I am not as stupid as my grades at the examinations showed, but I have bad study habits," we would not explore this at either Kvale's "factual" level or his "meaning" level. Instead, we would express interest only in the experience at the moment of the beep, perhaps saying something like, "At the moment of the beep what were you experiencing?" or "At the moment of the beep, were you experiencing something about an examination?" or "Are you saying that you were feeling stupid?" We would specifically instruct the subject to *avoid* speculating about things like whether grades are adequate measures of competence unless it happened that at the precise moment of the beep he was specifically thinking / feeling / imaging that his grades were not an adequate measure of his competence.

A theme may well emerge from a series of random beeps. The DES task is to describe the theme – that is, to provide a real generalization about a series of actual experiences. We do not speculate about *why* that theme emerges or anything else that might be said to be *behind* the theme.

DES follows Skinner's (among many others') critique of meaning as being not directly observable, and that what is held to be meaning changes from situation to situation and from person to person. Moxley (2002) summarized Skinner's position:

> Skinner withheld approval of the term *meaning*. It was a word that did not have a constant meaning in its use and was the kind of word that Bacon objected to. Skinner said, "It is safer to drop the term altogether."
> (Skinner 1948: 14; Moxley 2002: 78)

DES takes no particular position on whether it is possible to elucidate meanings as essential characteristics – the essential meaning of learning, for example. DES itself, however, explicitly avoids trying to elicit or elucidate meanings. Perhaps it is possible, but certainly it is much more problematic than describing experience.

Qualitative Research Interview aspect:

3. *Qualitative.* The qualitative research interview aims at obtaining nuanced descriptions from the different qualitative aspects of the interviewee's life world; it works with words and not with numbers. Precision in description and stringency in meaning interpretation correspond in qualitative interviews to exactness in quantitative measurements. (Kvale 1996: 32)

The DES analog:

3. *Qualitative.* DES aims at obtaining nuanced descriptions of experiences, and at describing salient characteristics should they emerge. Salience is a judgment based on both words and numbers.

DES seeks to obtain nuanced descriptions of different qualitative aspects of the subject's experience, and it does work with words. But DES also works with numbers. When DES describes a "salient" or "emergent" feature of experience, it is because that feature has occurred frequently in the subject's descriptions. That is, those labels are based in part on frequency data. In contrast, the qualitative interviews as Kvale describes them do not use frequency data to determine the salience of a topic/feature/characteristic. Every single conversation in Giorgi's study referred to above is about learning; every single conversation in Kvale's study is about grades. That is simply not true in DES. When we say that a subject has frequent *X*, whatever the characteristic *X* is has been counted and that count has been compared to the counts of other possible salient characteristics.

Qualitative Research Interview aspect:

4. *Descriptive.* The qualitative research interview aims at obtaining uninterpreted descriptions. The subjects describe as precisely as possible what they experience and feel, and how they act.... The question of

> why the subjects experience and act as they do is primarily a task for the researcher to evaluate. (Kvale 1996: 32)

The DES analog:

4. *Descriptive.* DES aims at obtaining uninterpreted descriptions of actual experience. The interviewer and the subject together seek to discover what the subject actually experiences. The question of why the subjects experience and act as they do is not considered.

Perhaps the most important distinction between DES and qualitative interviewing lies here: How does the interviewer deal with experience? DES is extremely precise and consistent about experience: it defines experience as that which occurs "before the footlights of consciousness" at some specific moment, nothing more, nothing less. Qualitative interviewing as Kvale and most others describe it seems to have a looser definition of experience, sometimes specific-moment-based (like DES) but sometimes general. For example, Kvale seems to intend a specific-moment focus when he writes, "The subjects describe as precisely as possible what they experience and feel."

However, at other times Kvale seems to mean by "experience" something much more general. For example, in Kvale's summary of Giorgi's interview cited above ("This interview gives a good picture of a semistructured research interview focusing on the subject's experience of a theme. The purpose was to investigate the subject's experience of learning") it seems that Kvale means by "experience" a general characterization, understanding, or interpretation. The "experience of a theme" probably does *not* refer to any specific moment's experience: it is likely that Giorgi's subject never had a specific experience of learning during her interactions with Myrtis. Giorgi's subject was not interested in learning, focused on learning, aimed at learning; she was interested in, focused on, aimed at horizontal/vertical lines, clunky furniture, husband's reaction. Learning can of course be said to have occurred, but, technically, that is a general construct that should be applied after the fact.

DES specifically avoids asking about or speculating about such generalities. It is interested in conscious experience at the moment of the beep and nothing else.

We might speculate that Kvale and other qualitative researchers are loose about their specific and general meanings of experience because their method is entirely retrospective and thus incapable of adequately exploring specific experiences. For the reasons discussed throughout this book, a retrospective account is unlikely to get to the specificity of a phenomenon as it was actually experienced at the moment it occurred. Retrospective accounts are therefore necessarily infused with substantial unspecified generalities, and therefore the distinction between the specific and the general is necessarily blurred by the retrospectiveness of the specific. Giorgi's subject is not describing what she experiences and feels; at best she is describing what she now, some substantial time later, believes she may have experienced and felt.

Thus both Kvale and DES say that their interviews are aimed at experience; however we mean very different things. The DES expositional interview is concerned with a series of relatively immediately, directly apprehended conscious events; the qualitative research interview is concerned with some unspecifiable admixture of retrospective accounts of conscious events and interpretations thereof.

> Qualitative Research Interview aspect:
>
> 5. *Specificity*. The qualitative research interview seeks to describe specific situations and action sequences from the subject's world. It is not general opinions that are asked for. (Kvale 1996: 33)
>
> The DES analog: the same.

DES can use the same words to express its concern with specificity, but as we have seen, we think DES takes far greater pains to ensure the accuracy of the description of the specific situations. Retrospective accounts simply cannot be trusted in the details. Some might hold that the inaccuracy of the details from any particular account will not be problematic when accounts are aggregated across subjects. That, in our view, is an overly optimistic point of view. Accounts gathered in similar situations are likely to have similar inaccuracies, and the aggregation cannot eliminate them.

> Qualitative Research Interview aspect:
>
> 6. *Deliberate Naïveté*. The qualitative interview attempts to gather descriptions of the relevant themes of the interviewee's life world that are as rich and presuppositionless as possible. Rather than the interviewer having preformulated questions and ready-made categories for analysis, the deliberate naïveté and absence of presuppositions advocated here implies an openness to new and unexpected phenomena. (Kvale 1996: 33)
>
> The DES analog:
>
> 6. *Deliberate Naïveté*. The DES interview attempts to gather descriptions of experience that are as rich and presuppositionless as possible. Rather than the interviewer having preformulated questions and ready-made categories for analysis, the deliberate naïveté and absence

> of presuppositions advocated here implies an openness to new and unexpected phenomena.

Thus DES replaces "descriptions of the relevant themes of the interviewee's life world" with "descriptions of experience." That slight rewording reveals, in our view, an important limitation on the qualitative interviewer's deliberate naïveté that we discussed in section 1 above. When the qualitative interviewer sets out to "gather descriptions of the relevant themes," that carries within it a large presupposition that is quite possibly unwarranted. Kvale assumed, presuppositionally, that grades were an important theme for his students; Giorgi assumed, presuppositionally, that learning was important for his subjects. Those assumptions may be correct, but they may be mistaken; that should be at important issue in the investigation. Therefore, DES prefers to let such themes *emerge out of the naïve perspective*, whereas Kvale interjects the themes *prior to the naïve perspective.* There is no way that Kvale's subjects can somehow report that grades are not important, or that Giorgi's subjects can report learning isn't important.

DES, on the other hand, takes no position on grades or learning or anything else. If grades or learning is an important feature of the subject's experience, it will emerge as a pattern in the beeped responses. If not, not.

> Qualitative Research Interview aspect:
>
> 7. *Focus.* The qualitative research interview is focused on certain themes in the interviewee's life world. It is neither strictly structured with standardized questions, nor entirely "nondirective," but is focused on certain themes.... The interviewer leads the subject toward certain themes, but not to certain opinions about these themes. (Kvale 1996: 34)
>
> The DES analog:
>
> 7. *Focus.* The DES interview is focused on the subject's experience. It is neither strictly structured with standardized questions, nor entirely "nondirective," but is focused on experience.... The interviewer leads the subject toward his or her experience, nothing more and nothing less.

Above, in Sections 1 and 6, we have discussed the dangers of focusing on predetermined themes.

> Qualitative Research Interview aspect:
>
> 8. *Ambiguity.* A subject's statements are sometimes ambiguous. An expression can imply several possibilities of interpretation, and the sub-

ject may also give apparently contradictory statements during an interview. It becomes the task of the interviewer to clarify, as far as possible, whether the ambiguities and contradictory statements are due to a failure of communication in the interview situation, or whether they reflect real inconsistencies, ambivalences, and contradictions in the interviewee. (Kvale 1996: 34)

The DES analog:

8. *Ambiguity/incorrectness.* A subject's statements are sometimes ambiguous or totally wrong. An expression can imply several possibilities of interpretation, and the subject may also give apparently contradictory statements during an interview. It becomes the task of the interviewer to help the subject, as far as possible, to resolve ambiguities and correct wrong statements. This clarification / correction may not be possible to apply to the samples being discussed in any single expositional interview since the observations of the experience have already taken place; however, it may lead to improved accuracy in subsequent observations / expositional interviews. In those situations where ambiguities and contradictory statements cannot be resolved, it becomes the task of the interviewer to clarify whether the ambiguities and contradictory statements are due to a failure of communication in the interview situation, a failure to understand the sampling task, a lack of skill in observing experience, to real inconsistencies, ambivalences, and contradictions in the interviewee's experience, or to the inability of the subject to apprehend his or her own experience.

Qualitative Research Interview aspect:

9. *Change.* It may happen in the course of an interview that subjects change their descriptions of, and meanings about, a theme. The subjects may themselves have discovered new aspects of the themes they are describing, and suddenly see relations that they had not been conscious of earlier. (Kvale 1996: 34)

The DES analog:

9. *Change.* It usually happens in the course of the series of DES interviews that subjects change the way they describe their experiences. The subjects may have improved their observational skills, or improved their reporting skills, or altered their way of experiencing itself.

As we have seen throughout this book, to observe experience accurately requires training in such things as bracketing presuppositions, understanding what counts as experience, avoiding faux generalizations, and the like. Therefore DES is deliberately a multi-day procedure so that later sampling observations can be informed by earlier sampling and expositional-interview experience. Subjects learn what we are asking, what we want them to attend to. The ability to observe is a skill, involving quickly apprehending the beep and immediately paying attention to the ongoing experience. Many subjects require a few sampling days of practice to become adequately proficient.

DES subjects frequently do change their descriptions of similar experiences during the course of their early interviews; often they do so with a conviction that "now I have it right!" We don't take a position on the truth of such claims, but we do discard the first sampling day's results (often we discard several days) as being too unreliable for our purposes. We prefer instead to look to the future: if a similar experience occurs on a subsequent sampling day, the training that the subject received during the first interview days will make it more likely to be described accurately.

DES does not go back and "repair" descriptions of samples from prior sampling days – that would inject retrospectiveness difficulties that we specifically seek to avoid. Subjects do occasionally ask to go back and reconsider a previous sample; we decline, saying that if the phenomenon is important, it will occur on subsequent beeps and we can deal with it then. If it's not important, there's no reason to go back.

And as stated in #2 above, we never are interested in the subject's meanings about a theme, whether stated in the first go around or if they should change later.

Qualitative Research Interview aspect:

10. *Sensitivity*. Interviews obtained by different interviewers, using the same interview guide, may be different due to varying levels of sensitivity toward, and knowledge about, the topic of the interview. Thus an interviewer who has no ear for music may have difficulties obtaining nuanced descriptions of musical experiences from his or her interviewees. (Kvale 1996: 35)

The DES analog:

10. *Sensitivity*. Interviews obtained by different DES interviewers may be different due to varying levels of sensitivity toward, and knowledge about, the characteristics of the reported experience. Thus an interviewer who has no ear for music may have difficulties obtaining nuanced descriptions of musical experiences from his or her interviewees.

DES interviews have no interview guide and no topic of the interview. Other than that, we agree.

> Qualitative Research Interview aspect:
>
> 11. *Interpersonal Situation.* The research interview is an inter view, an interaction between two people. The interviewer and the subject act in relation to each other and reciprocally influence each other....
>
>   The interview situation may, for both parties, be characterized by positive feelings of a common intellectual curiosity and a reciprocal respect. The interview may also be anxiety provoking and evoke defense mechanisms in the interviewee as well as in the interviewer. (Kvale 1996:35)
>
> The DES analog: the same.

We agree in principle, but would note that it is quite striking how often subjects are willing to report anxiety arousing, embarrassing, or otherwise problematic events. It seems that the specificity of the interview combined with the understanding that what is being reported may or may not be typical of the subject frees many subjects to report in precise detail what would be quite difficult or impossible to report in general.

> Qualitative Research Interview aspect:
>
> 12. *Positive experience.* A qualitative research interview can be a favorable experience for the interviewee. An interview is a conversation in which two people talk about a theme of mutual interest. A well-conducted qualitative interview can be a rare and enriching experience for the interviewee. It is probably not a very common experience in everyday life that another person – for an hour or more – is interested only in, sensitive toward, and seeks to understand as well as possible another's experiences and views on a subject. (Kvale 1996:36)
>
> The DES analog:
>
> 12. *Positive experience.* DES is usually a favorable and often an intensely favorable experience for the interviewee. DES is a series of conversation in which two people talk as honestly and forthrightly as possible about the inherently private experiences of one of them. Such interactions are extremely rare, and are sometimes seen as life-changing for the subject.

DES and phenomenological psychology

Without question, Amedeo Giorgi has been the principal proponent of phenomenological psychology, as well as being influential in many qualitative research approaches such as Kvale's. Because Kvale borrowed heavily from Giorgi, we have used some aspects of Giorgi's phenomenological psychology to illuminate DES. However, there remains much of the heart of phenomenology that will serve as an effective way of highlighting some additional characteristics of DES. We turn to those aspects now.

DES has great sympathy for phenomenology and phenomenological psychology. It counts as its major influences phenomenologists such as Husserl, Heidegger, and Merleau-Ponty, and phenomenological psychologists such as Giorgi. It can fairly be said that DES emerged from Hurlburt's attempt to build on the phenomenological psychology practiced at Duquesne by Giorgi and his students and colleagues. DES shares with phenomenology and phenomenological psychology the centrality of the phenomenological reduction, the importance of description, the mistrust of theory, and the value of bracketing presuppositions. However, DES departs substantially from phenomenological psychology in important ways.

The starting point

Giorgi (1989) revisited the phenomenon of learning that we cited above in our discussion of Kvale (Giorgi 1975). As you may recall, subjects were asked to provide descriptions of past events where learning had taken place; subjects were allowed to use "learning" in whatever way seemed appropriate to them. "Thus, the exclusive data in the research project consisted of retrospective reports by subjects concerning situations that *they* defined as experiences of learning" (Giorgi 1989: 100).

There are three related issues here: (a) the retrospectiveness of the report; (b) the use of descriptions as the starting point; and (c) the before-the-study-began choice of learning as the topic. We have discussed (a) and (c) in our consideration of qualitative research, so we need not repeat them.

Issue (b) is expressed by Giorgi's "the exclusive data in the research project consisted of ... reports by subjects." By contrast, the primary data in DES are the specific (beeped) experiences. Certainly DES subjects give reports about those experiences, but it is the subjects' experiences themselves, not the reports, that are the DES starting point. This is a subtle but extremely important distinction. If one uses retrospective accounts, as Giorgi does, as the starting place of the phenomenological study, no amount of analysis can penetrate behind those accounts to the experience itself. Thus we believe that Giorgi is correct when he says that his phenomenological accounts begin with reports. The experiential phenomena have already been lost forever.

However, DES believes that it is the experience itself, *not* the accounts of it, that are of primary interest. DES can properly make that claim because DES accounts are given immediately after the experience, and that experience can be consulted by the subject to shape the account of that experience. It is the job of the DES investigator to help reshape, rephrase, correct, refine, dismiss, or otherwise alter the descriptions so they accurately mirror the still-recalled experience, and to build the subject' observation skills to improve future DES experiential data gathering. Such improvements are simply impossible for the phenomenological psychology description, which must stand exclusively on the reports as Giorgi avers; these reports are unimprovable because directly accessing the long-past phenomenon is impossible. For example, without the combination of immediate retrospection and the ability to improve subjects' ability to report, it would be impossible to examine the forms of naturally occurring inner experience (inner speech, unsymbolized thinking, and so on) that we have found important and to which we return in Chapters 13 and 14.

The phenomenological reduction

The phenomenological reduction is perhaps the most important concept in phenomenology. Edmund Husserl, the principal founder of phenomenology, created the phenomenological reduction as a way of stepping out of the "natural attitude," the point of view where people take the "thingness" of things and the world for granted. Husserl originally, and Giorgi after him, advocated the phenomenological reduction as a radical departure from the natural attitude, wherein the phenomena themselves were examined to determine if or how they themselves have conveyed the attribute of "thingness" or existence.

> Even when one encounters in experience things and events that "obviously" have existence, the [phenomenological] reduction directs one to step back and describe and examine them [merely] as a presence. Husserl claims that nothing about the object is lost in this way, except its existential status. Everything that was present in the natural attitude is retained within the phenomenological reduction, except that one refrains from saying that the object is as it presents itself: one only says that the object presents itself as such and such. Thus, if I am perceptually present to a real table, within the phenomenological reduction I would say, "the table presents itself to me as a really existing table." That is more rigorous than saying "it is a real table." (Giorgi 1997:239–240)

Giorgi departs from Husserl in that while Husserl requires a thoroughgoing phenomenological reduction, Giorgi allows his subjects to remain in the natural attitude:

> The descriptive step becomes a detailed concrete description of specific experiences from an everyday attitude from others. The major change introduced to the method in order to conform more readily with scientific practices is that descriptions are obtained from others from the perspective of the natural attitude.... The natural attitude is utilized because, practically, one cannot expect all of the persons in the whole world to be phenomenological and thus be capable of assuming the attitude of the reduction. (Giorgi 1997: 243)

By allowing his subjects to adopt the natural attitude, Giorgi allows his subjects to blur, obliterate, or ignore the distinction between precise subjective experience that may or may not be of real objects (images, hallucinations, and the like; Husserl referred to this broad category as "intuition") and assumptive experience of real objects. His logic is that subjects are incapable of assuming the attitude of the phenomenological reduction – that is, are incapable of reporting phenomena with indifference as to whether the phenomena intend real or imaginary objects. We believe that that is not true. DES subjects can and routinely do adopt the attitude of the phenomenological reduction. We ask DES subjects to report what they experience without regard for whether this experience corresponds or does not correspond to anything in reality. Here are some common examples: Subject A reports a sadness as a twisting, descending feeling in her heart; she acknowledges that she doesn't know whether her real heart is in any way twisting or descending. Subject B reports an inner seeing of herself wearing a dress that she in fact doesn't own and has never seen before. Subject C reports innerly speaking at a fast rate of speed that would be impossible in the real world but that seems entirely natural in the inner speaking. Like good phenomenologists, they bracket that knowledge and carefully describe what they experience unconfounded with what they take to be the known reality. We believe that experienced DES subjects can learn to be quite good at that.

Thus a main difference between DES and phenomenological psychology is in determining who makes the phenomenological reduction: in DES both the subject and the researcher do so, whereas in phenomenological psychology it is only the researcher. We believe that it is desirable for the subject him or herself to perform the reduction because it is unlikely that a researcher can restore the reduction if it hasn't been made by the subject.

Generalization or essence?

Phenomenology is generally considered "eidetic" in the sense that it seeks essential features of consciousness. Thus, Giorgi writes

> The important result of phenomenological analyses is not to [identify] concrete, individual objects given to an individual's consciousness as such...but rather to present to the community of scholars a finding that is more durable. To do this, Husserl suggests that one seek the essence of the phenomenon being researched through a method he calls free imaginative variation.... As the name implies, the [free imaginative variation] method means that one freely changes aspects or parts of a phenomenon or object, and one sees if the phenomenon remains identifiable with the part changed or not.(Giorgi 1997:242)

This process of using free imaginative variation to discover essential features is often called the eidetic reduction. For example, Husserl discusses the essence of a table:

> Starting from this table-perception as an example, we vary the perceptual object, table, with a completely free optionalness, yet in such a manner that we keep perception fixed as perception of something, no matter what. Perhaps we begin by fictively changing the shape or the color of the object quite arbitrarily, keeping identical only its perceptual appearing. (Husserl 1960:70)

This imaginative variation of the essence of a table would discover that a table could be any color, could be made out of a variety of hard materials, but could not be made out of water or other fluids, would have a horizontal surface but the shape is not important, and so on. The characteristics of the table that remain stable, however, are what constitute the essentialness or eidos of table.

DES does not use free imaginative variation or anything that approaches an eidetic reduction. This is because the aim of DES is not to distill the essentialness from the non-essentialness of experience. Instead, DES seeks to discover all the main characteristics of the observed moments of experience. Free imaginative variation leads *away* from the observations by breaking them up, asking which features of the observations can be dropped or otherwise distorted while leaving the essential feature(s):

> We. . .shift the actual perception into the realm of non-actualities, the realm of the as-if, which supplies us with "pure" possibilities, pure of everything that restricts to this fact or to any fact whatever.... Perception [of essences], the universal type thus acquired, floats in the air, so to speak – in the atmosphere of pure phantasiableness. Thus removed from all factualness, it has become the pure "*eidos*" perception. (Husserl 1960:70)

By contrast, the DES focus on all salient characteristics – essential or not – leads *toward* the observations. By doing so, DES can eventually determine which features of experience are similar across several or many observations. The main difference here is that the eidetic reduction uses a subject's phenomenological data to hunt for objective essences, whereas DES uses that same data to discover characteristics of the subject's experience. Said another way, DES does not seek essences but contents itself with salient characteristics. It accepts that those characteristics may well be features important only in some limited subrange of the subject's environments; it accepts that subject A's salient characteristics may not apply to subject B or to anyone else. It is a fact that often the salient characteristics seem to be important and far reaching, but that seeming is an empirically derived conclusion rather than an a priori assumption.

Thus the aim of DES is substantially different from the aim of phenomenological psychology. DES tries to produce true generalizations of sampled experiences, whereas phenomenological psychology tries to produce essences.

Summary

This chapter has covered a wide range of material, so perhaps it would be useful to recapitulate an overview of the main differences between DES and qualitative / phenomenological psychological methods:

- DES clearly defines what is meant by "experience" as whatever is present to consciousness at a particular moment.
- DES begins with actual experiences, not with reports thereof.
- DES tries to be as nonretrospective as possible.
- DES does not start with a preconceived topic.
- DES relies on randomness as a means of bracketing presuppositions.

CHAPTER 13

Everyday inner experience

Psychologists use the term "idiographic" to refer to the characteristics of a particular, unique individual; they use the term "nomothetic" to refer to general laws or universal characteristics of people. Thus Chapter 2 was an idiographic study of Amy, the college student who believed herself to be an obsessive liar. We said, for example, that Amy lacked clarity of inner experience. That is an idiographic characteristic of Amy because it is characteristic of her as an individual person, regardless of whether other students, other obsessive individuals, or any other persons have or don't have the same lack of clarity. We also observed that when Amy's inner experience became clearer, she became more effective in a variety of different ways, interpersonally, as a student, and so on. That is another idiographic characteristic – it is true for Amy regardless of whether it is true for anyone else.

Most of psychological science, by contrast, is nomothetic, concerned with general laws or general characteristics. For example, social psychologists seek to establish the general laws of human behavior under various situations, such as the conditions under which there is pressure for conformity or obedience. Most of psychological science is focused on identifying these types of general principles, and therefore psychology is considered a nomothetic science. History, on the other hand, is often considered an idiographic enterprise as its primary concern is studying the unique set of circumstances that gave rise to a particular event.

DES is primarily an idiographic enterprise – it is about understanding the unique characteristics of each subject's inner experience, one person at a time. Nonetheless, it is possible to draw nomothetic generalities from DES results. We have examined many DES individual investigations, each of which is an idiographic description of the features of a particular individual person, and identified five characteristics of inner experience that occur frequently across many of these individuals: inner speech, images, unsymbolized thinking, feelings, and sensory awareness. In this chapter we summarize our understanding of these five characteristics and two related circumstances: the occurrence of multiple characteristics of inner experience and the occurrence of essentially no inner experience. We do not argue that our categories or conceptualizations are definitive; others may develop different ways of slicing the pie of inner experience. What follows, however, is based on carefully examining the inner experience of several hundred individuals.

Roughly speaking, each of the five characteristics occurs in about a quarter of all of our DES samples, although there are wide individual differences. Some people's experience is characterized by large frequencies of all these characteristics. However, it is more frequently the case that for a particular individual, one or the other of these characteristics occurs with substantially higher frequency that the others. We'll describe each characteristic in turn.

Inner speech

Inner speech is the experience of speaking words in your own voice but with no external (real) noise or motion. For example, you are saying to yourself, "That is a very strong odor – maybe it is a gas leak!" It was just as if you had said this aloud, but no noise was actually made and your mouth and throat were not actually moving.

The phenomenon

Usually, inner speech has the same vocal characteristics as your own external speech: same timbre; same rate of speaking; same inflection for commas, question marks, etc.; same pauses, accents, stutters; and so on. In its purest form, inner speech is experienced as being identical to external speech except that the mouth does not move and no external production of sound is produced.

Occasionally, some characteristics of the inner speaking are not identical to external speech. For example, some subjects report that their inner speaking is faster than their external speech; others report that their inner speaking has less inflection (is more monotonous) than their external speech; others report that the inner voice has a somewhat different timbre (perhaps a higher pitch) than their external speech. Nonetheless, even with these discrepant features, the experience is of themselves as speaking.

There is a range of meaningfulness of inner speech. Sometimes the speaking is directly related to ongoing activity. For example, the person may be "rehearsing" what she is about to say, or innerly saying the words currently being read. However, at other times inner speaking may be only loosely or apparently not at all related to known activities. For example, an inner speaking may be "left over" in the sense that a few seconds or minutes before, the speaking was meaningful, but now it is being mindlessly repeated (sometimes with unanticipated transformations). Occasionally the person will have no idea what the inner speaking relates to.

Discriminations

Inner hearing is the paying attention to the auditory characteristics of an inner phenomenon. For example, "I was hearing the Beatles 'Penny Lane' playing in my head. It was just like hearing it on a CD, as far as I could tell." Subjects do sometimes experience their own voice as if heard, rather than spoken. They might say that their voice "sounded like it had been recorded and was now being played back," or "was like an echo," or "was as if someone else is speaking it." If the inner voice is experienced as primarily being spoken, we call it inner speech. If the inner voice is experienced as primarily being heard, rather than spoken, we call it inner hearing. Often in inner speaking, there is the awareness both of speaking and hearing, but the speaking seems primary (just as in most real external speech). There is a quite clear phenomenological distinction between inner speech and inner hearing, but subjects need to be trained to distinguish it.

Partially unworded speech is the experience of inner speech that has "holes" or missing words or parts of words embedded in the speech production. For example, you experience yourself as speaking, "That is a very strong ______ – maybe it is a gas leak!" with a temporal space reserved for the word "odor" but the word "odor" itself is not actually in your experience. This "hole" often has the same rhythm (number of syllables, etc.) as the actual missing word. Typically in such cases you know the meaning of the missing word, even though the word itself is not present. The sensation is as if the speech-making process has two separate aspects, one that produces the rhythm of the speech and another that drops the actual words / phonemes into the rhythmic structure. When all goes well, rhythm and phoneme production happens in a coordinated manner, and smooth meaningful speech is experienced. Sometimes, however, the two processes get separated and the rhythm is incompletely merged with the phonemes. Novice samplers usually overlook this "holes" phenomenon. It takes practice to be directly aware of what was actually happening at the moment of the beep, and novices usually do not make a crystal clear distinction between what they *actually said* in inner speech and what they *knew they meant to say*.

Unworded speech is the experience of speaking in your own inner voice except that you have no experience of words at all. You have the sense of speaking, and are directly aware of the vocal characteristics of that speaking (rate, inflection, timbre, rhythm, etc.), and are directly aware of the meaning of what is being "said," even though no words are present. Unworded speech is experienced like partially unworded speech except that the holes predominate.

Unsymbolized thinking is the experience of thinking without the experience of speaking or hearing (or images or any other symbols). Subjects initially often (incorrectly) use the language of inner speech to report unsymbolized thinking ("I was saying to myself that I should...."), when there is no experience of speaking, words, or hearing at all. Careful questioning is necessary; see the section below on unsymbolized thinking.

DES skill considerations

As with all the characteristics of inner experience, the DES practitioner has to be careful to distinguish between what people say and what the characteristics of their inner experience actually are. Neophyte DES subjects often use "I was saying to myself" to refer to *any* inner phenomenon (images, unsymbolized thinking, feelings, and so on), whether or not that phenomenon is experienced to be a speaking.

Thus the DES examiner has to help the subject describe the phenomenon with accuracy and not assume that the original words actually reflect speaking. The examiner might say, "Could you please describe this in more detail?" and that might elicit a response that definitively establishes the speaking nature of the phenomenon (e.g., "I was saying the words 'I should go get lunch' to myself, and the beep came right at the word 'get'"). Sometimes it is useful to ask, "Were words a part of this experience or not?" and "If so, what were those words?"

Except in those rare instances of unworded speech, the experience of inner speech always includes words, and subjects are almost always able to tell the examiner what the precise words were. If subjects report they are saying something in inner speech and cannot report exactly what the words were, careful questioning is in order. It is often useful to inquire, "Are you having difficulty telling me what the words were because the words weren't clearly defined at the moment of the beep? Or were the words clear then but you have just forgotten them in the interim?"

The distinction between inner speech and inner hearing can be difficult because people often use the language of hearing to describe the phenomenon of speaking. For example, subjects often say, "I hear the words in my head." Certainly that locution implies an inner hearing phenomenon, but more often that not, the actual experience is primarily of speaking the words. Most often, careful examination reveals that the experience behind such a locution has no aspect of hearing whatsoever; sometimes, the words are both said and heard with the saying aspect primary. Sometimes, of course, the subject's experience is primarily of hearing, but that is somewhat less common. To tease apart the options, the DES examiner may say, "Is your experience of the words more of creating them or receiving them?" or "Is it more like you are producing the words, or more like you are hearing a recording of those words being played back?" The good news is that the phenomenon is usually quite robust; once the typical subjects have zeroed in on the actual phenomenon, (a) their descriptions will be pretty unshakable; and (b) they will quite confidently report that they had been misleading when they originally said the "heard."

Inner seeing (aka images)

Inner seeing is the experience of seeing something that is not actually present.

For example, you have the experience of seeing your mother's face. You can provide many of the visual details of the seeing; for example, you may report that you see the face without the body; you are viewing the face from the front and a little to the right; the face appears as in a photograph taken a few years ago; you can see her smile; you can see her neck and a hint of the blue blouse, but that is indistinct and disappears quickly away from the face; there is no background in the seeing; and so on.

The phenomenon

Usually inner seeing has the same characteristics as seeing an external object: the center is in clearer focus, the focus or attention becomes less clear at the periphery; there is no distinct border or edge to the experience, and so on.

We often refer to the experience of inner seeing as "seeing an image," and refer to the thing seen as "the image." For example, the first sentence of the previous paragraph is often phrased as "you are seeing an image of your mother's face." This is a natural way of speaking, and one that comports quite well with many of the characteristics of the inner-seeing phenomenon. However, "seeing an image" does have the major drawback of implying that there is a thing seen (the image) separate from the seer, and that can lead to distortions of the phenomenon, to which we will return in the "DES skill considerations" section below. For the moment, we will use the term "image" to refer to the thing seen in an inner seeing, thus avoiding awkward phrases such as "The thing seen in an inner seeing can be experienced in color or black and white."

Images can be experienced in color or black and white, in motion or still, in focus or out, and may or may not be accompanied by sounds. Occasionally the content of an image is a word, seen as if printed or typed or hand written. Images are often of things that have actually been seen in the real world, as if you were "seeing again" what you had actually seen. However, images are often of impossible or never-before-seen things. For example, people very often view themselves from the back, view rooms as if through a wall had been removed allowing otherwise impossible perspectives, and so on.

As we saw in the case of inner speech, there is a range of meaningfulness in images. Often the meaningful relationship of images to ongoing activities of stream of thought is perfectly obvious, but occasionally images seem to exist "left over" from some past activity, or whose source is not known.

For example, Margie Koch and RTH sampled with Hans, a college student whose inner experience was almost entirely visual images (Koch 1997). At one beep Hans was sitting in an economics class where the professor was lecturing about how price was related to supply and demand. Hans had an inner image of a used car lot as if viewed from across the street and about 20 feet above the ground – that is, Hans was looking down slightly on the lot. There were colored pennants flapping in the breeze all around the car lot. Hans' main focus was on a car salesman standing in front of a red car that had a price of $1,000,000 marked across the front window. The car dealer was dressed in a blue suit and was standing on gray concrete. Hans could hear the salesman shouting "used cars" and the background noise of traffic from the street next to the car lot. The car with the $1,000,000 price tag was Hans' way of representing the notion that if a commodity was priced too high, the demand would be lowered. The lecturer was talking about the effect of price on demand in general, and had not been talking about automobiles. Thus the automobile price was Han's own creative example of the price-demand concept.

Images are usually (but not always) in color, often (but not always) in motion, and often (but not always) floridly complex. The pennants and the street noise of Hans' image, for example, do not seem to be essential to the image of price and demand, and yet those details were vividly present in the image. Images often (but not always) include modes other than visual. The used car image included auditory features (the salesman's voice and the traffic noise) as well as visual features; some images do include auditory experience, some don't. Images can include features other than visual and auditory as well. For example, in another of Hans' images, he imagined that he was on a European railroad train, standing in the space between two passenger cars, with his head out the window looking forward as the train rounded a bend. He could see the green train on the left of his image, curving to the right, and the landscape alongside the tracks. He could also feel the cool wind on his cheeks and in his hair, sensations that were imagined just as clearly as the visual aspect of the image.

Just as we saw with inner speech, there is a range of clarity or completeness of inner seeing. Some visual images are seen perfectly clearly. As in Hans' images, the details are clear, colors are bright and vibrant, the point of view or perspective is unambiguous, and so on. Frequently not all the details of an image are actually seen at the moment of the beep but are instead simply known to be a part of the image. For example, Angeline was sitting at her desk at work. Her eyes were aimed at the computer monitor in front of her, but instead of seeing the monitor display, she was innerly seeing bottles of body lotion arranged on a department store shelf. In the center of her seeing she saw a few individual bottles, and to the left she saw some pinkness that she knew represented the bottles of another brand of body lotion. This pinkness was not an array of indistinct bottles, just some seen pink that Angeline knew represented bottles.

Discriminations

Imageless seeing is an inner experience that is understood clearly to be a seeing, but the thing being "seen" is not present in experience. This phenomenon is apparently in parallel with the phenomenon of unworded speech we described above. For example, Jennifer reported that she was seeing her friend Sally, but no visual details of Sally were present. It could not be determined whether Sally was seen in profile or full face, which way she was looking, what she was wearing, and so on. Despite this lack of visual detail, careful questioning revealed that Jennifer apprehended her experience to be a definitely visual phenomenon: Jennifer was unshakably confident that she had the experience of *visually seeing* Sally, even though Sally herself was not actually seen.

DES skill considerations

Note that we use the term "images" to refer to a primarily visual phenomenon. What might be called an "auditory image" we call inner hearing; what might be called a "sensory image" we call sensory awareness.

As with inner speech, the DES practitioner has to be careful to distinguish between what people say and what the characteristics of their inner experience actually are. Neophyte DES subjects often say "I had an image of..." to refer to phenomena that include no experience of seeing whatsoever.

To help the subject describe the phenomenon with accuracy, the examiner might say, "Could you please describe this experience in more detail?" and that might elicit a response that definitively establishes the image nature of the phenomenon (e.g., "I was seeing an inner picture of my history book. I was seeing the front cover, which was the same blue color as my car; I could see the picture of the Great Pyramid, just like my book actually has."). To establish the visual nature of an experience, it is often useful to ask, "What exactly were you seeing at the moment of the beep?" and "From what perspective or point of view did you see this?"

Except in those rare instances of imageless seeing, the experience of inner seeing always includes the thing seen, and subjects should be able to tell the examiner at least some of its visual characteristics (perspective, color, what is and is not seen, etc.). If such details are not forthcoming, then careful but non-leading questioning has to be employed to determine whether the experience is actually of seeing.

Imageless seeing is a quite different phenomenon from merely using visual language to described nonvisual inner events. For example, it is common for a person to say something like, "I was seeing the house where I grew up," but when questioned carefully it turns out that the person had no visual experience whatsoever – no image and no experience of seeing. Instead, he was remembering the house in some nonvisual way. By contrast, imageless seeing *is* a visual experience – the person does in fact have the experience of visually looking at something. However, the thing looked at is not seen. This is entirely analogous to the existence of unworded speech, where the rhythm of speech and the sense of speaking are experienced, but the words themselves are not present.

Many (perhaps most) images are of familiar objects or things that the subject has actually seen. The skilled DES examiner tries to help the subject make a clear distinction between the thing innerly seen and the actual thing. That is often difficult, because subjects often lapse into the description of the object rather than the description of the inner seeing. It is often useful to say, "Let's make sure we talk about the seeing that was ongoing at the moment of the beep," or "The thing you were innerly seeing may or may not look like the real thing. Let's try to focus on the inner seeing." If the DES examiner is consistent, subjects usually soon learn to make this distinction confidently.

As we have seen, it is often natural to say, "I was seeing an image of..." to describe an inner seeing (and we ourselves often use that "image" terminology), there is a substantial risk in that terminology. Saying "I was seeing an image" implies the existence of the seer and (separately) the thing seen (the image). DES takes no position on such existential questions; our aim is to describe the phenomenon, not to determine the answers to questions such as whether there are separate neural substrates for the seer and the image.

Here's an example that illustrates the issue. Leonore's parents owned a hardware store and lived in a house across the street from the store. At the moment of the beep, Leonore was innerly seeing the store and the house. Both store and house were seen clearly, as if viewed from the intersection a few hundred feet away. At the moment of the beep, Leonore was *not* seeing anything between the store and the house. In reality, there is a street with parked cars on both sides. But Leonore was not seeing any of the street, the cars, or the adjacent houses and stores; she was seeing her parents' house and the store, and nothing else.

Now if there were an image separate from the seeing, then there would have to be *something* in between the house and the store – otherwise they would be right next to each other, which they were not. In an image, this intermediate material would have to be there in some form, perhaps indistinct but there nonetheless. But that was not the phenomenon that presented itself to Leonore. There was the house, and there was the store, and they were not separate seeings, and there was nothing in between

If one accepts that Leonore was innerly seeing the house and the store, there is no problem here; she is simply seeing the house and the store and not seeing anything else. Her inner seeing sees whatever it is interested in at the moment (in this case, the house and the store) and does not see that which it is not interested in at the moment (the street and the cars). By contrast, if one requires that Leonore was innerly seeing *an image* of the house and the store, then the image has to include details (at some level of differentiation) that are not of current interest. That is certainly true of real images such as photographs; a photograph of Leonore's house and store taken from the same perspective would include the street and cars. At any particular moment, Leonore might be looking at the photograph and seeing the house and store and not seeing the street and cars, *but the street and cars would be there in the photograph just the same.*

The risk is that if Leonore (and/or her DES examiner) were to assume that all inner seeings include the existence of images separate from the seer, then that assumption would demand the existence of things (such as streets and cars) that may not actually have been a part of the phenomenon at the moment of the beep.

It is sometimes held that imagery is difficult or impossible to observe. For example, Schwitzgebel (2002) held, "Participants in these historical debates were right to mistrust their opponents' reports of their imagery experiences: Imagery is difficult to introspect accurately, and even in favorable circumstances people can make large mistakes about their own current, conscious imagery" (p. 38). Whereas we agree with Schwitzgebel's general thesis that people, even sophisticated people, are often substantially mistaken about their inner imagery experience, we disagree with the implication that therefore DES reports about images are to be discounted. DES subjects who describe images usually do so with total confidence, and this includes those subjects who prior to sampling thought it would be difficult or impossible. Subjects' DES reports about images are unshakeable, even by a highly skeptical inquirer.

Unsymbolized thinking

Unsymbolized thinking is the experience of thinking some particular, definite thought without that thought's being represented in awareness in words, images, or any other symbols.

For example, you are wondering whether you should have a peanut butter sandwich or a ham sandwich. This wondering presents itself to you clearly as a cognitive or mental process (not as a feeling or a bodily inclination, for example). It is specifically a choosing between the peanut butter and the ham alternatives (not between salami or roast beef). However, there is no image of a peanut butter or a ham sandwich, no words "peanut butter" or "ham" or any other word. In fact, no symbols whatsoever are present in your experience. At the moment of the beep it is clear that you are wondering or trying to decide or choosing between a peanut butter sandwich and a ham sandwich, but there are no sensory characteristics that support or surround that thinking/wondering/deciding process.

The phenomenon

Whereas inner speech and images are familiar phenomena, unsymbolized thinking requires some discussion. First, unsymbolized thinking is a specific mental event, every bit as specific as saying to yourself, "That is a very strong odor – maybe it is a gas leak!" or seeing your mother's face as she was a few years ago. Second, there is nothing vague about unsymbolized thinking. The choice in our example is clearly between peanut butter and ham. Third, unsymbolized thinking can be as differentiated as any other kind of thought process. Our example differentiates between two kinds of sandwiches, but the list could be longer.

Fourth, our DES research shows that unsymbolized thinking is just as robust an inner phenomenon as is inner speech or visual images. However, many people (including most psychologists) mistakenly believe that unsymbolized thinking is not possible. It's beyond our scope to explain why, but we speculate that the western philosophical tradition that associates thinking with inner verbalization is largely to blame.

Perhaps most striking is that even those people who themselves frequently engage in unsymbolized thinking often believe that unsymbolized thinking is impossible! It's as if the power of the tradition outweighs their own self-observations, even though they have spent literally thousands of hours engaged in unsymbolized thinking. Additionally, it may well be that the lack of recognition of unsymbolized thinking compared to inner speech and images stems from the difficulty observing mental events that are experienced without symbols. The salience of the actual thought may draw attention, leaving the lack of symbolization of the thought unrecognized.

Discriminations

It is often the case in inner seeing that details of not-fully-realized elements in images are immediately known to the person. We do *not* refer to such known or implied characteristics of inner seeings as unsymbolized thinking. Recall, for example, Angeline's inner seeing of body lotion described above. In that seeing, there was a pinkness that Angeline knew or understood to represent body lotions of other brands. We consider that kind of knowing to be a part of the inner seeing process, and it is phenomenally much different from unsymbolized thinking. In unsymbolized thinking, the thought process itself is directly present in experience: you understand yourself to be thinking a particular thought. By contrast, Angeline understood herself to be seeing pinkness, and understood in some what that that pinkness represented other brands; but she was not thinking about those other brands or about the pinkness that represented them.

People are almost unanimously very clear about the difference between the experience of a thought and a feeling or inclination. An *unsymbolized thought* is clearly, unshakably a thought, and is not a feeling or inclination.

Unworded speech, as we saw above, involves the experience of speaking (sense of control, linear sequence, rhythm, pace, etc.) even though the words being spoken are not present to awareness. Unsymbolized thinking has none of these temporal characteristics. However, it does seem that for some subjects, unsymbolized thinking seems "almost" to be innerly spoken. In other subjects, unsymbolized thinking seems "almost" to be seen.

DES skill considerations

As in the example of Sam in Chapter 10, DES is often initially difficult for those people who experience frequent unsymbolized thinking but who themselves believe that thinking without words or symbols is impossible. On the first sampling day they typically report that "I was saying to myself...," but then on questioning cannot describe the words or any vocal features of the sentence they said they were saying. On the second sampling day, their inability to report words is distressing – they feel inadequate, anxious, or unfit as participants in the sampling study and often want to quit. Reassurance is often necessary. For example, we might say, "It's OK to have a thought but not to be able to describe its features – perhaps we will be better able at a subsequent sample. But perhaps we won't get any better – that would be OK too." On the third day they become confident that they were in fact thinking something but there were no words or images or other symbols.

Subjects often use the term "wondering" to describe unsymbolized thinking. However, "wondering" is also used to describe inner speech and images, so careful interviewing is necessary.

Subjects often use the term "feeling" to describe unsymbolized thinking, or in the interview alternate back and forth between saying they were "feeling" or "thinking" something. The fact is that even in these cases, the experience is definitely a thought, "cognitive," "mental," and the lack of precision in the language subjects use does not reflect an unclarity in their experience. If the examiner asks whether the experience was more a thought-type process or a feeling-type process, the typical response is that it is definitively a thinking, but the subject is quizzical about how that could be.

In order for an experience to be called unsymbolized, it must clearly be a thought recognized as taking place in experience, and that thought must not include words, images, or other symbols.

Feelings

A feeling is an emotional experience, including sadness, happiness, humor, anxiety, joy, fear, nervousness, anger, embarrassment, and so on.

For example, you are anxious. There's no doubt about whether you are experiencing anxiety, but it's hard to describe. It seems like maybe a tight feeling in your chest and a little shakiness in your hands, but you're not sure.

The phenomenon

Emotional experience, when it occurs, is often quite differentiated. That is, people usually have absolutely no doubt that at this moment the emotion is anger, at that moment anxiety, at another moment anger mixed with anxiety, and so on. People typically recognize their emotions clearly.

However, many people have great difficulty describing the details of how these emotions present themselves. That is, people often cannot easily answer questions such as, "What does this anger feel like?" or, "How do you know you are anxious?" You can say with confidence that you are angry or anxious, but the characteristics of how that anger presents itself to you are often far from clear.

There are, broadly speaking, four ways in which feelings are typically experienced: (1) they seem to be localized somewhere in the body (most often at least partly in the chest); (2) they seem to be physically experienced in the head; (3) they are experienced as mental events; and (4) they seem to have no phenomenal features at all – you are angry, and it is clear that you are angry, but you can't say how you experience that anger (you're angry, that's all that can be said).

Whereas for many people the bodily representation of emotion is vague, shadowy, or nonexistent, there are some people for whom the phenomena of feelings are extremely clear. For example, a person might report that a feeling of sadness was "exactly as if a blunt knife has been thrust directly into my heart." This was a clear, bodily sensation. The "as if" portion of this description referred to the fact that she knew that no such knife wound actually existed, but other than that she was reporting a sensation that was just as real, just as excruciatingly painful, as that caused by an actual wound.

Often, perhaps most often, those individuals who report clear bodily sensations report them to exist in the heart. For them, the sensation of their "heart breaking" is a real experience, as is "heavy hearted," "warm hearted," "hard hearted," "big hearted," "whole hearted," "heart on fire," "heart uplifted," and so on. Those phrases should not be understood to apply directly to the physiology of the body – the heart as a physical organ probably does not become heavy or warm or big in certain emotional situations – but those phrases should be understood to be accurate descriptions of experienced sensations in the chests of these individuals.

Discriminations

Subjects often use the word "feelings" to describe both what we call feelings and also unsymbolized thinking. However, once the terminology is clarified, there is usually no confusion between the experience of feelings and the experience of unsymbolized thinking. Unsymbolized thinking is clearly a thought, whereas a feeling is clearly an emotion. Most people make that distinction readily, unhesitatingly, and confidently. There are two additional distinctions to be made with feelings that are not necessary for the four other main characteristics of inner experience (inner speech, images, unsymbolized thinking, and sensory awareness). First, emotion can be present in experience at the moment of the beep (in which case, as we have been describing, we call it a "feeling"), or an emotion can be present in the body but not be experienced at the moment of the beep (in which case we call it a "feeling-fact-of-body"). For example, prior to the beep, Mary had been experiencing a warm, loving feeling toward her friend Dave, primarily experienced as a warm/bubbly sensation that seemed to originate deep in her chest and radiate outward toward the surface of her body and culminate as a tingling sensation on her skin. But at the exact moment of the beep, she was preparing her grocery list and was seeing an image of the paper towels she needed to purchase. When the beep occurred, she confidently reported that the imaged paper towels occupied her entire experience at that precise moment, and yet, as she 'took stock' of what was going on with her, it was clear that the emotional warm/loving was continuing in her body.

The task of DES is to explore the phenomena of experience, and because the emotion was not in her experience at the moment of the beep, we cannot legitimately call it a feeling. However, because the emotional process is clearly ongoing, it seems illegitimate to say there is no feeling. Our solution is to identify the ongoing but not experienced feeling as "feeling fact of body."

The second distinction is between emotional experience and emotional behavior. We have seen many instances of emotional behavior that is accompanied by no emotional experience whatsoever, whether at the beep or just before or after it. For example, Jerry was red in the face and yelling at his wife; to any onlooker he was "obviously" angry. However, Jerry had no experience whatsoever of anger. There was no feeling of anger; furthermore, even when beeped an experience of anger did not seem to be present for Jerry (and thus this was not feeling-fact-of-body). Jerry simply had no anger experience whatsoever despite his obviously angry appearance and behavior.

DES skill considerations

When someone says "I feel...," he or she may mean:

– I'm reporting an emotional awareness that is a strong, clear, vivid, real sensation in my heart;

- I'm reporting an emotional awareness that seems to be in my body, but I'm not really clear about it;
- I'm reporting a hyperclear emotional awareness that exists in a well defined but seemingly arbitrary region of my body;
- I'm reporting an emotional awareness that seems to be in my head, but I'm not really clear about it;
- I'm reporting on an emotional process that seems to be ongoing in my body but which is not present in my awareness at all;
- I'm reporting a cognitive event that has no emotional significance at all;
- I'm reporting a general characteristic of my situation; or
- Some other meaning.

All these meanings can be expressed *in identical language*, typically beginning "I feel. . ..". The DES examiner has to tease apart these meanings.

People often have difficulty describing any of the phenomenal characteristics of emotion. It is sometimes useful to ask, "Well, does this anger seem to be in your head, or your body, or neither one, or does this question not make sense?"

If people have difficulty describing a feeling (as is often the case), it is often useful to wait until the second appearance of a feeling and then ask how the two were the same or different: "How does this anger present itself in ways that are different from that anxiety, so that you can know the difference between them?"

The DES examiner needs to accept that while it is generally easy for subjects to give the "perceptual" details of thoughts (what words are part of an inner speaking, or what is seen in an inner seeing), it is often difficult or impossible to give the perceptual detail of a feeling. "It's in my head, and it's an emotion, not a thought, but beyond that I can't say."

Sensory awareness

A sensory awareness is a sensory experience (itch, visual taking-in, hotness, pressure, sound) that is in itself a primary theme or focus for the subject. Such a sensory awareness may be bodily (itch, tingle, pain, pressure, hotness, coldness, shiver, stiffness, etc.) or external (noting the color of a flower, smelling gasoline, seeing the orange of a sunrise, hearing the scratching of the cat at the door, etc.).

Here are some examples. Paula was brushing her teeth and noticing the cool gooiness of the toothpaste. Sam had just quit his job and was seeing an image of his boss crying. He was paying particular attention to the shimmering streak of the tear on the imaged boss' cheek. Florence was seeing a can of 7-Up and noticing the particular green of the can.

The phenomenon

By sensory awareness we do *not* mean merely a perception. If the subject's interest at the moment is primarily in the thing itself, then this is a perception, not a sensory awareness. But if a primary interest is in the sensory features of the thing, than we do consider the experience a sensory awareness. If the center of awareness when hearing the cat scratching at the door is the *cat*, then the scratching is *not* sensory awareness. If the center of awareness is the peculiar dry raspiness of the cat's scratches at the door, then the hearing of the scratching *is* sensory awareness. Thus the following are *not* sensory awarenesses: Paula was brushing her teeth and noticing that she didn't have enough toothpaste (she is not interested in the sensory aspects of the toothpaste but in the utility of the toothpaste). Sam was seeing an image of his boss who was crying (he is not interested in the sensory aspects of the tear but in the emotion of the boss). Florence was reaching for a green can of 7-Up because it was non-diet (she was not interested in the greenness but in the non-dietness).

Discriminations

Feelings are recognized for their emotional significance, whereas the experience of sensory awareness is not primarily emotional. It is often difficult to make that discrimination. For example, if you were feeling anxiety that was manifested by a tightness in your chest, we call the chest tightness part of the feeling and not a sensory awareness. Here the chest tightening was being appreciated *not* as a thematic experience in itself, but was merely the manifestation of the feeling. On the other hand, if you were feeling anxiety and paying particular attention to the way the tightness in your chest seemed to move from left to right, then the chest tightness *would* be considered a sensory awareness. The question is whether your experience was thematically one of sensation or of emotion. The question of emotional significance is decided on the basis of your direct experience. For example, a heart palpitation may be a part of a feeling (e.g. "I was scared and I could feel my heart palpitating"); or it may be a sensory (bodily) awareness (e.g. "I was noticing a strange palpitation in my heart").

Sometimes people have an inner seeing and note the particular sensory qualities of something in the image. We consider that both an inner seeing and a sensory awareness. Sam's boss' glistening tear above is one example. Another example: Carlos was innerly seeing a parrot and was paying particular attention to the reddish-purpleness of the parrot's wings. We consider that both an image and a sensory awareness.

DES skill considerations

Those new to DES often have a mistaken view of what we mean by sensory awareness. The fact that a subject is paying attention to some perceptual aspect of the environment does *not* imply the presence of sensory awareness. "I was seeing a man in a purple shirt" may or may not (but probably not) be sensory awareness as we define it. It is often useful to ask, "Are you particularly interested in the purpleness of the shirt, or are you simply describing an aspect of the man?" If the answer is something like, "I was looking at the purple, which I was noticing was the same color purple as Barney the dragon," then we would call this sensory awareness. But if the answer is something like, "I was interested in the man and to identify him I said he had on a purple shirt" then it is not sensory awareness as we define it.

To qualify as sensory awareness, the interest / focus of the experience has to be on the sensory aspect of the experience *per se*.

A subject's initial reporting of an experience is rarely adequate to decide whether the experience involves sensory awareness. If the subject says, "I was reading the yellow highlighted part of my psychology textbook," you cannot know whether the "yellow" reference is meant to be a description of the book (in which case it is not sensory awareness) or whether the subject is noting the particular shade of yellow (in which case it is a sensory awareness). It is often useful to ask, "Are you paying attention to the yellowness of the highlight or the highlighted text?"

On the next page are a few examples for your practice. We suggest you cover up the right-hand column and then uncover one item at a time.

Multiple awareness

Multiple awareness is two or more separate, substantially unrelated processes experienced to be ongoing simultaneously.

For example, you're seeing an image of your brother, and at the same time you are thinking, in inner speech, "I need to paint my house." If your brother is not involved in your house repainting (he didn't tell you it needed painting; he's not going to paint it; etc.) then this is considered to be a multiple awareness. However, if they are related (perhaps you are directing the inner speech to your brother), then this is not considered to be multiple awareness.

	Description of experience	Sensory awareness?
1.	I was trying to get out a splinter, which was hurting my hand. *What are you paying attention to right at the moment of the beep?* I can see the end of the splinter, and I'm trying to get the tweezers around it.	No
2.	I was trying to get out a splinter, which was hurting my hand. *What are you paying attention to right at the moment of the beep?* It hurts, a sharp pain as I try to get it out.	Yes
3.	I was cold, and I was thinking I should get my green sweater. *What are you paying attention to right at the moment of the beep?* I was shivering and feeling the cold on the surface of my arms.	Yes (the coldness)
4.	I was cold, and I was thinking I should get my green sweater. *What are you paying attention to right at the moment of the beep?* I was trying to remember where I put my green sweater.	No
5.	I was cold, and I was thinking I should get my green sweater. *What are you paying attention to right at the moment of the beep?* I was remembering the green of the sweater – it would go well with my pants.	Yes (the greenness)
6.	I was seeing a blue car that was about to make a left turn in front of me. *When you say the car was blue, are you interested in the blueness? Or are you simply describing the car?* The car was about to make a left turn, and I had to slow down.	No
7.	I was seeing a blue car that was about to make a left turn in front of me. *When you say the car was blue, are you interested in the blueness? Or are you simply describing the car?* It was a really bright blue, not like most cars.	Yes
8.	I was feeling insecure. *What do you mean?* I didn't know what to do, and it was like my shoulders were hunching and I didn't feel very strong. *Are you paying particular attention to your shoulders and/or your strength?* Yes. It was like I was trying to straighten up but I couldn't.	Yes
9.	I was feeling insecure. *What do you mean?* I didn't know what to do, and it was like my shoulders were hunching and I didn't feel very strong. *Are you paying particular attention to your shoulders and/or your strength?* No. I couldn't figure out what to do, and I was feeling bad.	No
10.	I was tired and about to fall asleep. *How does this tiredness present itself?* My eyelids were heavy. *And are you paying attention to your eyelids?* No. I'm just sleepy, that's all.	No
11.	I was tired and about to fall asleep. *How does this tiredness present itself?* My eyelids were heavy. *And are you paying attention to your eyelids?* Yes, the lids were heavy and I was feeling a burning sensation. *Right at the moment of the beep?* Yes.	Yes

We also consider two separate, distinct images to be multiple awareness even if they relate to the same topic. For example, you're seeing an image of your house that needed to be repainted, and at the same time you're seeing a separate image of a can of Sherwin Williams paint.

The phenomenon

The object of the Multiple Awareness characterization is to notice that some people apparently have very complex inner experience, where several or many things happen simultaneously or asynchronously, whereas many other people's inner experience is primarily one thing at a time.

The complexity of one single experience does *not* count as Multiple Awareness. For example, Mary was looking at a fellow student's drawing of a tree, noticing the pleasing curve of the branch (sensory awareness). As she looked, she was wishing she could draw like that (unsymbolized thinking). Because the sensory awareness and unsymbolized thinking are related aspects of the same situation, this is *not* multiple awareness.

Note that DES takes no position on whether things are actually simultaneous or actually so close together in time that they only appear to be simultaneous. The DES issue is of experience, not reality. If two disparate things are experienced as being simultaneous, then we consider it to be multiple awareness regardless of the underlying real simultaneity or lack thereof.

DES skill considerations

On the next page are a few examples for your practice. We suggest you cover up the right-hand column and then uncover one item at a time.

No inner experience

In addition to the characteristics of inner experience that we have discussed, and the occurrence of multiple, simultaneous, independent characteristics which we call multiple awareness, it occasionally happens that subjects report that there was essentially nothing ongoing in inner experience at the moment of the beep. The most common reports of this type accompany the subject's being actively engaged in some activity, such as speaking, reading, or watching TV. For example, at the moment of the beep Estelle was buttering toast. She was engaged in the activity with no awareness of any particular aspect of the experience. Clearly her eyes were aimed at the toast, and she was engaged in some active processing that resulted in the toast being buttered, but there was

	Description of experience	Multiple awareness?
1.	I was seeing an image of my room at home, noting particularly the green of the walls that seemed to stand out as if greener than usual. I was feeling safe, as if the room were a haven.	An image, a sensory awareness, and a feeling, but *not* a multiple awareness.
2.	I was angry and was shouting at my wife, and at the same time noting how strident my voice sounded.	A feeling and sensory awareness, but *not* a multiple awareness.
3.	I was saying to myself in inner speech, "I should make an appointment with the Dean." At the same time, I was saying aloud to my wife, "Let's go have lunch."	Inner speech, external speech, and multiple awareness
4.	I was seeing an image of my sister holding her son. At the same time I was feeling a strong twinge in my neck on the left side.	Image, sensory awareness, and multiple awareness

no particular characteristic of experience that was ongoing at that moment – she was not feeling hunger, she was not noticing the particular characteristics of the butter, she was not noting the sensations in her hands, she was not saying anything to herself, and so on. She was "just buttering." In general, therefore, we call this type of experience *just doing*.

Thus just doing refers to moments when there is no particular characteristic of experience that emerges in some thematic way. That doesn't necessarily mean that there is nothing happening, only that there is nothing happening *in particular* that has formed itself into a coherent or noticeable experience.

This kind of experience occurs occasionally, but by no means always, while watching TV. Thus, if the beep occurs while watching TV, and at the moment of the beep the subject is noticing the tone of voice of the actor, we would consider that sensory awareness, not just doing. If the watching-TV beep catches the subject saying to himself, "Oh No!" we would consider that inner speech, not just doing. If the watching-TV beep catches the subject feeling empathy for the character on the TV show, we would consider that a feeling, not just doing. But if the subject was just watching the TV show, without any such particularized experience, we would consider that just doing (or, specifically, just watching TV).

Similarly, this kind of experience occurs occasionally, but by no means always, while speaking aloud. Often when speaking aloud, the subject is unable to report any particular experience, saying, for example, "I was talking, that's all." We consider that a form of just doing (specifically, just talking).

It does occasionally happen that a beep catches subjects when there was neither an attention-occupying activity nor noticeable inner experience of any kind. Subjects typically describe these moments as "blank" or "empty," as if they were experientially "shut down" when the beep occurred. We refer to this as *no inner experience,* a phenomenon quite different from just doing. In no inner experience, nothing is happening; in just doing, something comprehensible is ongoing but no particular feature of experience coalesces.

Comments

We have described five frequently occurring characteristics of inner experience (and their combination, multiple awareness, and absence, just doing or no inner experience). As we said at the outset, we don't claim that these are necessarily the only frequently occurring characteristics or even the most frequently occurring characteristics – other nomothetic characteristics are assuredly possible. We have assiduously tried, however, to "slice experience at its knuckles," separating characteristics where divisions seemed naturally to occur. The adequacy, utility, and longevity of these categories will have to be judged by others.

The features that we have described here are all characteristics of what might be called the form of experience, as distinct from its content. That is, we have described the "how" of experience, not the "about what." We did not set out initially in that direction; instead, the focus on the form is the *result* of our DES investigations. It simply turns out that form seems more important than content. There are some exceptions; for example, the inner experience of anxious individuals is often critical of self or others, and there we are referring to the content of experience. However, such exceptions are rare in our work. Most often, form emerges as much more noteworthy than content. Whether others find the same thing remains to be seen.

As we have said, the characteristics that we have described here are nomothetic – they apply across many individuals and abstract out the single individual idiosyncrasies. We will return to a discussion of the features of this nomothetic analysis in Chapter 14.

Ontological postscript

Let's review. We have said that there are five or seven (or 12, 14, or more if you consult our web site) characteristics of experience that seem robust across people. The concepts "inner speech," "images," "unsymbolized thinking," "feelings," "sensory awareness," and so on apply to many people, perhaps to most or even all people if you accept locutions such as "he has no inner speech." We have said that these characteristics of experience across people emerged organically over time; they were not hypothesized to exist and then confirmationally discovered. We have said that these characteristics are identifiable with great reliability – not perfect reliability to be sure. We have claimed that these characteristics are not figments of the Hurlburt/Heavey imagination, but are characteristics of the subject; that the aim of the expositional interview is to allow characteristics of the subject to emerge relatively untainted by the investigator. We believe that there are usually right and wrong answers to questions such as, "At the moment of this beep, was Juan experiencing inner speech?", "At the moment of this beep, was Juan experiencing an image?", and so on. We believe that if you claim to be using the DES method, you should be able to spot unsymbolized thinking in the same places that we spot it, and so on. We believe that it is sometimes correct to say, "Mary was experiencing sensory awareness at the moment of the beep," and sometimes not correct to say that, and that the correctness is not an artificial imposition of ours.

Does all that imply that inner speech, images, unsymbolized thinking, and so on, are real existing entities; that Adam has a "pile of these entities," that is, a variety of experience types (inner speech, images, unsymbolized thinking, etc.) with which to populate his awareness, and (through whatever process) at any given moment he selects one or some small number of those? The answer is that DES takes no particular position on this matter. We personally think it likely that the answer is No, but DES doesn't care about that answer one way or the other. DES merely tries to describe the phenomena of experience, whatever those phenomena happen to be and from wherever they come. Others may use the DES results and try to discern something about the fundamentals of consciousness, or about cognitive elements, or about whatever. We have no quarrel with them – what they do may well be valuable – we don't do it ourselves because it is difficult (or impossible) to do so and bracket presuppositions at the same time.

What, then, is the ontological status of inner speech, images, and so on? Certainly it is possible that people are neurologically wired to be able to engage in inner speech, images, unsymbolized thinking, and so on. We wish neither to affirm nor refute that. But we do wish to observe that it is quite likely that people's experience can occur in a multidimensional continuum of ways, and that inner speech, images, unsymbolized thinking and so on are the terms with limited ranges of convenience that we believe "slice experience at the knuckles" as best we have been able to do.

Perhaps an example will be useful. There are (let's say) five kinds of storms: tornados, hurricanes, ice storms, thunder storms, snow storms. Meteorologists can reliably distinguish among the kinds of storms, and there are right and wrong answers to whether this particular storm is a hurricane, a tornado, a thunderstorm, and so on. But that doesn't really mean there five kinds of storms, and that a weather pattern will produce either a hurricane or a tornado or whatever. In fact, there are doubtless an infinite variety of actual existing storms, which for convenience meteorologists divide into five. These storm categories have existed for quite a while, which doubtless indicates that they "slice weather phenomena at the knuckles," that is, that there are natural divisions between the storm types based on recognizably similar patterns (even though there is substantial overlap between them).

In fact, storm specialists who have narrower focus subdivide the categories; hurricane experts distinguish among Category I, II, III, IV, and V hurricanes on the basis of wind speed, for example. Snowplow drivers distinguish among five kinds of snowstorms, and on that basis determine how much salt to apply to the roads and when. Similarly, DES distinguishes among inner speech, partially worded speech, and unworded speech, and so on.

Ocean temperatures and land temperatures and jet streams and humidity and air temperature and many other factors combine to produce weather patterns of more-or-less infinite variety. It has proven convenient to speak of these patterns in five categories, and then to subdivide those categories. Similarly, genetics and history and situation and many other factors combine to produce inner experience of more-or-less infinite variety. It has proven convenient to us to divide these patterns into five categories, and then to subdivide them. But just as there is no "pure" or "perfect" hurricane, but instead are storms that more or less match our definition of a hurricane, there is no "pure" or "perfect" inner speech.

Whether the DES categories (inner speech, images, etc.) withstand the test of time as well as have the storm-type categories remains to be seen; that will reflect *whether* experience can be sliced at the knuckles as well as can weather patterns, and *how good a job* we have done in doing so.

CHAPTER 14

Implications of inner experience

with Sarah A. Akhter

In Chapter 13 we described phenomena that occur frequently across people as discovered by DES: inner speech, images, unsymbolized thinking, feelings, and sensory awareness. In Chapter 11 we showed that these characteristics can be described reliably, in fact, very reliably, and we reviewed evidence for the idiographic validity of DES observations. Now we turn to the "so what?" question: What difference does it make whether I have frequent inner speech, or frequent sensory awareness, and so on?

In this chapter we will speculate about the answers to those questions, based on the belief that people's patterns of inner experience could influence (and be influenced by) how they encounter the world. These speculations about the "so what?" question are based on sampling with several hundred people over many years. Nonetheless, it is still early in the game, so to speak, of understanding how (or *if*, for that matter) inner experience relates to the way people exist in the world. Thus what follows should be understood as a preliminary foray into the attempt to understand how the careful observation of inner experience might inform our understanding of people. Much of what we say here may turn out to be incorrect or in need of revision, and that is the purifying process of science we wish to stimulate.

Our first observation is that there is substantial variability across people in the frequency of the five characteristics of inner experience that we presented in Chapter 13. There are some people whose inner experience is almost entirely inner speech; others whose inner experience is almost entirely images; others sensory awareness; and so on. There are other people who experience a mix of some subset or all five of the characteristics. We are quite sure that these differences are not merely variations in reporting style. That is, we are quite sure that people are quite different from each other in their way of experiencing the world.

That may seem totally unsurprising to some readers, but to others, it will be met with strong resistance. There is a well entrenched point of view that sees people as having basically the same form of inner experience. DES shows that that is not true.

Modern psychology generally accepts that characteristics of inner experience play a large role in behavior and adjustment. For example, cognitive psychotherapy, currently the dominant force in psychological treatment, is based on the premise that what you think influences how you feel and what you do (ancient thinkers expressed somewhat similar views, see Chapter 1). We will see that our views are in some ways quite different from that of mainstream psychology, but we agree in a general sense about the importance of inner experience. We think that there are probably similarities among, say, people whose experience is predominantly inner speech, and a different (but sometimes overlapping) set of similarities among those whose experience is predominantly, say, sensory awareness.

Form vs. content

As we noted near the end of Chapter 13, the five main characteristics of inner experience that we have identified (inner speech, inner seeing, unsymbolized thinking, feelings, and sensory awareness) are all characteristics of the form (or manner, structure, conformation, style) of inner experience, not its content. There is no single best word for what we are calling here "form." We use that word in its central Merriam-Webster senses: "1a: the shape and structure of something as distinguished from its material; 2: the essential nature of a thing as distinguished from its matter." We did not set out to discover the various forms of inner experience, and we wish to emphasize that DES does not inherently prefer form to content. The fact that Chapter 13 focused on form is not a predisposition but an empirical *result* of DES: form emerged from the data to be more important, in most cases, than content. (As we mentioned, anxiety is an exception, where criticism of self and others, a content characteristic, is salient. That exception demonstrates that DES would be open to content categories.)

The fact that formal characteristics have emerged as salient for us in no way implies that future DES examiners should ignore content in favor of form. The object here (as in all of DES) is to provide a level playing field where form or content (or some other as yet unnamed facet of experience) can freely emerge as salient if driven thus by the data. However, we note that when psychology thinks of inner experience as being important, it almost always thinks of content. For example, when cognitive psychotherapy asks about thinking, the question is almost always "*What* were you thinking *about*?" (a content question) and almost never "*How* were you thinking it?" (a form question). New DES investigators will have to bracket that penchant. Psychology's disinterest in form is not the result of an examination of the phenomena and a conclusion that content is important and form isn't; rather it is the result of never having had a method that could adequately examine the form of experience. Content analysis is well known to psychology (e.g., Neuendorf 2001), whereas form analysis is totally unknown.

Inner experience is important

An hour before the beep, Ann had read a letter from Julia to Ann's boyfriend. That two-page letter included the sentences "I love you" and "I want to spend the weekend with you" in the text near the top and the bottom of the second page. Now, at the moment of the beep, Ann is arguing with her boyfriend, and while doing so is seeing an image of this letter's second page with the two offending sentences in clearer focus than the rest of the page. She "couldn't shake" this image – the letter is there, vividly right in front of her, its two incendiary sentences the focal point of her inner seeing. At the moment of the beep, Ann was actually screaming at her boyfriend, "She said 'I love you' and 'I want to spend the weekend with you'!" but Ann wasn't actually paying attention at all to the fact that she was screaming or to the content of what she was screaming; her attention had been totally preempted by the inner seeing of the letter. Also at the moment of the beep, the boyfriend was saying something, probably trying to give some explanation, but she wasn't hearing what he was saying because of her absorption in the imaged letter.

This sample vividly illustrates how Ann (like most of us most of the time) is focused on things of her own construction rather than on external reality. She is absorbed in her inner seeing to the almost complete exclusion of all else. Her external speech (or yelling) does not come from anywhere in her awareness, but is merely accompaniment for the image, so to speak. Her boyfriend's talk is totally without effect not because she doesn't believe him, but because she literally doesn't even hear what he is saying. She doesn't hear her own words, much less his.

Since Freud, we have focused on how people distort reality. What is particularly dramatic in this example is that Ann wasn't *distorting* objective reality;

she had literally no bit of that reality in her experience at all. Her "I love you" letter image, while historically related to the situation, is not at all perceptually related to either the surrounding external stimuli (boyfriend trying to explain) or her own proprioceptive stimuli (screaming). In that moment we get a glimpse of Ann creating her own world, populated by letters that say "I love you," not by the people explaining or screaming that an external "objective" observer might notice.

Inner experience form impacts people

We have seen that inner experience can be observed with substantial accuracy and that it is important: Ann was paying much more attention to her own inner experience than the external reality. In fact, most of our subjects most of the time are paying primary attention to some aspect of their own creation rather than to features of the external world. As we shall see below, the form of Ann's experience is important. It is easier to be absorbed in an image than in other forms of experience.

Here is one more example to make the case that it is reasonable to believe that the form of inner experience has an important impact on people. Consider James, whose inner experience is almost entirely sensory awareness. Here are glimpses of his inner experience: At one beep, he was eating a ham sandwich, paying attention to the sensation of his teeth slicing through the leaves of lettuce that were piled high in the sandwich: crunch/tingle – crunch/tingle – crunch/tingle – crunch/tingle as the teeth smashed through the leaves one at a time. All that took a quarter of a second, or so, but James was experiencing the sequential one-after-another individual leaf crunchings. At another beep, he was washing his hands and observing the shine on the silver faucet – the silver's brightness seemed to attract and fascinate his attention. At another beep his coworker was talking to him and James was noticing the slight crackle in the coworker's voice. James had no idea what the coworker was saying – he was focused entirely on the crackly sound of the voice.

Now consider John, whose inner experience was almost entirely inner speech. At one beep, he was eating a ham sandwich and saying to himself in his own inner voice, "I should have gotten 26." Earlier in the day he had received a package that had 24 parts, and now, while eating, he was remembering opening the package. John apparently had no awareness whatsoever of eating the sandwich; his entire awareness was aimed at the package. At another beep, John was washing his hands. He had just noticed that the restroom was out of towels and at the moment of the beep was innerly saying to himself "No towels." At another beep, his coworker was talking to him and John was hearing what the coworker was saying as well as saying to himself, "I did the same thing!" The inner speech was a preparation for what he would say when it became his turn in the conversation.

Let's assume that the beeps are typical of James and John. Is it reasonable to suppose that James and John would have different characteristic ways of acting in the world, somehow related to the fact that James is almost always absorbed in the sensations of the inner and outer world whereas John is almost always creating words and paying attention to them? We think so.

However, there is almost no research that is adequate to address this question. Because inner experience has never been examined carefully in the Western tradition, what research exists is based on analysis, armchair introspection, or retrospection; none of those approaches is adequate for science. The lone exception is a study we did with Margie Koch a few years ago that showed that people who talk at fast rates are likely to have complex or "rich" inner experience (Hurlburt, Koch, & Heavey 2002).

Thus there is little hard knowledge about the ramifications of inner experience on people's lives; in this chapter we intend to enter that void with a series of speculations. Over many years, we have taken a careful look at the inner experience of hundreds of individuals, and made some casual observations along the way. Now we draw on those observations and attempt to paint what seems to us to be a reasonable picture of the connections between inner experience and the characteristics of the people who have them. We wish to emphasize that what follows are speculations, not facts, much less corroborated or replicated facts. We write this chapter with a look to the future, not to the past. We call for these speculations to be investigated and refined, improved, or discarded.

Thus this chapter is quite different from all others in this book. Everywhere else, we have written about things that we take to be quite well established to our satisfaction. Here, we allow ourselves considerable speculative latitude, constrained by our observations but not by confirmatory science.

Inner speech

What we have said so far about inner speech (in the entire book up to now) have been (we believe) true observations of actually-occurring phenomena. Now, we permit ourselves to speculate about the function / ramifications / implications / correlates of inner speech, the characteristics of people who have frequent inner speech, how people who frequently engage in inner speech might encounter the world / experience reality. These speculations are based on casual and non-systematic observations that we have made over years of sampling, no doubt flavored by other non-sampling influences, so the connections between the underlying observations and the speculations are quite loose and perhaps, even, incorrect.

Why do we permit ourselves such speculations? Wouldn't it be better to stick to the facts, as we have done so far? Perhaps it would. However, part of the aim of this book is to demonstrate why it might be important to know about inner experience, and one reason is this: it appears that patterns of inner experience exert a significant influence on how people encounter reality / the world. By clearly marking the following as speculations, we hope to maintain the integrity of the previous descriptions while at the same time laying out some directions that future validation research might take.

With that caveat, we now describe what, based on casual observation, we take to be how people who have frequent inner speech negotiate certain tasks. For convenience, let's call these people "inner speakers," although many "inner speakers" also experience other forms of inner phenomena as well.

- Inner speakers are likely to be fluent in their external speech. It is as if the inner speech provides a substantial amount of practice. If you're constantly (or very frequently) engaging in speech "in your head," you will be constantly (or very frequently) practicing the skills necessary to speaking. Furthermore, inner speech is often an explicit preparation for what is about to be spoken aloud.
- Inner speakers are likely to value logic and to have a capability for logical, analytical skills. Logic and analysis are by nature verbal undertakings: the logician wants to determine whether a statement (expressed in words) is true or false. Practice with inner words facilitates practice with logic.
- Inner speakers are likely to be good at planning sequential operations. "First this, then this, then if X happens do Y,..." is made particularly easy through the use of language. Imagine, for example, attempting to create a wordless cartoon that represents that sequence of activities – it's quite difficult, if not impossible.
- Inner speakers are likely to be prosaic: factual, ordinary, everyday, not particularly imaginative. The term "prose" derives from the Latin *prosa*, which means straightforward. People who spend most of their lives paying attention to their own prose are likely to be straightforward.

- Inner speech leads to shallow over confidence. Speech always expresses one point of view (is always "in a manner of speaking"), but often doesn't recognize this fact. That often leads speakers to believe (incorrectly) that they have expressed something the way it is, rather than to recognize that they may have expressed one small dimension of the way it is.
- Inner speakers are likely to value facts over relationships or artistry.
- Inner speakers can be very focused, which can lead to narrow-mindedness.

We do not mean to imply that all inner speakers are the same. Certainly people whose inner speech is predominately negatively self-critical might be different in important ways from people whose inner speech is predominately positive and optimistic. Certainly people whose inner speech is complexly differentiated and nuanced might be different in important ways from those whose inner speech is simple and straightforward. However, we do think that within this diversity there are likely to be commonalities among people who have the proclivity (for whatever genetic, historical, situational reason) predominately to generate inner speech rather than to generate images, or unsymbolized thinking, and so on.

At the risk of over-repetition, those are all speculative based on far too little direct evidence. Substantial validation studies need to be mounted to determine whether some, none, or all of those statements are true, and to what extent, and the extent to which other personality characteristics not mentioned here are related to inner speech.

Inner seeing (aka images)

As we did with inner speech, we will refer to people whose inner experience is predominantly images as "imagers" or "inner seers." We now describe what, based on casual observation, we take to be how people who have frequent images negotiate certain tasks. As we noted in the inner speech section above, many (probably most) "inner seers" also experience other forms of inner phenomena as well.

- Inner seers often have high energy levels. They need less sleep, they move quickly, and so on. We are not sure whether it's the high energy level which causes the inner seeing, whether it's the inner seeing that causes the high energy, or whether some third factor causes both.

- Inner seers are likely to be creative, inventive. The reason? People who see images are skilled at seeing things *that are not there*, and therefore skilled at imagining alternative realities.
- It is, we think, no coincidence that we use *imag*inative, *vision*ary, forward *look*ing, *see*r to describe creative, inventive people. The possibilities of the future are most easily portrayed in visual images. The ability to create complex detailed scenes quickly and easily, to modify them and transform them, to represent easily things never before seen, are second nature to people who frequently create images in their inner experience.
- Inner seers often have difficulty taking the point of view of another person. Pretend you are a cartoonist and you wish to convey *in pictures only* the notion that I am looking at the world from a perspective that is different from yours. It is very difficult for a pictorial-only representation to convey that. Inner seers therefore often have an inflated view of the value / pre-eminence of their own perspective, as if it were impossible for any other perspective to exist.
- Inner seers are often self absorbed. The high level of detail that is possible in images make images fascinating, engrossing, and enthralling, perhaps much more fascinating than the external world and the people in it.
- Inner seers are often optimistic, perhaps even euphoric or hypomanic. Things seem to go their way, and the future looks bright. Language reflects this connection of visual phenomena with optimism: we say that the optimistic person "sees the world through rose colored glasses" or is "in the pink."
- Inner seers are likely to be impatient. Perhaps because high-energy people move fast, people who frequently see inner images often are impatient with their peers.
- Inner seers are likely to be unrealistic. The inner world is so vivid and attractive that it often preempts reality.
- Inner seers are likely to speak rapidly. If a picture is worth 1000 words, and the pictures are changing rapidly, speech has to be hurried to keep up with the visual complexity. Unlike the other speculations in this chapter, this one has some support (Hurlburt, Koch, & Heavey 2002).
- Inner seers are likely to have affective cycles. We don't know why, but people who see frequent images often go through periods where they lose the image-making ability (usually replacing it with unsymbolized thinking). At the same time, their high energy level and optimism vanishes (see Hurlburt 1993).

Unsymbolized thinking

We refer to people whose inner experience is predominantly unsymbolized thinking as "unsymbolized thinkers." Here are our casual observations about personality characteristics of unsymbolized thinkers.

- Unsymbolized thinkers are likely to be emotional. They may be depressed, anxious, blush easily, cry easily.
- Unsymbolized thinkers may be slowed down. There is no temporality, no rhythm to unsymbolized thinking. Inner speech, for example, comes to the end of the sentence; if the same thought process is to continue, the inner speech has to be restarted. Unsymbolized thinking does no such thing; the same topic may be thought for a long time without stopping or starting over.
- Unsymbolized thinkers may dwell on one thing, be stuck in a rut.
- Unsymbolized thinkers may appear inert or listless, have no "sparkle." Words and images have double meanings, connotations, implications, references that enliven and refresh, provide hooks or entrees for other thoughts. Unsymbolized thinking has one and only one meaning and is therefore not generative.
- Unsymbolized thinkers may have an accurate view of the world, and are not likely to be misled by words or captivated by pictures.
- Unsymbolized thinkers may have memory difficulties because it is more difficult to encode.
- Unsymbolized thinkers may find it hard to "change gears."
- Unsymbolized thinkers may have speech that is halting with no emotion between words.
- Unsymbolized thinkers may have no transitions between sentences or thoughts or meanings.

Feelings

Here are our casual observations about feelings. There are people who have emotion frequently and those who have emotion rarely or not at all. Of those who have emotion frequently, there are, broadly speaking, two kinds of people: those who experience their emotions directly as part of their ongoing stream of experience and those whose emotions play out in their bodies for the most part *outside* of awareness. Of those who experience emotions directly, there are, broadly speaking, four kinds of people: those whose experiential concomitants of emotion are primarily in the body, those whose experiential concomitants are primarily in the head, those whose emotion seems more a mental than a physical process, and those who apparently have no concomitants of emotion at all. Of those whose emotional experience is primarily in the body, there are, broadly speaking, two kinds of people: those whose bodily experience of emotion is very clear and those whose bodily experience is quite diffuse or general.

In our DES subjects, those distinctions are quite robust. Further, we believe that those distinctions are of fundamental importance for understanding emotion, and that understanding emotion is fundamental to understanding the human condition. However, as far as we know, the science of emotion has not explored those distinctions nor even recognized that they exist.

To appreciate why these distinctions may be important, let's consider some examples. Ted was feeling self-critical, unsure of himself. Whereas he was quite sure that the feeling was primarily self-critical and to a lesser extent unsure (that is, he was unshakably confident about the emotional phenomenon), he had a difficult time pinning down exactly how that self-criticism and unsureness presented itself or themselves to him. Yes, there seemed to be something bodily about it; yes, this bodily aspect seemed more in his chest than in, say his arms or his head; no, there didn't seem to be some bodily aspect that was self-critical and another that was unsure, and yet somehow those two aspects were distinct in the emotion; yes, it is clearly an emotion, not a thought.

By comparison, Bob experienced a self-critical, unsure feeling that was clearly located in a teardrop-shaped region centered in his chest. This region was about three inches wide at the top and about 14 inches wide at his waist. This region was teardrop shaped in depth also: at the top it began at the surface of his skin and extended about an inch into his body, and became gradually thicker until at the waist it extended about four inches into his belly.

Certainly it is true to say that both Ted and Bob were experiencing self-criticism and unsureness. However, the experiences are dramatically different from each other. Let's assume that such experiences are frequent for Ted and Bob. It is hard for us to imagine that Ted and Bob would have similar personality characteristics.

It turns out that Bob has been diagnosed as having a schizophrenic disorder, as described in Hurlburt, 1990, and Ted's emotional experience is quite commonplace. Therefore Ted and Bob are in fact much different from each other. But the distinctions between the characteristics of emotional experience are not necessarily a matter of psychiatric diagnosis.

The existence of hyper-clear emotions such as Bob's is a relatively unknown characteristic of schizophrenia. Most psychiatrists and psychologists believe that schizophrenics typically have "blunted" emotions – feelings that are flat and not vivid. However, DES research leads us to think that that is a mistaken view. Our schizophrenic samplers often have hyper-vivid, hyper-clear emotions as aspects of their inner experience, but they control the expression of these emotions, so that externally they *appear* to have blunted emotions. To have clear emotions but not to express them is very different from not having clear emotions in the first place. If our findings are in fact true of many schizophrenics, science's understanding of the role of emotion in schizophrenia will have to change dramatically.

Distinctions between emotional experience are not merely between those who are and are not diagnosed with schizophrenia. Here's another example, this time in non-diagnosable individuals. Sally is reading about the humanitarian crisis in the Sudan and is "heartsick." This is experienced as a distinct, painful, mushy yet powerful pressure on and in her heart. As she reads, the heart-pressure feeling increases to the extent that she cannot physically bear it, and she lies down to let the pressure pass.

Mary is also reading about the Sudan crisis, and is also heartsick. This emotion is experienced as a primarily mental process that is difficult to describe. There is some mental sense that the Sudan situation is very grave, that Mary is helpless, that Mary must do something, that Mary doesn't know what to do, that the Sudan situation is horrible.

Sally and Mary both describe themselves as "heartsick," and it is our opinion that both are absolutely correct in their descriptions. And yet the phenomena they describe are very different. Both heartsicknesses are felt emotions; both are extremely strong; and yet one is clearly experienced to be a bodily process and one is experienced to be a mental process.

Certainly Sally's version of "heartsickness" is closer to the etymology of the term, but we see no reason at this point to believe that Sally's heartsickness is real while Mary's is sham or that Sally's is deep while Mary's is shallow. But clearly they are different. Let's assume that Sally's experience of emotion is usually strongly, clearly in her body, and that Mary's experience of emotion is mental. We think it likely that Sally and Mary have personality differences that are related to the differences in emotional experience, but so far science has little or no evidence.

We must be clear that DES does not concern itself with the actual bodily processes involved in emotion. Whether Sally's bodily process is actually in her heart as a bodily organ, whether it is elsewhere in her chest that simply appears to be in her heart, or whether it is not in her body at all but projected there from some neuronal pattern in the brain does not concern us at all. We are concerned with Sally's experience, which is a bodily sensation in the chest/heart. Similarly, whether Mary has or doesn't have an actual bodily process of emotion but doesn't directly experience it is of no concern to us. We are concerned with Mary's experience, which is of a mentally understood emotion.

How frequently emotion is a factor at a particular moment varies dramatically from individual to individual. There are many people who never or only rarely have any kind of emotion, either directly experienced or indirectly as part of a bodily process. There are others who have only the bodily process kind of emotion, with emotion never or only rarely occurring directly in awareness at the moment of the-beep experience. And there are others who have the direct awareness of emotion as the focus or as part of the focus of nearly all their samples. The result of this variety is that people may refer to dramatically different things when they speak of their emotions.

We wish to point out that with emotion, it is the experience, not the behavior, that is important. Consider two kinds of people: One kind experiences feelings so bodily acutely that they avoid emotional situations. The other kind feels emotions not at all and therefore is bored by emotional situations. Behaviorally the two people are similar – they both avoid emotional situations. Focusing only on behavior thus misses the point altogether: these people are very different from each other.

In the previous sections of this chapter, we have listed speculations about personality relationships with inner speech, images, and unsymbolized thinking. Because emotional experience comes in such substantial variety (as we have just seen), speculations about the personality / emotional experience relationships are difficult to make. Research on emotion must first explore the differences in emotional experience before it can profitably explore personality relationships. That said, here are a few ballpark speculations.

- People who experience frequent, clear emotions are likely to be quite judgmental or evaluative: good/bad, like/dislike, right/wrong. It is easy for them to mistake their own feelings of, say, good or bad for actual goodness or badness.
- People who experience frequent, clear emotions are likely to be stubborn and intolerant, because emotional experience does not easily change or react to one new incident or fact.

- People who experience frequent, clear emotions are likely to react to the deepest human characteristics. Excellent artists (painters, sculptors, musicians, poets) have clear access to their emotions.
- People who experience frequent, clear emotions are not likely to be fluent speakers.
- People who experience frequent, clear emotions are likely to think in categorical terms, not in gradations. The sense of proportion is difficult (something is felt to be good or bad, and it doesn't matter whether it is a major thing or a minor thing).
- People whose experience of emotion is too frequent and too clear are likely to have chaotic lives.
- People who have anger management problems don't experience emotions in situations that others would find emotional "until it is too late." They do not react skillfully to small emotional cues; they do not "see confrontational situations coming."

Sensory awareness

First, we remind the reader that sensory awareness, as we define the concept, is the paying particular attention to specific sensory qualities. Thus sensory awareness is not merely paying attention to things in the environment, a process we might call perceptual awareness. Seeing a sandwich as part of the process of deciding to have lunch is not sensory awareness; feeling the crunch-crunch-crunch of your teeth going through the lettuce, as in the James example above, is sensory awareness.

Sensory awareness can facilitate multiple awarenesses and fragmentation of attention. For example, it is possible to have a sensory awareness of the coldness on your left arm and at the same time to have a separate but simultaneous sensory awareness of the "bite" of the lemonade you are drinking, and perhaps to have other entirely independent but simultaneous sensory awarenesses. Such multiple simultaneous sensory awarenesses are much easier than, for example, simultaneous multiple inner speech, where you are saying one thing to yourself and at the same time saying something entirely different to yourself. (Simultaneous separate inner speech occurs occasionally, but is rare.)

It has been our observation that sensory awareness is often associated with psychological disturbance, as if sensory awareness is a kind of "raw impact" that leaves the person "at the mercy" of the environment. People who have frequent sensory awareness are often disorganized and emotionally labile, perhaps because they become absorbed by some sensation to the exclusion of many of the more important aspects of a situation, perhaps because of the fragmentation of awareness often seen in sensory awareness. By contrast, healthier people somehow process the sensory aspects of the things and organize them into perceptual wholes, and then operate more constructively on those perceptual realities.

However, we know of substantial exceptions to this rule – people who seem quite emotionally healthy who nonetheless experience frequent sensory awareness. We have sampled, for example, with an adept Zen meditator whose inner experience was often predominantly sensory awareness. He reported that one of his favorite meditation practices, engaged in over many years, was the bare attention to sensory qualities, and sampling seemed clearly to indicate that this meditation practice had generalized to his everyday being. Another exception was a non-meditating college student, who seemed quite healthy despite frequent pure sensory awarenesses. Our current, highly tentative, thinking is that sensory awareness is a "razor's edge": it may well be a high state of achievement, a direct connection to the world unencumbered by distraction. But in an individual who is not well balanced, whatever that may mean, sensory awareness can lead to disorganization and selectivity that is decidedly counterproductive.

Clarity

An overall observation based on our DES research is that people's experience is only rarely directed mainly at the real world. Most of the time, the most central features of inner experience are things of the person's own construction: inner speech, images, feelings, unsymbolized thinkings, and so on.

Sensory awareness is an exception; many sensory awarenesses are direct apprehensions of the internal or external world. But even here, most sensory awarenesses are of particular features of a small portion of the world: the shininess of the tear streak, the muscle tension in my arms.

Certainly people are paying meaningful attention to things that do not occupy any or much of their experience. For example, people who are driving when beeped often report that they had no awareness of the road or the cars around them – their awareness was entirely occupied by an inner image, say – and yet they negotiate the traffic without incident.

In short, people are occupied by their experience much more than by the real world. However, we have sampled with a number of people whose experience is not clear – Amy of Chapter 2 is an example. We think that has an impact on people's lives and personalities.

So far, we don't have a set notion about exactly how that impact gets played out, except to say that unclear inner experience seems to have been problematic in every case that we have observed it. The type of problem has varied considerably: obsessive lying in Amy's case, true obsessive compulsive disorder, dyslexia, schizophrenia, interpersonal dysfunction, and so on. As best we can say at this time, clarity of inner experience is generally (always?) good, and unclarity is generally (always?) bad.

Communication and relationships

The speculations we have been discussing so far in this chapter apply to individuals one at a time. Here we speculate that communication and relationships are likely to be strongly affected by the inner-experience characteristics of the people involved. We are in no position to sketch a complete theory of communication or relationship, but we provide the following to whet the appetite for further studies of the impact of inner experience on relationships.

Imagine a married couple where his inner experience is primarily inner speech while hers is primarily feelings and sensory awareness. Like most people, they have little awareness of the characteristics of their own inner experience, much less that of their partner's or how these patterns may affect each other. Now let's speculate about their communication and relationship. Inner experiences are skills; because of his substantial practice in inner speech, he's likely to be relatively good at task-oriented and logic-requiring things but relatively bad at interpersonal nuance. Because of her substantial practice experiencing feelings and sensory awarenesses, she's likely to be relatively good at being in-the-moment and skilled at the non-linearity that in-the-momentness implies but relatively bad at sequential operations.

As a result of their differing experiential abilities, he's likely to be frustrated by her inability to get things done in a straightforward, timely fashion; she's likely to be frustrated by his seeming mechanical shallowness. In a conversation where he is trying to persuade her of something, she may not be listening at all because she's observing how the light from the lamp plays on the shininess of his hair. In a conversation where she's trying to describe her feelings, he may not be hearing the meaning she intends because he doesn't have much experience with and therefore little practice in differentiating the emotional aspects she's describing. As illustrated in the first conversation, the difficulty in communication can be that while one person talks, the other may be having an experience entirely other than hearing (that is, the form of people's experience may determine *whether* they hear). As illustrated in the second conversation, the difficulty in communication can be that while one person talks, the other may be having a related experience but one that is substantially different because of the level of skill in the experience being conveyed (that is, the form of people's experience may determine *how* people hear what the other is saying).

His inner-experiential strengths are in fact her inner-experiential weaknesses, and vice versa. She is in fact stubbornly immaturely chaotic from the point of view of the inner-speech sequential-logic skill set that creates the only world he knows. He is in fact stubbornly immaturely shallow from the point of view of the feeling/sensory-awareness-immediacy skill set that creates the only world she knows. If they could appreciate each others' strengths, they might see that they complement each other, and together they can be effective in ways that neither of them might be alone. But that will be difficult because the other's experiential strengths are their own experiential weaknesses, and people are not in general very good at recognizing, much less accepting, their own weaknesses.

Postscript

We close this chapter by re-emphasizing that the speculations sketched in this chapter are largely unsubstantiated and many are likely to be false. For example, in the couple we sketched in the previous section, we spoke as though inner speech *causes* task-orientedness. We recognize that if there is a relationship between inner speech and task-orientedness, the direction of causation could go the other way (or some third factor might underlie both), and that much work remains to be done. We have allowed ourselves the liberty to make such speculations to illustrate the potential of the method, and the fact that some or even all of our speculations may be false shouldn't be held against the method any more than van Leeuwenhoek's mistaken belief in animalcules should be held against his invention of the microscope.

CHAPTER 15

Idiographic science

Throughout this book, we have made a distinction between the "idiographic," referring to the characteristics of unique individuals, and the "nomothetic," referring to general laws or universal characteristics of people. We have said that DES is fundamentally an idiographic procedure. For example, when we described Amy in Chapter 2, we concluded that her who-am-I bewilderment and frequent lying were likely the result of her inability to focus on, or to have, inner experience. That was an idiographic conclusion, a statement that applies to Amy *as a particular individual* regardless of whether it applies to other people diagnosed as obsessive compulsive, other college women, or to any other group, or to any other individual, for that matter.

However, for the more recent chapters, we have for the most part treated DES as a nomothetic tool. We identified (Chapter 13) five forms of inner experience that apply in important ways *across people* (regardless of whether they apply to any particular person such as Amy); we showed (Chapter 11) that these five forms of inner experience could be identified with high reliability *across people*; we speculated (Chapter 14) on the relationships between these forms of inner experience and personality characteristics *across people*.

Thus it is clear that DES can be both an idiographic and a nomothetic tool. We think the distinction between idiographic and nomothetic is vitally important to the future of DES and psychological science, so we focus on it directly now.

Idiographic science is rare

By far the most influential psychologist in the idiographic / nomothetic distinction was Gordon Allport, who observed in 1937 that psychological science was much more nomothetic, interested in general laws, than idiographic, interested in the individual:

> There is a typical procedure the scientist feels compelled by convention to follow.... First, he makes a critical discrimination of his subject matter, isolating from the individual who confronts him a chosen segment of behavior. This procedure is called *abstraction*. He then observes the recurrence of this segment and its conditions in many members of a hypothetical class. Finding uniformity in the event and its attendant conditions, he makes a *generalization* or law, and then, if he is a thorough investigator, he will submit his law to repeated tests and so establish it securely by *empirical verification*....
>
> The piling of law upon law does not in the slightest degree account for the pattern of individuality which each human being enfolds. The *person* who is a unique and never-repeated phenomenon evades the traditional scientific approach at every step. (Allport 1937:4–6, italics in original)

That passage is often cited as evidence that Allport favored the idiographic over the nomothetic, but that is an incorrect decontextualization of Allport's position (Hurlburt & Knapp 2006). Actually, Allport thought both were important:

> The dichotomy [between nomothetic and idiographic], however, is too sharp: it requires a psychology divided against itself.... It is more helpful to regard the two methods as overlapping and as contributing to one another. In the field of medicine, diagnosis and therapy are idiographic procedures, but both rest intimately upon a knowledge of the common factors in disease determined by the nomothetic sciences of bacteriology and biochemistry. Likewise, biography is clearly idiographic, and yet in the best biographies one finds an artful blend of generalization with individual portraiture. A complete study of the individual will embrace both approaches. (Allport 1937:22)

Allport's own career reflected to some extent both approaches: the nomothetic, for example, was represented in his discussion of common traits (Allport 1937) while the idiographic was represented in his analysis of the personality of one particular woman, the writer of 301 letters in *Letters from Jenny* (Allport 1965).

However, despite the efforts of Allport and others, the idiographic approach has never been influential in psychology:

> Historically, the single most persistent response to previous proponents of idiography has been that whatever descriptive advantages idiography might have, it would ultimately undermine the overriding objective of establishing general principles of personality (cf. Beck 1953; Eysenck 1954; Falk 1956; Holt 1962; Kleinmuntz 1967). ...Because this view has so thoroughly dominated empirical personality psychology for so long, very little research of a truly idiographic nature has been reported in the literature – even by those who have advocated such research most earnestly (cf. Hall & Lindzey's [1978] discussion of Gordon Allport's career). Moreover, it has never been made clear how to reconcile what little idiographic research has been done (cf. Allport

> 1965; Levinson, Darrow, Klein, Levinson, & McKee 1978; White 1972) with the nomothetic objectives of a science of personality. (Lamiell 1981:285)

That passage was from an *American Psychologist* article of a generation ago in which Lamiell tried to rekindle an interest in the combination of idiographic and nomothetic (an approach he called "idiothetic"). However, Lamiell and the others who have advocated idiographic approaches have not been successful: the interest in idiographic methods remains low. In the two decades before Lamiell's 1981 review, about 2 out of every 10,000 articles indexed in PsycINFO contained "idiographic" as a keyword; in the two decades after his review, about 4 out of every 10,000 articles contained "idiographic" as a keyword; however, many of those articles that do use the keyword "idiographic" are actually not at all idiographic in Allport's (or Lamiell's) sense. Thus, idiographic science is not substantially more frequent now than it was in 1937 when Allport embraced the concept or in 1981 when Lamiell reviewed it.

Why is idiographic science rare?

It is beyond the scope of this book to give a complete historical account of the idiographic / nomothetic conflict, but we can sketch a few of the recurring themes. First, idiographic science was attacked by nomothetic scientists (by far the majority) for the reasons that Lamiell noted above: nomothetic scientists held (and still hold) that idiographic science would undermine the attempt to establish general psychological principles. For ideological, political, and economic reasons, the nomothetic science attack on idiographic science has often been acrimonious.

Second, the idiographic approach was often conflated with the clinical approach, in that clinical psychologists often state that their aim is to understand the individual. However, as we saw in Chapter 1, there has been a heated conflict between clinical and experimental psychologists that Tavris (2003) characterized as a "war." Clinicians had difficulty defending themselves from the claim that they often injected their own points of view or predilections into the characterizations of their clients and that they failed to employ the best findings of nomothetic psychology, and as a result, the experimental psychologists discredited the idiographic method along with the clinical approach.

Third, most of those few who claim to practice an idiographic approach do not actually embody the core aim of idiographic psychology: the attempt to understand a person as he or she really is, to apprehend the person in his or her intimate, personal uniqueness. That core was evident in Allport's introduction to the idiographic approach:

> In daily life, in our direct contacts with our fellows, the pre-eminence of individuality is recognized readily enough.... The man in the street is never in danger of forgetting that individuality is the supreme characteristic of human nature.... But with the scientist the case is different. Of the several sciences devoted to the study of life-processes, none, peculiarly enough, recognizes as its central fact that life processes actually occur only in unified, complex, individual forms. (1937:3)

Allport emphasized this unique personal intimacy core of idiographic science even more strongly five years later:

> No nomothetist can tell what his wife would like for a Christmas present by applying the general laws of psychology. He can make this prediction correctly only by knowing his wife's particular patterns of interest and affection. If the reply is made that such knowledge is itself generalization from the wife's past behavior, well and good, but be it noted *it is the single life that is generalized*: in other words, it is purely idiographic knowledge that is employed.
>
> (Allport 1942:59, italics in original)

Allport's Christmas gift metaphor seems to have been meant to exemplify the truly idiographic method. Certainly nomothetic research fails Allport's Christmas-present test. However, we believe that much of the research that is now called idiographic also fails to embrace the core of the idiographic ideal. That is, most modern idiographic research doesn't pass the Christmas-present test either. Clinical interviews are often said to produce idiographic knowledge of the client. However, there is substantial evidence that the results of clinical interviews are a fusion of the characteristics of the client and the characteristics of the clinician, which, in Allport's metaphor, would be like giving your spouse a present that reflects some unspecifiable combination of your desires and hers. Techniques such as the Role Construct Repertory (REP) test (Kelly 1955) or the Q-sort (Stephenson 1953) give individualized measurements, but Lamiell (1981) noted that

> even those studies which have used individualized assessment devices, such as role construct repertory (REP) tests and Q-sorts, have tended to end in the assessment and study of individual differences. For example, the information contained in REP test protocols has been used to define individual differences

> in such attributes as cognitive complexity (Crockett 1965) and cognitive differentiation/integration (Landfield 1976). Similarly, Q-sort protocols have been used in personality research as the basis for identifying typological or dimensional differences between persons. (cf. Block 1961; Stephenson 1953).
> (Lamiell 1981:278)

Studies of individual differences are not studies of particular individuals, and such studies also fail the Christmas-present test: they would be like giving your spouse a present that people who are said to be somewhat similar to your spouse generally want. Thus the sad fact is that Allport's stinging attack on nomothetists applies equally well to idiographers: Most *idiographers* can't tell what their spouse would like for a Christmas present by applying the results of their idiographic methods.

Idiographic research is difficult but possible

True (Christmas-present-test-passing) idiographic research is difficult because of two conflicting aims: you have to know the person intimately, but you have to be objective. There is the risk of the clinician on the one side, building intimate relationships but collusively allowing well-entrenched but incorrect views to be elaborated. There is the risk of the nomothetist on the other side, obtaining objective information that is impersonal. True idiographic researchers must walk the narrow path between those two risks.

DES, we think, is a tool (perhaps among others) that allows that path to be walked. The skilled DES interviewer does get to know the subject intimately. Many subjects, after four or five sampling days, report the conviction that they have revealed more intimate, deeper, more incisive aspects of themselves than they have ever revealed to their psychotherapist, their spouse, or to any other person. They report, usually with considerable surprise, the belief that the DES interviewer knows them better than does anyone else. It is a striking realization for them. They marvel at how the discussion of a mere 24 or 30 extremely brief moments, moreover randomly selected mundane moments as distinct from events they supposed were important, could be so profoundly revealing. Thus we think that DES is in fact intimately idiographic in the Christmas-present sense.

Furthermore, we think that DES can be highly objective. The moments of experience are chosen randomly rather than according to presuppositions about what is important or relevant; the expositional interview is aimed at finding the truth (no more, no less); demand characteristics and the imprecision of language are minimized. In Chapter 11 we showed that skilled DES interviewers can arrive at the same characterizations of the subjects' inner experience. In Chapter 10 we discussed how the bracketing of presuppositions is a goal that is attainable to a quite high level by many practitioners (although certainly not by all who might attempt the method).

Besides its intimacy and objectivity, there is one additional feature of DES that leads us to the belief that DES may provide a better chance at successful idiographic science than previous methods: it is renewable. By renewable, we mean that DES observations can be made repeatedly with little or no loss (and in fact, in most cases, gain) in fidelity. That is a rare feature of psychological tools. A psychological test might be administered a second time, but there is no reason to believe that the second administration is better than the first (in fact, there is good reason to believe that the second administration is worse). Certainly there can be repeated clinical interviews, but each subsequent interview is likely to be substantially contaminated or constrained by prior interactions. By contrast, DES always starts at a new place – the moment of a never-before-encountered beeped experience. Certainly the freshness of the new moment does not provide a guarantee against importing the contaminations of presuppositions, but the concreteness of each unique moment provides some support in the battle against inadvertent contamination and jumping to unwarranted conclusions.

Truth

How can the discussion of 24 or 30 randomly selected mundane moments be so intimately revealing? Such reactions are doubtless multiply determined, and the emphasis may vary somewhat from one person to the next, but we think there are two central reasons. First, DES effectively aims at discovering some actually existing truth about the person. Most interactions, be they with friends, psychotherapists, spouses, or whomever, are a complex mix of the truth-about-experience and narrative, mask, defense, avoidance, exaggeration, minimization, sugar-coating, attempts not to hurt the other's feelings, inattention, repetition, convenience, counter-balancing of the other's misunderstandings, misleadings, and so on. All that is not necessarily bad, but it does imply that in nearly all human interchange, the truth about experience is mixed up with many other motives, and thereby the person's apprehension of the truth is cloudy, mistaken, misdirected, uneven.

By contrast, DES provides a forum in which the expectation is that narrative, mask, defense, avoidance, and so on are to be suspended, leaving the truth about the person's experience laid bare. Granted we discuss only extremely brief moments, but we penetrate effectively to the majority of the truth of those moments. That is a very rare occurrence in most people's lives, and most people have a natural apprehension of its value: "This is the real me." Most people recognize that the truth about themselves is uniquely precious, the diamond among the polished glass heap of narrative, mask, defense, and so on. Most people, when they apprehend 24 or 30 diamonds, particularly after they have observed the glass being swept away by the DES questioning, recognize that 24 or 30 small diamonds are far more valuable than the pile of glass.

The second reason that 24 or 30 mundane moments can be revealing is that randomly chosen moments are not as unrelated to each other as might be expected. Important themes in a person's life get played out in some way in many mundane activities such as buttering toast, making a left turn, washing your face, watching TV, watering the lawn, going to work. Important themes are not always present, of course, but they are (a) more present than most people think; and (b) present often enough that they occur in several of the 24 or 30 moments. In the effort to make those moments clear, the facet of the moment that is related to the important theme has also to be made clear. That is, the bit of the important theme that is present in the buttering of the toast is revealed truly, along with the toast and the butter. This revealing entails disentangling that aspect of the important theme from the narrative, mask, defense, avoidance, and so on, and that is recognized as valuable.

Do all important themes get revealed in 24 or 30 beeps? No. Do all aspects of the important themes get revealed in 24 or 30 beeps. No. But some aspects do get revealed in precious clarity, and that is often apprehended as a big deal. Furthermore, the aspect that is revealed is the truth without much distortion from the narrative; it is the truth behind the mask, shared with an outside observer without disastrous effects (in fact, with supportive acceptance). That is also often apprehended as a big deal.

Clinical impression is not necessarily truth

Clinicians and their clients frequently report that their psychotherapy interviews reveal deep truths about the client. It certainly is the case that there are excellent therapists who are capable of observing aspects of their clients that may be unknown to the client, to bring those aspects into the open, and to practice alternative behaviors.

But we wish to observe the impediments that make that endeavor difficult. Clinical interactions start with clients telling their stories (that is, with an amalgam of truth and narrative, mask, defense, avoidance, exaggeration, minimization, sugar-coating, etc.) to therapists who have their own idiosyncrasies, presuppositions, blind spots, hypersensitivities, and so on. Good therapists may pay attention to their clients' presentations and behaviors as well as their stories, and so may be able to reduce their clients' and their own distortions. However, that is often difficult, and there is no generally accepted way of acquiring such skills.

Psychotherapy is very often a very useful endeavor, but it should be recognized that it does not necessarily depend on truth for its success. A plausible yet untrue theory may well be enough to motivate a client to substantial and constructive change. Certainly we are not claiming that all psychotherapy is divorced from the truth. We believe that most therapists most of the time are aiming at the truth, and sometimes they hit the mark. However, we do believe that their methods for discerning whether they are close to or far from the truth in any particular case are substantially flawed because it is difficult to disentangle reality from the mix of other factors at play.

Validity is not truth

It might be argued that the clinician's objectivity would be improved by using objective tests, such as personality measures, which do not depend on the clinician's idiosyncrasies, and we agree. However, validity does not actually guarantee truth.

Suppose that the clinician administers a valid test of Extraversion and the client scores high. That means that the client has endorsed items such as "I find public speaking easy," "I have many friends," and "I like large parties"; in fact, it means that she has endorsed more of such items than the average person endorses. But that does *not* mean that the client does in fact find public speaking easy; or actually has many friends; or actually likes large parties. A person scoring high on Extraversion is more likely to find public speaking easy than is a person who scores low, but validity does not speak to whether George, an individual who scores high on Extraversion, does or does not find public speaking easy. Perhaps George likes parties but not public speaking; perhaps George doesn't like either parties or speaking but endorsed those items in an attempt to please the investigator; perhaps George thinks he likes public speaking but is mistaken. The test of Extraversion does not and cannot distinguish between those very different alternatives. That is, a test of Extroversion, even though valid, does not discover a personal truth about George but only a pattern of probabilities about George compared to some validation sample.

We are not at all critical of validity *per se*; validity is a useful tool in the service of truth. But we do believe that modern psychological science has blurred the distinction between validity and truth, that it values validity and has largely forgotten that truth is what is really at issue. We think that trend will have to be reversed if psychology is to reach its potential. We believe that the future of psychological science depends on the ability of science to develop objective techniques that are truly idiographic in the Christmas-present sense. There will doubtless be techniques other than DES, better than DES, aimed at other aspects of the subject than is DES. But the criticisms that have been levied against nomothetic science are fully justified and unavoidable. Nomothetic science can never do much better than the validity coefficients of .2 or .3 that Mischel (1968) and many others have discussed. Certainly it can do somewhat better than .2 or .3, but not enough better to come anywhere near passing the Christmas-present test. Psychological science has an enormous amount of talent and resources, a substantial portion of which should be aimed at idiographic science.

Questions and answers

Q: DES is in the same situation as clinicians: people telling stories that are an amalgam of truth and distractions to people who have their own peculiarities. On what basis can you think that DES can do better?

A: There is one important difference: there is a very objectively correct answer to the "what was ongoing at the moment of the beep?" question. By contrast, there is not a similarly objectively correct answer to the "What is going on?" question of the therapist. That makes the acquisition of the DES skill a different matter from the acquisition of the therapeutic skill.

Q: I worry that important characteristics will be missed by a random sampling strategy that uses as few samples as you typically do.

A: It is certainly possible that sampling will miss something important, but we can confidently say that if there is some important characteristic, it is usually striking how soon that characteristic appears in the samples. It turns out that for many people, what seem like rare or hidden features of experience are actually quite pervasive and occur as aspects of many if not all samples. It is a common sampling result that people turn out to be preoccupied with something but are unaware of that preoccupation when they retrospectively examine themselves, even though they are aware of it moment-by-moment. The case of Donald that we discussed in Chapter 1 is an example.

Q: But still, DES cannot examine those events that are extremely important but relatively rare.

A: Yes, but we believe that most important events are important because they are frequent, not because they are rare. Certainly a traumatic event can have a lifelong alteration of a personality, but it is not the event itself that is important, it is the fact that the event colors every or many subsequent activities. Sampling will in fact discover those frequent colorations if they exist. As Pete Carrill, basketball coach for Princeton University and the Sacramento Kings, said, *As a player, you want to be good at those things that happen a lot–that cannot be overstated.*

Q: Sometimes you say that inner experience is robust – that it is relatively insensitive to the way questions are asked. But other times you say that the method is delicate – it is highly sensitive to things like presuppositions, and so on. You can't have it both ways!

A: Actually, we believe that both are true, and are not as contradictory as they appear. We believe that skilled practitioners of the method *will* discover largely the same features of a person's inner experience – that was the point of the interrater reliability study described in Chapter 11 and also a large number of less formal interrater comparisons. But those comparisons presuppose a high level of skill on the part of both investigators. If one or the other of the investigators is not so skilled, then all bets are off. Perhaps this metaphor will be instructive. Suppose you have before you two violins, a Stradivarius and a Wal-Mart special. The tone producible by the Stradivarius is robustly better than the tone from the Wal-Mart special, but only when played by a skilled performer.

Q: Does DES get to undisturbed awareness?

A: No. It gets to a complex admixture of the ongoing awareness, the perception of the beep, the task to respond, and so on.

Q: But doesn't that mean that you may always get to some artifact rather than to awareness itself?

A: We don't think so. If sampling always leads to some artifact, then it seems likely that sampling would always produce the same result – it would always discover whatever that artifact is. But that's not what typically happens.

DES reports are typically rather different from each other, both within participants and between participants. Therefore it seems that what is being "caught" has something importantly to do with what was going on before the beep disturbed it.

Q: Is the DES task to discover the truth about or essence of a person?

A: No. Our task is *not* to discover the truth about Sam, or the essence of Sam. To try to discover the truth or essence implies that there really is such a truth or essence. We are agnostic about that. We don't know whether there is a true Sam or an essential Sam.

Q: Then what do you mean when you say that DES tries to help subjects speak truly about their experiences?

A: Our task is to help Sam to speak truly about his inner experience, but that does *not* imply that there is a Truth about his experience and we are helping him to match his words to that Truth. On the contrary, our use of "truly" is more analogous to that of the archer, who tries to make his arrows true, who tries to aim truly. The master archer teaches the student how to fletch, to select the proper kinds of feather and wood, to examine them carefully without distraction, to observe accurately what combinations lead to true flight. But that does *not* imply that the master knows the Truth about arrows; he is simply skilled in their use. He is focused on making arrows fly true, but that does not mean that he is comparing this arrow to some True or essential arrow. DES is analogous. We teach Sam how to apprehend his inner experience truly – to select specific moments, to observe them without distraction, to practice detachment from his self-theories, and so on. But that does not imply that we should try to discover the Truth about Sam or to help Sam discover his own Truth. On the contrary, we simply try to help Sam to apprehend as accurately as possible his inner experience, and then to speak as truly about it as possible.

Q: In your archery analogy, the target is out of sight for the master archer. Doesn't that make it impossible for him to teach archery skills (and therefore, by analogy, impossible for you to teach inner experience observation)?

A: No. It might slow it down a bit, but the master archer can watch how the student shoots, and the student can report where the arrow went. The master can instruct the student how to watch carefully the path of the arrow, and whatever else is important to good archer skill.

Q: If you can't observe someone else's experience, how do you know whether what someone says is true?

A: That question is analogous to, If he can't see the target, how does the master archer know if a particular shot by the student archer hit it? The answer to that is, he doesn't know for certain. We accept that any particular response might be mistaken.

A better question would be, How do you know when a person is skilled at observing and reporting inner experience? Or, by analogy, If you can never see the target, how do you know if an archer is skilled? If the archer selects the proper kinds of feathers, and he trims them the proper way, and he selects the proper kinds of wood, and he correctly rejects some pieces of wood as being not as good as the rest of the batch, and his arrows are all consistently carved and balanced, and.... And the same for the bow, and the same for the string... And the same for the stance and the approach and the draw and the release.... And if on some particular shot the master observes that the archer twisted to the left and the archer says "I missed to the left."... And this list could be expanded indefinitely. If each of those objective qualities pass the test, then it seems reasonable to conclude that this archer is skilled. The alternative is that he can do everything correctly, down to the gnat's eyebrow, but still not be able to hit the target. That's possible, but it might be more difficult to train that skill than to train to hit the target.

Q: But still, you concede that what the subject says might not be true.

A: Yes we do. But to be fair, you should ask the same question of all other psychological endeavors. How do we know that the psychologist's impression at the end of a clinical interview is true? How do we know whether a diagnosis made on the basis of the MMPI or some other test or tests is true? The answer to those questions, it seems to us, is that psychologists don't know whether what they conclude is true, and they don't take as careful steps to maximize the probability that what they conclude is true as does DES.

Q: You have identified five important characteristics of inner experience (inner speech, images, unsymbolized thinking, feelings, and sensory awareness). Is the object of DES to be able to identify correctly which of the five characteristics are currently being experienced?

A: No. Identifying those five characteristics correctly is an important skill, but it is *not* the object of DES, it is *not* DES's highest skill, and it is likely that overemphasizing such a skill will *stand in the way* of mastering DES's highest skill.

Here's another metaphor. Suppose we are interested in the cities of the world. Suppose we examine them and discover five characteristics that are important in understanding how cities function: (1) Whether the population is over 2 million; (2) whether there is proximity to an ocean/river; (3) whether the mean height of buildings is over 40 feet; (4) whether the average income if over $30,000; and (5) whether there are multiple educational opportunities.

Now let's say you want to tell your friend about Las Vegas. Would you say, its population is over 2 million, it has no ocean or river, its mean building height is more than 40 feet, its average income is over $30,000, and there are multiple educational opportunities? No, you wouldn't. You'd say, its main industry is gaming, it's justifiably called the entertainment capital of the world, it's very hot, when you get away from the Strip it's much like most other southwestern communities, and so on.

Why didn't you want to use the five categories that had been judged to be important for cities? Because the important characteristics of Las Vegas do not happen to coincide with those five categories. The categories that are judged to be important across many instances are not necessarily important in any particular instance.

That same conclusion applies to DES. It *is* important to know what the rest of us mean by unsymbolized thinking, and to be able to recognize it when it occurs. The same holds for the other main characteristics. But that isn't the *aim* of DES, it's the *beginning* of DES. The object of DES is to reveal the characteristics of the individual subject before you. If those characteristics happen to include inner speech, unsymbolized thinking, and so on, then report them. But don't let the commonality of those characteristics blind you to the very real possibility that they simply may not be important for the single person you are currently examining.

Epilogue

This book has tried to demonstrate that it is in fact possible to explore inner experience with accuracy and to report those observations with precision. We are convinced that that is true and that science can work out the details such as the problem of determining who can and cannot be trusted to employ DES properly.

Once one accepts that inner experience is important and that it can be observed, the world of psychological science becomes a dramatically different place where possibilities seem endless. Are there specific characteristics of inner experience in Alzheimer's disease? If there are, can they be observed before the clinical symptoms of Alzheimer's disease become apparent? There is substantial evidence that Alzheimer's disease patients have some manifestations of the disorder decades before the memory loss is observed, and it seems possible, even likely, that those manifestations would appear in inner experience if a method to explore it were sufficiently incisive. If that is so, that would be a great good in the sense that all observers agree that early detection of Alzheimer's disease would be beneficial to the patients and families involved.

Everything that was said about Alzheimer's disease in the previous paragraph could have been said about schizophrenia or other major disorders.

It is well known that even in highly heritable disorders such as schizophrenia, many more people who are at risk for the disorder do not manifest it than do manifest it over the course of their lifetimes. Why not? is an important, currently unanswered question. Early detection of inner experience precursors may dramatically improve science's ability to answer that question.

We have seen that inner experience is likely to be a skill that has to be acquired and practiced. It is possible that people who are at risk for schizophrenia but who do not develop it have acquired some inner experiential skill that alters or forestalls that development. Once one accepts that inner experience is observable, it becomes possible to investigate such issues directly.

Once one accepts that inner experience is observable, then most retrospective reports become highly unacceptable. Certainly gathering DES-type reports is much more labor intensive than using retrospective questionnaires or clinical interviews, but the fidelity is far better. Psychological science will have to reorganize itself to facilitate the gathering of such data. It can be done, but it may take something of a revolution.

Thus we are extremely optimistic about the future of psychological science. We can't predict what the experiential findings will be any better than van Leeuwenhoek could predict the biological findings when he looked through his first few microscopes, but it does seem that the findings will be interesting and beneficial.

References

Allport, G. W. (1937). *Personality; a psychological interpretation.* New York: Holt.

Allport, G. W. (1942). *The use of personal documents in psychological science.* New York: Social Science Research Council.

Allport, G.W. (1965). *Letters from Jenny.* New York: Harcourt, Brace, Jovanovich.

Altmann, J. (1971). Observational study of behavior: Sampling methods. *Behavior, 49,* 227–267.

American Psychiatric Association. (2000). *Diagnostic and Statistical Manual of Mental Disorders DSM-IV-TR (Text Revision).* Washington, DC: Author.

Anastasi, A. (1988). *Psychological testing* (6th ed.). New York: Macmillan.

Aneshensel, C. S., Estrada, A. L., Hansell, M. J., & Clark, V. A. (1987). Social psychological aspects of reporting behavior: Lifetime depressive episode reports. *Journal of Health and Social Behavior, 28,* 232–246.

Arntz, A., van Beijsterveldt, B., Hoekstra, R., Hofman, A., Eussen, M., & Sallaerts, S. (1992). The interrater reliability of a Dutch version of the Structured Clinical Interview for DSM-III-R personality disorders. *Acta Psychiatrica Scandinavica, 85,* 394–400.

Aronson, E. & Carlsmith, J. M. (1968). Experimentation in social psychology. In G. Lindzey & E. Aronson (Eds.), *Handbook of social psychology* (Vol. 2, pp. 1–79). Reading, MA: Addison-Wesley.

Aronson, G., E., Wilson, T. D., & Brewer, M. B. (1998). Experimentation in social psychology. In D. T. Gilbert, S. T. Fiske, & G. Lindzey (Eds.), *The handbook of social psychology, 4th ed.* (Vol. 1, pp. 99–142). New York: McGraw-Hill.

Atkinson, R. C., & Shiffrin, R. M. (1968). Human memory: A proposed system and its control processes. In K. W. Spence & J. T. Spence (Eds.), *The psychology of learning and motivation: Advances in research and theory* (Vol. 2, pp. 89–195). New York: Academic Press.

Baars, B. J. (2003). How brain reveals mind: Neural studies support the fundamental role of conscious experience. *Journal* of *Consciousness Studies, 10,* 100–114.

Barrett, L. F., & Barrett, D. J. (2001). An introduction to computerized experience sampling in psychology. *Social Science Computer Review, 19,* 175–185.

Beck, S. J. (1953). The science of personality: Nomothetic or idiographic? *Psychological Review, 60,* 353–359.

Berkeley, G. (1710/1965). A treatise concerning the principles of human knowledge. In C. M. Turbayne (Ed.), *Principles, dialogues, and philosophical correspondence.* New York: Macmillan.

Block, J. (1961). *The Q-sort method in personality assessment and psychiatric research*. Oxford, England: Thomas.

Bower, G. H. (1970). Organizational factors in memory. *Cognitive Psychology, 1*, 18–46.

Brewer, W. F. (1988). Memory for randomly sampled autobiographical events. In U. Neisser & E. Winograd (Eds.), *Remembering reconsidered* (pp. 21–90). New York: Cambridge.

Brooks, R. B., Baltazar, P. L., McDowell, D. E., Munjack, D. J., & Bruns, J. R. (1991). Personality disorders co-occurring with panic disorder with agoraphobia. *Journal of Personality Disorders, 5*, 328–336.

Brown, R., & Kulik, J. (1977). Flashbulb memories. *Cognition, 5*, 73–99.

Bruck, M., & Ceci, S. J. (1999). The suggestibility of children's memory. *Annual Review of Psychology, 50*, 419–439.

Campbell, D. T., & Stanley, J. C. (1963). *Experimental and quasi-experimental designs for research*. Chicago: Rand McNally.

Ceci, S. J., & Bruck, M. (1993). The suggestibility of the child witness: A historical review and synthesis. *Psychological Bulletin, 113*, 403–439.

Chalmers, D. (1996). *The conscious mind*. New York: Oxford.

Connors, E., Lundregan, T., Miller, N., & McEwen, T. (1996). *Convicted by juries, exonerated by science: Case studies in the use of DNA evidence to establish innocence after trial.* Washington, DC: U.S. Department of Justice, National Institute of Justice.

Cooper, L. A., & Shepard, R. N. (1973). Chronometric studies of the rotation of mental images. In Chase, W. G. (Ed.), *Visual information processing* (pp. 75–176). New York: Academic Press.

Craik, F. I. M., & Lockhart, R. S. (1972). Levels of processing: A framework for memory research. *Journal of Verbal Learning and Verbal Behavior, 11*, 671–684.

Crockett, W. H. (1965). Cognitive complexity and impression formation. In B. Maher (Ed.), *Progress in experimental personality research* (Vol. 2). New York: Academic Press.

Cronbach, L. J., & Meehl, P. E. (1955). Construct validity in psychological tests. *Psychological Bulletin, 52*, 281–302.

Csikizentmihalyi, M., & Larson, R. (1987). Validity and reliability of the experience-sampling method. *Journal of Nervous & Mental Disease, 175*, 526–536.

Damasio, A. R. (1999). *The feeling of what happens: Body and emotion in the making of consciousness*. New York: Harcourt Brace.

Danziger, K. (1980). The history of introspection reconsidered. *Journal of the History of the Behavioral Sciences, 16*, 240–262.

Davison, G. C., Vogel, R. S., & Coffman, S. G. (1997). Think-aloud approaches to cognitive assessment and the articulated thoughts in simulated situations paradigm. *Journal of Consulting and Clinical Psychology, 65*, 950–958.

Delespaul, P. A. E. G. (1992). Technical note: Devices and time-sampling procedures. In M. deVries (Ed.), *The experience of psychopathology: Investigating mental disorders in their natural settings* (pp. 363–376). Cambridge: Cambridge University Press.

Doucette, S. (1992). *Sampling the inner experience of bulimic and other individuals.* Unpublished master's thesis, University of Nevada, Las Vegas.

Dreesen, L., & Arntz, A. (1998). Short-interval test-retest interrater reliability of the Structured Clinical Interview for DSM-III-R personality disorders (SCID-II) in outpatients. *Journal of Personality Disorders, 12*, 138–148.

Ebbinghaus, H. (1885). *Memory: A contribution to experimental psychology*. Translated by H. A. Ruger & C. E. Bussenius, 1913. New York: New York Teacher's College, Columbia University.

Eich, J. E. (1995). Searching for mood dependent memory. *Psychological Science, 6*, 67–75.

Eich, J. E. (1980). The cue-dependent nature of state dependent retrieval. *Memory and Cognition, 8*, 157–173.

Eich, J. E., Weingartner, H., Stillman, R. C., & Gillin, J. C. (1975). State-dependent accessibility of retrieval cues in the retention of a categorized list. *Journal of Verbal Learning and Verbal Behavior, 14*, 408–417.

Ericsson, K. A., & Simon, H. A. (1980). Verbal reports as data. *Psychological Review, 87*, 215–251.

Ericsson, K. A., & Simon, H. A. (1984/1993). *Protocol Analysis: Verbal reports as data*. Cambridge, MA: Bradford Books/MIT.

Eysenck, H. J. (1954). The science of personality: Nomothetic! *Psychological Review, 61*, 339–342.

Falk, J. (1956). Issues distinguishing idiographic from nomothetic approaches to personality theory. *Psychological Review, 63*, 53–62.

First, M. B., Spitzer, R. L., Gibbon, M., Williams, J. B. W., Davies, M., Borus, J., Howes, M. J., Kane, J., Pope, H. G. Jr., & Rounsaville, B. (1995). The Structured Clinical Interview for DSM-III-R personality disorders (SCID-II). Part II: Multi-site test-retest reliability study. *Journal of Personality Disorders, 9*, 92–104.

Fisher, R. P., & Geiselman, R. E. (1992). *Memory-enhancing techniques for investigative interviewing: The cognitive interview*. Springfield, IL: Thomas.

Giele, J. Z., & Elder Jr., G. H. (1998). *Methods of life course research*. Thousand Oaks, CA: Sage.

Gilbert, D. T., Pinel, E. C., Wilson, T. D., Blumberg, S. J., & Wheatley, T. P. (1998). Immune neglect: A source of durability bias in affective forecasting. *Journal of Personality and Social Psychology, 75*, 617–638.

Giorgi, A. (1975). An application of phenomenological method in psychology. In A. Giorgi, C. Fischer, & E. Murray (Eds.): *Duquesne studies in phenomenological psychology, II* (pp. 82–103). Pittsburgh: Duquesne University Press.

Giorgi, A. (1989). Learning and memory from the perspective of phenomenological psychology. In R. S. Valle & S. Halling (Eds.), *Existential-phenomenological perspectives in psychology* (pp. 99–112). New York: Plenum Press.

Giorgi, A. (1997). The theory, practice, and evaluation of the phenomenological method as a qualitative research procedure. *Journal of Phenomenological Psychology, 28*, 181–205.

Goodenough, F. L. (1928). Measuring behavior traits by use of repeated short samples. *Journal of Juvenile Research, 12*, 230–235.

Goodman, W. K, Price, L. H., Rasmussen, S. A., Mazure, C., Fleischmann, R. L., Hill, C. L., Heninger, G. R., & Charney, D. S. (1989). The Yale-Brown Obsessive Compulsive Scale: I. Development, use, and reliability. *Archives of General Psychiatry, 46*, 1006–1011.

Greenwald, A. G., McGhee, D. E., & Schwartz, J. L. K. (1998). Measuring individual differences in implicit cognition: The implicit association test. *Journal of Personality and Social Psychology, 74*, 1464–1480.

Hall, C. S., & Lindzey, G. (1978). *Theories of personality* (3rd ed.). New York: Wiley.

Hilgard, E. R., & Loftus, E. F. (1979). Effective interrogation of the eyewitness. *International Journal of Clinical & Experimental Hypnosis, 27*, 342–357.

Holt, R. (1962). Individuality and generalization in the psychology of personality. *Journal of Personality, 30*, 377–404.

Hormuth, S. E. (1986). The sampling of experiences *in situ*. *Journal of Personality, 54*, 262–293.

Hurlburt, R. T. (1976). *Self-observation and self-control.* Unpublished doctoral dissertation, University of South Dakota.

Hurlburt, R. T. (1990). *Sampling normal and schizophrenic inner experience.* New York: Plenum Press.

Hurlburt, R. T. (1993). *Sampling inner experience in disturbed affect.* New York: Plenum Press.

Hurlburt, R. T. (1997). Randomly sampling thinking in the natural environment. *Journal of Consulting and Clinical Psychology, 65*, 941–949.

Hurlburt, R. T. (2000). V.3.x random interval generator ("beeper"). University of Nevada, Las Vegas. Retrieved January 16, 2000 from the World Wide Web: http://www.nevada.edu/~russ/beeper.html.

Hurlburt, R. T., Happé, F., & Frith, U. (1994). Sampling the form of inner experience in three adults with Asperger syndrome. *Psychological Medicine, 24*, 385–395.

Hurlburt, R. T., & Heavey, C. L. (2000). Descriptive Experience Sampling manual of terminology. University of Nevada, Las Vegas. Retrieved January 16, 2000 from the World Wide Web: http://www.nevada.edu/~russ/codebook.html.

Hurlburt, R. T., & Heavey, C. L. (2001). Telling what we know: Describing inner experience. *Trends in Cognitive Sciences, 5*, 400–403.

Hurlburt, R. T., & Heavey, C. L. (2002). Interobserver reliability of Descriptive Experience Sampling. *Cognitive Therapy and Research, 26*, 135–142.

Hurlburt, R. T., & Heavey, C. L. (2004). To beep or not to beep: Obtaining accurate reports about awareness. *Journal of Consciousness Studies, 11*, 113–128.

Hurlburt, R. T., & Knapp, T. J. (in press). Münsterberg in 1898, not Allport in 1937, introduced the terms idiographic and nomothetic to American psychology. *Theory & Psychology.*

Hurlburt, R. T., Koch, M., & Heavey, C. L. (2002). Descriptive Experience Sampling demonstrates the connection of thinking to externally observable behavior. *Cognitive Therapy and Research, 26*, 117–134.

Hurlburt, R. T., & Melancon, S. M. (1987). How are questionnaire data similar to, and different from, thought-sampling data? Five studies manipulating retrospectiveness, single-moment focus, and indeterminacy. *Cognitive Therapy and Research, 11*, 681–703.

Hurlburt, R. T., & Sipprelle, C. N. (1978). Random sampling of cognitions in alleviating anxiety attacks. *Cognitive Therapy and Research, 2*, 165–169.

Husserl, E. (1960). *Cartesian meditations: An introduction to phenomenology.* (Trans. D. Cairns). The Hague: Martinus Nijhoff.

Hutchins, L. L. (2003). *Sampling inner experience in individuals with anxiety.* Unpublished Masters Thesis, University of Nevada, Las Vegas.

Jack, A. I., & Roepstorff, A. (2002). Introspection and cognitive brain mapping: From stimulus-response to script-report. *Trends in Cognitive Sciences, 6*, 333–339.

Jack, A. I., & Roepstorff, A. (2003). Why trust the subject? *Journal of Consciousness Studies, 10*, v–xx.

James, W. (1890/1950). *The principles of psychology*. New York: Dover.

Jones-Forrester, S. (2006). *Inner experience in bulimia.* Unpublished master's thesis, University of Nevada, Las Vegas.

Kahneman, D. (1999). Objective happiness. In D. Kahneman, E. Diener, & N. Schwarz (Eds.), Well-being: The foundations of hedonic psychology (pp. 3–25). New York: Sage.

Kahneman, D., & Tversky, A. (1982). The simulation heuristic. In D. Kahneman, P. Slovic, & A. Tversky (Eds.), *Judgment under uncertainty: Heuristics and biases* (pp. 201–210). New York: Cambridge.

Kelly, G. A. (1955). *The psychology of personal constructs*. New York: Norton.

Kessler, R. C., McGonagle, K. A., Zhao, S., Nelson, C. B., Hughes, M., Eshleman, S., Wittchen, H.-U., & Kendler, K. S. (1994). Lifetime and 12-month prevalence of DSM-III-R psychiatric disorders in the United States: Results from the National Comorbidity Survey. *Archives of General Psychiatry, 51*, 8–19.

Klatzky, R. L. (1975). *Human memory: Structures and processes*. New York: Freeman.

Klayman, J., Ha, Y-W. (1987). Confirmation, disconfirmation, and information in hypothesis testing. *Psychological Review, 94*, 211–228.

Kleinmuntz, B. (1967). *Personality measurement: An introduction.* Homewood, IL: Dorsey.

Klinger, E. (1978–1979). Dimensions of thought and imagery in normal waking states. *Journal of Altered States of Consciousness, 4*, 97–113.

Koch, M. G. (1997). *Descriptive experience sampling of individuals with high natural rates of speech*. Unpublished master's thesis, University of Nevada, Las Vegas.

Kvale, S. (1996). *InterViews: An introduction to qualitative research and interviewing.* Thousand Oaks: Sage.

Lamiell, J. T. (1981). Toward an idiothetic psychology of personality. *American Psychologist, 36*, 276–289.

Landfield, A. W. (1976). Interpretive man: The enlarged self-image. *Nebraska Symposium on Motivation, 24*, 127–177.

Larson, R., & Csikizentmihalyi, M. (1983). The Experience Sampling Method. *New Directions for Methodology of Social & Behavioral Science, 15*, 41–56.

Levinson, D. J., Darrow, C. N., Klein, E. B., Levinson, M. H., & McKee, B. (1978). *The seasons of a man's life.* New York: Knopf.

Leys, S. (Tr.). (1997). *The analects of Confucius*. New York: W. W. Norton.

Locke, J. (1689/1975). *An essay concerning human understanding.* Oxford: Clarendon.

Locke, L. F., & Jensen, M. K. (1974). Thought sampling: A study of student attention through self-report. *The Research Quarterly, 45*, 263–275.

Mack, M. (Ed.), (1997). The Norton anthology of world masterpieces. New York: Norton.

Mascaro, J. (Tr.). (1973). *The Dhammapada: The path of perfection*. New York: Penguin.

McWhorter, J. (2003). *Doing our own thing.* New York: Gotham.

Mill, J. S. (1882/1961). *Auguste Comte and Positivism*. Ann Arbor: University of Michigan.

Miller, G. A. (1956). The magical number seven, plus or minus two: Some limits on our capacity for processing information. *Psychological Review, 63*, 81–97.

Mischel, W. (1968). *Personality and assessment*. New York: Wiley.

Misiak, H., & Sexton, V. S. (1966). *History of psychology: An overview.* New York: Grune & Stratton.

Monson, C. K., & Hurlburt, R. T. (1993). A comment to suspend the introspection controversy: Introspecting subjects did agree about imageless thought. In Hurlburt, R. T. (1993). *Sampling inner experience in disturbed affect* (pp. 15–26). New York: Plenum.

Moxley, R. A. (2002). The selectionist meaning of C. S. Pierce and B. F. Skinner. *The Analysis of Verbal Behavior, 18,* 71–91.

Murdoch, B. B., Jr. (1962). The serial position effect of free recall. *Journal of Experimental Psychology, 62,* 618–625.

Myers, D. G. (2004). *Psychology* (7th ed.). New York: Worth.

National Institute of Justice (1999). *National Institute of Justice Guide: Eyewitness evidence: A guide for law enforcement.* Washington, DC: U.S. Department of Justice.

Neisser, U., & Harsch, N. (1992). Phantom flashbulbs: False recollections of hearing the news about Challenger. In E. Winograd & U. Neisser (Eds.), *Affect and accuracy in recall: Studies of "flashbulb" memories. Emory symposia in cognition* (Vol. 4, pp. 9–31). New York: Cambridge University Press.

Neuendorf, K. A. (2001). *The Content Analysis Guidebook.* Thousand Oaks: Sage.

Nisbett, R. E., & Wilson, T. D. (1977). Telling more than we can know: Verbal reports on mental processes. *Psychological Review, 84, 231–259.*

Nolen-Hoeksema, S., Morrow, J., & Fredrickson, B. L. (1993). Response styles and the duration of episodes of depressed mood. *Journal of Abnormal Psychology, 102,* 20–28.

Orne, M. T. (1962). On the social psychology of the psychological experiment: With particular reference to demand characteristics and their implications. *American Psychologist, 17,* 776–783.

Pearson, R. W., Ross, M., & Dawes, R. M. (1992). Personal recall and the limits of retrospective questions in surveys. In J. M. Tanur (Ed.), *Questions about questions: Inquiries into the cognitive bases of surveys* (pp. 65–94). New York: Russell Sage Foundation.

Pfungst, O. (1911). *Clever Hans (the horse of Mr. von Osten): A contribution to experimental, animal, and human psychology.* New York: Holt, Rinehart, and Winston.

Pope, K. S. (1978). How gender, solitude and posture influence the stream of consciousness. In K. S. Pope & J. L. Singer (Eds.), *The stream of consciousness* (pp. 259–299). New York: Plenum.

Popper, K. (1963). *Conjectures and refutations.* London: Routledge and Keagan Paul.

Redelmeier, D. A., & Kahneman, D. (1996). Patients' memories of painful medical treatments: Real-time and retrospective evaluations of two minimally invasive procedures. *Pain, 66,* 3–8.

Reisberg, D. (1997). *Cognition: Exploring the science of the mind.* New York: Norton.

Renneberg, B., Chambless, D. L., Dowdall, D. J., Fauerbach, J. A., & Gracely, E. J. (1992). The Structured Clinical Interview for DSM–III–R, Axis II and the Millon Clinical Multiaxial Inventory: A concurrent validity study of personality disorders among anxious outpatients. *Journal of Personality Disorders, 6,* 117–124.

Riskind, J. H., Beck, A. T., Berchick, R. J., Brown, G., & Steer, R. A. (1987). Reliability of DSM-III diagnoses for major depression and generalized anxiety disorder using the Structured Clinical Interview of DSM-III. *Archives of General Psychiatry, 44,* 817–820.

Robinson, M. D., & Clore, G. L. (2002a). Belief and feeling: Evidence for an accessibility model of emotional self-report. *Psychological Bulletin, 128,* 934–960.

Robinson, M. D., & Clore, G. L. (2002b). Episodic and semantic knowledge in emotional self-report. *Journal of Personality and Social Psychology, 83,* 198–215.

Roepstorff, A., & Jack, A. I. (2004). Trust or interaction? Editorial introduction. *Journal of Consciousness Studies, 11,* v–xxii.

Rosenthal R. (1976). *Experimenter effects in behavioral research.* New York: Irvington.

Rosenthal, R., & Jacobson, L. (1968). *Pygmalion in the classroom: Teacher expectation and pupils' intellectual development.* New York: Holt, Rinehart & Winston.

Rubin, D. C., & Wetzel, A. E. (1996). One hundred years of forgetting: A quantitative description of retention. *Psychological Review, 103,* 734–760.

Sacks, O. (1990). *The man who mistook his wife for a hat and other clinical tales.* New York: Harper.

Salovey, P., Sieber, W. J., Jobe, J. B., & Willis, G. B. (1994). The recall of physical pain. In N. Schwarz & S. Sudman (Eds.), *Autobiographical memory and the validity of retrospective reports* (pp. 89–106). New York: Springer-Verlag.

Schacter, D. L. (1996). *Searching for memory: The brain, the mind, and the past.* New York: Basic Books.

Schooler, J. W., Reichle, E. D., & Halpern, D. V. (2004). Zoning-out while reading: Evidence for dissociations between experience and meta-consciousness. In D. Levin (Ed.), *Visual meta-cognition: Thinking about seeing* (pp. 203–226). Westport, CT: Praeger.

Schwarz, N. (1990). Assessing frequency reports of mundane behaviors: Contributions of cognitive psychology to questionnaire construction. In C. Hendrick & M. S. Clark (Eds.), *Research methods in personality and social psychology: Review of personality and social psychology* (Vol. 11, pp. 98–119). Beverly Hills, CA: Sage.

Schwarz, N. (1999). Self-reports: How the questions shape the answers. *American Psychologist, 54,* 93–105.

Schwitzgebel, E. (2002). How well do we know our own conscious experience? The case of visual imagery. *Journal of Consciousness Studies, 9,* 35–53.

Schwitzgebel, E. (2004). Introspective Training: Reflections on Titchener's Lab Manual. *Journal of Consciousness Studies, 11,* 58–76.

Searle, J. (1990). Who is computing with the brain? *Behavioral and Brain Sciences, 13,* 632–642.

Shanon, B. (1984). The case for introspection. *Cognition & Brain Theory, 7,* 167–180.

Shepard, R. N. & Metzler, J. (1971). Mental rotation of three-dimensional objects. *Science, 171,* 701–703.

Shiffman, S. (2000). Real-time self-report of momentary states in the natural environment: Computerized ecological momentary assessment. In A. A. Stone, J. S. Turkkan, C. A. Bachrach, J. B. Jobe, H. S. Kurtzman, & V. S. Cain (Eds.), *The science of self-report: Implications for research and practice* (pp. 277–296). Mahwah, NJ: Erlbaum.

Simon, C. C. (2002). A change of mind. *Washington Post,* September 3, 2002, p. HE01.

Skinner, B. F. (1948). *Verbal behavior: William James lectures Harvard University 1948.* Available from the B. F. Skinner Foundation Morgantown Office, Room 507A Allen Hall, West Virginia University, Morgantown, WV 26507–6122. (e-mail: info@bfskinner.org)

Skinner, B. F. (1953). *Science and human behavior.* New York: Macmillan.

Skinner, B. F. (1974). *About behaviorism.* New York: Knopf.

Snowdon, D. A., Kemper, S. J., Mortimer, J. A., Greiner, L. H., Wekstein, D. R., & Markesbery, W. R. (1996). Linguistic ability in early life and cognitive function and Alzheimer's disease in late life: Findings from the Nun Study. *Journal of the American Medical Association, 275,* 528–532.

Sorabji, R. (Tr.) (1972). *Aristotle's On Memory.* London: Duckworth.

Spitzer, R. L., Williams, J. B. W., Gibbon, M., & First, M. B. (1990). *User's guide for the Structured Clinical Interview for DSM-III-R: SCID.* Washington, DC: American Psychiatric Association.

Stanley, M. A., Turner, S. A., & Borden, J. W. (1990). Schizotypal features in obsessive-compulsive disorder. *Comprehensive Psychiatry, 31,* 511–518.

Stephenson, W. (1953). *The study of behavior; Q-technique and its methodology.* Chicago: University of Chicago.

Stone, A. A., & Shiffman, S. (1994). Ecological momentary assessment (EMA) in behavioral medicine. *Annals of Behavioral Medicine, 16,* 199–202.

Stone, A. A., Schwartz, J. E., Neale, J. M., Shiffman, S., Marco, C. A., Hickcox, M., Paty, J., Porter, L. S., & Cruise, L. J. (1998). A comparison of coping assessed by ecological momentary assessment and retrospective recall. *Journal of Personality and Social Psychology, 74,* 1670–1680.

Stone, A. A., Kessler, R. C., & Haythornthwaite, J. A. (1991). Measuring daily events and experiences: Decisions for the researcher. *Journal of Personality, 59,* 575–607.

Stone, P. J., & Nicolson, N. A. (1987). Infrequently occurring activities and contexts in time use data. *The Journal of Nervous and Mental Disease, 175,* 519–525.

Suchan, B., Yagueez, L., Wunderlich, G., Canavan, A. G. M., Herzog, H., Tellmann, L., Hoemberg, V., Seitz, R. J. (2002). Neural correlates of visuospatial imagery. *Behavioural Brain Research, 131,* 163–168.

Tavris, C. (2003). Mind Games: Psychological warfare between therapists and scientists. *Chronicle of Higher Education,* February 28, 2003, pp. B7–B9.

Titchener, E. B. (1910/1980). *A Textbook of Psychology.* New York: Scholars' Facsimiles & Reprints.

Titchener, E. B. (1912). Prolegomena to a study of introspection. *American Journal of Psychology, 23,* 427–448.

Tourangeau, R. (2000). Remembering what happened: Memory errors and survey reports. In A. S. Stone, J. S. Turkkan, C. A. Bachrach, J. B. Jobe, H. S. Kurtzman, & V. S. Cain (Eds.), *The science of self-report: Implications for research and practice* (pp. 29–47). Mahwah, NJ: Erlbaum.

Tulving, E. (1984). Precis of elements of episodic memory. *Behavioral and Brain Sciences, 7,* 223–268.

Tulving, E. (1993). What is episodic memory? *Current Directions in Psychological Science, 2,* 67–70.

Ventura, J., Liberman, R. P., Green, M. F., Shaner, A., & Mintz, J. (1998). Training and quality assurance with the Structured Clinical Interview for DSM-IV (SCID-I/P). *Psychiatry Research, 79,* 163–173.

Vermersch, P. (1999). Introspection as practice. *Journal of Consciousness Studies, 6,* 17–42.

Watt, H. J. (1905). Experimental contribution to a theory of thinking. *Journal of Anatomy & Physiology, 40,* 257–266.

Wegner, D. M. (2002). *The illusion of conscious will.* Cambridge, MA: MIT Press.

Weiten, W. (2004). *Psychology: Themes and variations* (6th ed.). Belmont, CA: Wadsworth.

Wells, G. L., & Olson, E. A. (2003). Eyewitness testimony. *Annual Review of Psychology, 54,* 277–295.

Wertheimer, M. (1987). *A brief history of psychology* (3rd ed.). New York: Holt, Rinehart & Winston.

White, R. W. (1972). *Lives in progress: A study of the natural growth of personality* (3rd ed.). New York: Holt, Rinehart & Winston.

Williams, J. B. W., Gibbon, M., First, M. B., Spitzer, R. L., Davies, M., Borus, J., Howes, M. J., Kane, J., Pope, H. G. Jr., Rounsaville, B., & Wittchen, H-U. (1992). The Structured Clinical Interview for DSM-III-R (SCID) II: Multisite Test-retest reliability. *Archives of General Psychiatry, 49,* 630–636.

Wilson, J. (2003). Comments made as a panelist at the September 5, 2003 meeting of the President's Council on Bioethics. Transcript retrieved from http://www.bioethics.gov/transcripts/sep03/session5.html in February, 2004.

Wilson, T. D. (2002). *Strangers to ourselves: Discovering the adaptive unconscious.* Cambridge, MA: Belknap Press.

Wixted, J. T., & Ebbesen, E. B. (1991). On the form of forgetting. *Psychological Science, 2,* 409–415.

Wonderlich, S. A., Swift, W. J., Slotnick, H. B., & Goodman, S. (1990). DSM-II-R personality disorders in eating-disorder subtypes. *International Journal of Eating Disorders, 9,* 607–616.

Zaragoza, M. S., & Lane, S. M. (1994). Source misattribution and the suggestibility of eyewitness memory. *Journal of Experimental Psychology: Learning, Memory, and Cognition, 20,* 934–945.

Index

In the series *Advances in Consciousness Research* the following titles have been published thus far or are scheduled for publication:

65 **SHAUMYAN, Sebastian:** Signs, Mind, and Reality. A theory of language as the folk model of the world. ix, 343 pp. *Expected May 2006*

64 **HURLBURT, Russell T. and Christopher L. HEAVEY:** Exploring Inner Experience. The descriptive experience sampling method. 2006. xii, 276 pp.

63 **BARTSCH, Renate:** Memory and Understanding. Concept formation in Proust's *A la recherche du temps perdu.* 2005. x, 160 pp.

62 **DE PREESTER, Helena and Veroniek KNOCKAERT (eds.):** Body Image and Body Schema. Interdisciplinary perspectives on the body. 2005. x, 346 pp.

61 **ELLIS, Ralph D.:** Curious Emotions. Roots of consciousness and personality in motivated action. 2005. viii, 240 pp.

60 **DIETRICH, Eric and Valerie Gray HARDCASTLE:** Sisyphus's Boulder. Consciousness and the limits of the knowable. 2005. xii, 136 pp.

59 **ZAHAVI, Dan, Thor GRÜNBAUM and Josef PARNAS (eds.):** The Structure and Development of Self-Consciousness. Interdisciplinary perspectives. 2004. xiv, 162 pp.

58 **GLOBUS, Gordon G., Karl H. PRIBRAM and Giuseppe VITIELLO (eds.):** Brain and Being. At the boundary between science, philosophy, language and arts. 2004. xii, 350 pp.

57 **WILDGEN, Wolfgang:** The Evolution of Human Language. Scenarios, principles, and cultural dynamics. 2004. xii, 240 pp.

56 **GENNARO, Rocco J. (ed.):** Higher-Order Theories of Consciousness. An Anthology. 2004. xii, 371 pp.

55 **PERUZZI, Alberto (ed.):** Mind and Causality. 2004. xiv, 235 pp.

54 **BEAUREGARD, Mario (ed.):** Consciousness, Emotional Self-Regulation and the Brain. 2004. xii, 294 pp.

53 **HATWELL, Yvette, Arlette STRERI and Edouard GENTAZ (eds.):** Touching for Knowing. Cognitive psychology of haptic manual perception. 2003. x, 322 pp.

52 **NORTHOFF, Georg:** Philosophy of the Brain. The brain problem. 2004. x, 433 pp.

51 **DROEGE, Paula:** Caging the Beast. A theory of sensory consciousness. 2003. x, 183 pp.

50 **GLOBUS, Gordon G.:** Quantum Closures and Disclosures. Thinking-together postphenomenology and quantum brain dynamics. 2003. xxii, 200 pp.

49 **OSAKA, Naoyuki (ed.):** Neural Basis of Consciousness. 2003. viii, 227 pp.

48 **JIMÉNEZ, Luis (ed.):** Attention and Implicit Learning. 2003. x, 385 pp.

47 **COOK, Norman D.:** Tone of Voice and Mind. The connections between intonation, emotion, cognition and consciousness. 2002. x, 293 pp.

46 **MATEAS, Michael and Phoebe SENGERS (eds.):** Narrative Intelligence. 2003. viii, 342 pp.

45 **DOKIC, Jérôme and Joëlle PROUST (eds.):** Simulation and Knowledge of Action. 2002. xxii, 271 pp.

44 **MOORE, Simon C. and Mike OAKSFORD (eds.):** Emotional Cognition. From brain to behaviour. 2002. vi, 350 pp.

43 **DEPRAZ, Nathalie, Francisco J. VARELA and Pierre VERMERSCH:** On Becoming Aware. A pragmatics of experiencing. 2003. viii, 283 pp.

42 **STAMENOV, Maxim I. and Vittorio GALLESE (eds.):** Mirror Neurons and the Evolution of Brain and Language. 2002. viii, 392 pp.

41 **ALBERTAZZI, Liliana (ed.):** Unfolding Perceptual Continua. 2002. vi, 296 pp.

40 **MANDLER, George:** Consciousness Recovered. Psychological functions and origins of conscious thought. 2002. xii, 142 pp.

39 **BARTSCH, Renate:** Consciousness Emerging. The dynamics of perception, imagination, action, memory, thought, and language. 2002. x, 258 pp.

38 **SALZARULO, Piero and Gianluca FICCA (eds.):** Awakening and Sleep–Wake Cycle Across Development. 2002. vi, 283 pp.

37 **PYLKKÄNEN, Paavo and Tere VADÉN (eds.):** Dimensions of Conscious Experience. 2001. xiv, 209 pp.

36 **PERRY, Elaine, Heather ASHTON and Allan H. YOUNG (eds.):** Neurochemistry of Consciousness. Neurotransmitters in mind. With a foreword by Susan Greenfield. 2002. xii, 344 pp.

35 **Mc KEVITT, Paul, Seán Ó NUALLÁIN and Conn MULVIHILL (eds.):** Language, Vision and Music. Selected papers from the 8th International Workshop on the Cognitive Science of Natural Language Processing, Galway, 1999. 2002. xii, 433 pp.

34 **FETZER, James H. (ed.):** Consciousness Evolving. 2002. xx, 253 pp.

33 **YASUE, Kunio, Mari JIBU and Tarcisio DELLA SENTA (eds.):** No Matter, Never Mind. Proceedings of Toward a Science of Consciousness: Fundamental approaches, Tokyo 1999. 2002. xvi, 391 pp.

32 **VITIELLO, Giuseppe:** My Double Unveiled. The dissipative quantum model of brain. 2001. xvi, 163 pp.

31 **RAKOVER, Sam S. and Baruch CAHLON:** Face Recognition. Cognitive and computational processes. 2001. x, 306 pp.

30 **BROOK, Andrew and Richard C. DEVIDI (eds.):** Self-Reference and Self-Awareness. 2001. viii, 277 pp.

29 **VAN LOOCKE, Philip (ed.):** The Physical Nature of Consciousness. 2001. viii, 321 pp.

28 **ZACHAR, Peter:** Psychological Concepts and Biological Psychiatry. A philosophical analysis. 2000. xx, 342 pp.

27 **GILLETT, Grant R. and John McMILLAN:** Consciousness and Intentionality. 2001. x, 265 pp.

26 **Ó NUALLÁIN, Seán (ed.):** Spatial Cognition. Foundations and applications. 2000. xvi, 366 pp.

25 **BACHMANN, Talis:** Microgenetic Approach to the Conscious Mind. 2000. xiv, 300 pp.

24 **ROVEE-COLLIER, Carolyn, Harlene HAYNE and Michael COLOMBO:** The Development of Implicit and Explicit Memory. 2000. x, 324 pp.

23 **ZAHAVI, Dan (ed.):** Exploring the Self. Philosophical and psychopathological perspectives on self-experience. 2000. viii, 301 pp.

22 **ROSSETTI, Yves and Antti REVONSUO (eds.):** Beyond Dissociation. Interaction between dissociated implicit and explicit processing. 2000. x, 372 pp.

21 **HUTTO, Daniel D.:** Beyond Physicalism. 2000. xvi, 306 pp.

20 **KUNZENDORF, Robert G. and Benjamin WALLACE (eds.):** Individual Differences in Conscious Experience. 2000. xii, 412 pp.

19 **DAUTENHAHN, Kerstin (ed.):** Human Cognition and Social Agent Technology. 2000. xxiv, 448 pp.

18 **PALMER, Gary B. and Debra J. OCCHI (eds.):** Languages of Sentiment. Cultural constructions of emotional substrates. 1999. vi, 272 pp.

17 **HUTTO, Daniel D.:** The Presence of Mind. 1999. xiv, 252 pp.

16 **ELLIS, Ralph D. and Natika NEWTON (eds.):** The Caldron of Consciousness. Motivation, affect and self-organization — An anthology. 2000. xxii, 276 pp.

15 **CHALLIS, Bradford H. and Boris M. VELICHKOVSKY (eds.):** Stratification in Cognition and Consciousness. 1999. viii, 293 pp.

14 **SHEETS-JOHNSTONE, Maxine:** The Primacy of Movement. 1999. xxxiv, 583 pp.

13 **VELMANS, Max (ed.):** Investigating Phenomenal Consciousness. New methodologies and maps. 2000. xii, 381 pp.

12 **STAMENOV, Maxim I. (ed.):** Language Structure, Discourse and the Access to Consciousness. 1997. xii, 364 pp.

11 **PYLKKÖ, Pauli:** The Aconceptual Mind. Heideggerian themes in holistic naturalism. 1998. xxvi, 297 pp.

10 **NEWTON, Natika:** Foundations of Understanding. 1996. x, 211 pp.

9 **Ó NUALLÁIN, Seán, Paul Mc KEVITT and Eoghan Mac AOGÁIN (eds.):** Two Sciences of Mind. Readings in cognitive science and consciousness. 1997. xii, 490 pp.

8 **GROSSENBACHER, Peter G. (ed.):** Finding Consciousness in the Brain. A neurocognitive approach. 2001. xvi, 326 pp.

7 **MAC CORMAC, Earl and Maxim I. STAMENOV (eds.):** Fractals of Brain, Fractals of Mind. In search of a symmetry bond. 1996. x, 359 pp.

6 **GENNARO, Rocco J.:** Consciousness and Self-Consciousness. A defense of the higher-order thought theory of consciousness. 1996. x, 220 pp.

5 **STUBENBERG, Leopold:** Consciousness and Qualia. 1998. x, 368 pp.

4 **HARDCASTLE, Valerie Gray:** Locating Consciousness. 1995. xviii, 266 pp.

3 **JIBU, Mari and Kunio YASUE:** Quantum Brain Dynamics and Consciousness. An introduction. 1995. xvi, 244 pp.

2 **ELLIS, Ralph D.:** Questioning Consciousness. The interplay of imagery, cognition, and emotion in the human brain. 1995. viii, 262 pp.

1 **GLOBUS, Gordon G.:** The Postmodern Brain. 1995. xii, 188 pp.